LIE AFTER LIE

LIE AFTER LIE

*THE TRUE STORY OF A MASTER OF DECEPTION,
BETRAYAL, AND MURDER*

LARA BRICKER

BERKLEY BOOKS, NEW YORK

THE BERKLEY PUBLISHING GROUP
Published by the Penguin Group
Penguin Group (USA) Inc.
375 Hudson Street, New York, New York 10014, USA

Penguin Group (Canada), 90 Eglinton Avenue East, Suite 700, Toronto, Ontario M4P 2Y3, Canada
(a division of Pearson Penguin Canada Inc.)
Penguin Books Ltd., 80 Strand, London WC2R 0RL, England
Penguin Group Ireland, 25 St. Stephen's Green, Dublin 2, Ireland (a division of Penguin Books Ltd.)
Penguin Group (Australia), 250 Camberwell Road, Camberwell, Victoria 3124, Australia
(a division of Pearson Australia Group Pty. Ltd.)
Penguin Books India Pvt. Ltd., 11 Community Centre, Panchsheel Park, New Delhi—110 017, India
Penguin Group (NZ), 67 Apollo Drive, Rosedale, North Shore 0632, New Zealand
(a division of Pearson New Zealand Ltd.)
Penguin Books (South Africa) (Pty.) Ltd., 24 Sturdee Avenue, Rosebank, Johannesburg 2196,
South Africa

Penguin Books Ltd., Registered Offices: 80 Strand, London WC2R 0RL, England

The publisher does not have any control over and does not assume any responsibility for author or third-party websites or their content.

LIE AFTER LIE

A Berkley Book / published by arrangement with the author

PRINTING HISTORY
Berkley mass-market edition / November 2010

ISBN: 978-0-425-23778-6

BERKLEY®
Berkley Books are published by The Berkley Publishing Group,
a division of Penguin Group (USA) Inc.,
375 Hudson Street, New York, New York 10014.
BERKLEY® is a registered trademark of Penguin Group (USA) Inc.
The "B" design is a trademark of Penguin Group (USA) Inc.

PRINTED IN THE UNITED STATES OF AMERICA

10   9   8   7   6   5   4   3   2   1

Most Berkley Books are available at special quantity discounts for bulk purchases for sales, promotions, premiums, fund-raising, or educational use. Special books, or book excerpts, can also be created to fit specific needs.

For details, write: Special Markets, The Berkley Publishing Group, 375 Hudson Street, New York, New York, 10014.

ACKNOWLEDGMENTS

This book would not have been possible without the help of many people who helped me along the way. I would like to thank my agent, Jane Dystel, for her assistance in finding this book a home and graciously helping a first time book author navigate the world of publishing. I am extremely grateful to Waltham Police Officer Jon Bailey, who volunteered endless hours of his time to help with this book. Without his input and knowledge of this case I would never have been able to finish this project. I would also like to thank my editor, Shannon Jamieson Vazquez, for her insight and feedback as this book made its way through the editing process. Her suggestions greatly enhanced the final product. And lastly, thanks to my hometown support network of Jason Schreiber, Susan Nolan, and my husband, Ken, who endured countless phone calls when I needed help, offered their advice, and were there to read the latest draft of the chapters when I asked. Their support was invaluable.

The greatest trick the Devil ever pulled was convincing the world he didn't exist.

—Kevin Spacey as Verbal Kint in *The Usual Suspects*

CHAPTER 1

Spring 2004

Lana Koon-Anderson was thrilled when she saw her friend Julie Keown's name on the list of employees selected to travel on a company trip to Richmond, Virginia.

Yes! she thought to herself. Both Lana and Julie were nurses who'd previously worked in hospitals before taking jobs with the Kansas City, Missouri–based Cerner Corporation, known as one of the leading suppliers of health-care information technology in the United States. Though they were no longer working directly with patients in hospitals, the two women were part of a task force in the company made up of individuals with nursing backgrounds. Once a month, the nurses all got together to use their real-world experience to improve the quality of the software products Cerner supplied.

Despite an eighteen-year age gap between them, during her first meeting with the other nurses, Lana had

immediately felt a kinship with thirty-year-old Julie, a
pretty brunette with a warm smile and open personality.

"Julie just radiated friendliness," Lana would later recall
about the younger woman.

That friendliness made people gravitate toward Julie
when she was in a group. She had a good energy and
inviting manner that made people instantly comfortable
when they were around her. Raised on a soybean farm
north of Kansas City, Julie seemed to epitomize the word
wholesome.

"You could just sit down and talk to her; she was an
open book," Lana said. "You could be completely at ease
with her almost immediately after meeting her."

Although Lana and Julie didn't see much of each other
in their day-to-day work, because they worked on opposite sides of the building, Lana loved every chance she
had to work with her friend. So as soon as she saw Julie's
name on the list of employees going to Virginia, to help
bring a hospital online with software from Cerner, Lana
immediately sent her an e-mail.

Hey I guess we're going to be there together, Lana
wrote.

Lana was surprised when Julie e-mailed her back with
news that she had just moved to Waltham, Massachusetts,
and was telecommuting for her job with Cerner. Lana had
not seen Julie recently and was unaware that her friend
had moved, though it wasn't an unusual arrangement
for a number of employees at Cerner; employees were
often able to telecommute, and Lana even knew of one
employee who worked from home in Alaska.

The two women e-mailed back and forth several times
in the months leading up to their trip, which took place
over the Mother's Day weekend in May 2004. Once in
Richmond, they worked long days launching the software

in the hospital, usually starting work at 6 a.m. and then working through until dinner.

Lana was still familiarizing herself with Cerner's software, but Julie seemed to really get what Cerner was trying to do for hospitals and worked tirelessly to train the hospital staff. She was right there every time someone needed extra help or had a question, and Lana was struck by how "on top of it" Julie was with their assignment. At one point, a group of the hospital's residents was learning how to log on to the new system, but their passwords weren't working. Julie was on the phone almost instantly, getting the passwords straightened out and getting the group online.

During the time they spent in the hospital together, it became clear to Lana that Julie's first love was helping patients. At one point, the two women stood next to the neonatal ICU in the hospital. Lana watched Julie's face as she looked at the tiny babies. Her love of being a nurse and desire to help those little babies was written all over her face. Julie would do anything for anybody, give them the shirt off her back. That's what made her such a great nurse, Lana thought—her desire to help others before herself.

Lana, who considered herself a bit of a tomboy, was equally impressed by Julie's professional clothes. When she complimented Julie on how nice she looked, Julie smiled and explained that her husband of eight years, James, had suggested she get some new clothes for the trip. Lana, who had just packed the same clothes she usually wore to work, thought it was sweet that James had wanted his wife to get new clothes.

Julie also mentioned to Lana that she hadn't been feeling well before the trip; she'd had some sort of stomach bug that she couldn't seem to kick. James was concerned about her and had at first been nervous about Julie going forward with the trip. But eventually, he encouraged her to go because it was a good opportunity.

With two grown children and a husband who worked as a firefighter and paramedic, Lana was long past those idyllic early years of marriage herself, but although she didn't begrudge Julie for having such a considerate husband, she *was* a little envious.

Though the group had little downtime during the intense four-day trip to Richmond, they did get together for dinner one night. Away from the hospital and the busy days, Lana had a chance to ask Julie about her move to Waltham, a western suburb of Boston.

Julie practically gushed with pride as she explained that they had moved because her husband, James, had been accepted to the prestigious Harvard Business School. She just beamed as she talked about her husband. Julie's love for James was obvious to everyone.

"It is so great; he's just so wonderful," Julie said, adding that the couple was "doing so well financially that all of my paycheck is going into a savings account."

Lana couldn't help but again find herself a bit envious of her friend's situation. She rolled the numbers over in her head of how much she thought the couple was saving each year, and they were impressive.

God she's lucky, Lana thought to herself. Julie seemed to be truly living a real-life fairytale, complete with a great job, financial security, and Prince Charming. The life that every little girl dreams she'll find when she grows up. Unfortunately for Julie, her redheaded Prince Charming was not who he appeared to be . . . and her fairytale life would soon turn out to be a nightmare.

CHAPTER 2

For most residents of Waltham, Massachusetts, the morning of Tuesday, September 7, 2004, was their first day back to work after the Labor Day weekend holiday, which many residents around the Boston metro area had ended by battling the traffic along Route 3 on that last summer trip to the ocean off Cape Cod. Though James and Julie Keown had honeymooned on Cape Cod eight years before, they stayed home that holiday weekend because Julie had recently been battling a serious kidney illness. The couple had moved to Waltham in late January 2004 after James was accepted into Harvard Business School, though both continued to telecommute to their existing jobs in Missouri while on the East Coast. Julie was hoping to get pregnant but wasn't sure if that would be possible yet, because of her kidney illness.

Across the city, Jon Bailey was beginning not just his first day back to work, but also his first day as a detective with the Waltham Police Department. He had transferred to an open spot in the detectives division after nine years as the department's TRIAD officer, a special post that dealt with the elderly of the city, and was looking forward to a change of pace.

So far, that pace was slow. His new supervisor, Lieutenant Brian Navin, had briefed the detectives that morning about the weekend, which had been quiet. There wasn't much for them to follow up on. Navin told Bailey that some cases would be assigned to him once he settled in, but that morning he had none. He spent his time getting his new desk set up and finishing up a few lingering reports from his previous position.

Although he was a police officer by profession, Jon Bailey was a family man at heart. He and his wife, Doreen, took walks around the neighborhood almost daily and got together with her brother every weekend to play pool during the winter months. During the summer, they and their son, Brandon, spent most weekends out by their aboveground pool. The only thing that could tear Bailey away from the pool was watching the New England Patriots football team. The Baileys' Labor Day weekend had involved the traditional extended-family cookout at home, a time to relax and enjoy the pool for one last time before covering it up for the season.

Jon Bailey's path in life, and decision to become a police officer, still amazed his father, Parker Bailey. Parker, himself a career police officer in Waltham, had never imagined that Jon would follow in his footsteps. Parker liked to joke that although he'd always felt his son would be involved with the law, for the better part of Jon's teenage years, he hadn't been sure which side of the law his son would pick.

Bailey hadn't been that different from many teenagers. He'd tested limits and was often more interested in having fun than following rules. It wasn't that he wasn't intelligent; he just chose to do things his own way, such as his method of attending classes at Waltham High School. Bailey didn't skip school, but more often than not, he skipped class. If he liked a particular teacher, he'd go to that class, regardless of whether he was supposed to be there or not. His father received more than one call from teachers at the school about his son's habits.

As a teen, Bailey had spent his time cruising the blue-collar streets of Waltham in his 1970 blue Dodge Charger or hanging out smoking cigarettes on the corner with his friends. There were times when he and his friend ran into trouble with the local police, but the teens were always sent on their way with a stern warning. Every time the police found Bailey up to no good, they just reported back to Parker, who handled the situation at home.

When he wasn't out cruising, Bailey was playing bass guitar in a rock band. It was during that time that he met an attractive blond named Doreen, and it wasn't long before the two became inseparable—except that after the fourth KISS concert, she refused to attend any more. Bailey continued to follow the band on his own, and he has since been to almost forty concerts.

Jon Bailey's mother, Hilda, often asked when he was going to marry Doreen, to which he replied that he was never getting married because he wasn't cutting off his hair, which was down to his elbows. They did get married, but Bailey still refused to cut his long blond locks. Then, one day while working a job in a local department store, he decided it was finally time to cut it off. To those who knew him, it was typical behavior—he made decisions when he was ready, not when he was told. His parents had been trying to get him to cut his hair for years at that point, and on one occasion, Parker actually gave his son money for a haircut. Bailey returned home with his hair slicked back and combed but as long as ever. When Parker asked what he'd done with the money, Bailey replied simply: he had bought pizza for his friends. To his father, it was just another example of Bailey's aversion to being bound by traditional rules.

It wasn't that Jon Bailey had decided as a young man that he *didn't* want to be a police officer, but he'd wondered what else was out there. For a while, he worked in security at the regional Zayre Department Store before trying electrical assembly work, like one of his uncles. After he was laid off from the electrical job, he started to question his future plans. He decided to try police work and got a job as an officer at nearby Mount Ida College, a small liberal arts school in nearby Newton, Massachusetts. But as he dealt with routine patrol around the college, Bailey realized he was nearing the age limit to take the entrance test for the Waltham Police Department. He knew it was now or never. He took the test and passed.

On December 19, 1992, he got a card in the mail informing him that he was a candidate for a position in Waltham. He had only seven days to make a decision and wasn't sure what to do. On one hand, he had a good job at Mount Ida, where he was a day supervisor and made a good salary. Going to Waltham would mean a cut in pay, and he would have to work the night shift to start. His weekends would no longer be free. Bailey spent the weekend talking over his decision with Doreen, who told him she was behind him no matter what. First thing Monday morning, Bailey went to the police station and accepted the job.

When Parker Bailey learned that his son had quietly

gone about taking, and passing, the police entrance exam to join the Waltham Police Department, he was more than a little surprised. Being a police officer meant not only enforcing rules and laws, but following the directives of your supervisors. Nevertheless, despite his initial surprise, Parker was extremely proud when he heard the news about Jon joining the Waltham Police Department and following a family tradition in law enforcement. Back in 1929, Parker's grandfather Frederick Hansen had been one of the first state troopers in the state of Connecticut, and he had spent a good amount of his time breaking up speakeasies during Prohibition. Even Parker hadn't been sure about going into police work at first. Like his son, he took his entrance test without telling anyone other than his wife. But once on the job, Parker knew he'd made the right decision. He still remembered the first major accident he responded to, where a girl had gone through a windshield in a car wreck. He remembered standing at the scene, looking at the accident like the rest of the bystanders, before he suddenly realized that he had to step into gear and help.

"The bottom line is you get it under your belt and you go out and do it," Parker said.

The Waltham that Jon Bailey saw as a police officer, though, was a far cry from the working-class city he'd grown up in, and that his father had known as a police officer. Just ten miles northwest of downtown Boston, modern Waltham had a population of just under sixty thousand residents, and had the honor of being considered one of the top one hundred best cities in the country to live.

Often referred to as "Watch City" because of the Waltham Watch Company, which opened in 1854, the city was now known mostly for its two universities, Bentley and Brandeis. Waltham was also home to a number of major high-tech companies—including Adobe and Symantec, which owns Norton Antivirus—which helped keep residential taxes down. And those low taxes, along with the city's proximity to Boston and major highways like Interstate 95 and Route 128, drew a number of young professionals to live there in recent years.

The downtown underwent a major revitalization starting in the early 1990s. Gone were the days when rough-looking customers lined up outside the bars at 8 a.m., waiting for them to open, or when police responded to drunken brawls in the downtown bars and kept an eye out for motorcycle gangs like the Hells Angels who called the city home. Parker Bailey compared the times he had to break apart fights to scenes in old movies with "rip-roaring drunks." One infamous fight among some of the motorcycle-gang members was only brought under control with sixty police officers.

But those days were gone. People now came from miles around to eat on Moody Street, known for its seemingly endless array of restaurants and specialty ethnic food stores as well as high-end shops and bargain stores. Dentist offices shared the street with jewelers, thrift stores, grocers, and bookshops. Nearby high-end condominiums were home to movers and shakers in the area, including some players for the Boston Red Sox baseball team. But Waltham's more quaint New England traditions were still visible during the annual outdoor concert series on the town common, where people gathered every Tuesday during the summer to hear live music.

But among the many new residents who flocked to the city, there were still lifelong residents, like Jon and Doreen Bailey, who called Waltham home. Bailey's Protestant ancestors first came to the area fourteen generations back, when they arrived on the *Mayflower*, and had been there ever since. Bailey jokes that his path in life is like the theme song from the 1970s sitcom *The Jeffersons*, "Movin' on Up." After growing up in the crowded downtown area, Jon and Doreen now lived in a comfortable colonial-style house with a large backyard in a quiet neighborhood.

After going through the police academy, Bailey's first assignment had been night patrol, where he spent two years before transferring to the day shift. Soon after starting the day shift, all of the patrol officers, including Bailey, were charged with coming up with a community policing project. At the time, *community policing* was a buzzword heard in departments around the country, and there was a seemingly never-ending supply of grants to start up community policing programs. He had just gone through a two-week crime-prevention program where he heard about a program called TRIAD that advocated partnership between law enforcement and senior service agencies. At the time, Bailey's grandmother had recently been the victim of a robbery in Florida; she'd been in her car, stopped at a red light, when someone had smashed out her car window and grabbed her purse. That experience, coupled with the information about the TRIAD program, made Bailey realize there was a real need for a similar program in Waltham. He proposed a TRIAD program in Waltham, partnering the Waltham Police Department, the AARP, and the Waltham Council on Aging.

Before long, the Waltham program became a model for other departments around the country looking to do the same, and started receiving awards in recognition of the local effort. The TRIAD program received the Rose Award from the Executive Office of Elder Affairs in Massachusetts, while Bailey was lauded by numerous groups for his work for the elderly. He was presented with a citation and recognition from the Massachusetts State Senate, the Massachusetts House of Representatives, the

City of Waltham's City Council, the Waltham Council on Aging, and the Alzheimer's Association of Massachusetts. In 2001, he was named the state's officer of the year by the Crime Watch Commission. Along the way, Bailey was asked to take part in a training video for the National Alzheimer's Association and served on the state attorney general's Elder Abuse Project, where he helped to develop policies regarding elder abuse in the state. It seemed that Jon Bailey had found his calling, but after nine years as the TRIAD officer, he felt he needed a change.

He was hoping for a change in the detective division, but as he prepared to go home for lunch that first day, Bailey started to wonder if he was going to find his assignment with detectives as dull as he'd found patrol work. On patrol, he'd felt like he did a whole lot of nothing while waiting for something to happen. Bailey hated just sitting around and waiting for calls; he liked to be busy, doing something.

But Waltham had an extremely low crime rate, with the city perhaps seeing one murder a year, with most calls property crimes. Which made the phone call that came into the police station's business line that afternoon, on September 7, 2004, even more unusual.

CHAPTER 3

September 7, 2004

Kerri Doherty was just eighteen years old and a cadet with the Waltham Police Department, basically an officer in training, and she had a feeling she wasn't the one who should be taking this call. But at the same time she realized how serious the situation was and concentrated on taking extremely meticulous, detailed notes, as the woman on the other end of the phone made the report.

The report was horrifying, but Doherty continued to write.

_____

Kerri Doherty had grown up in and around the Waltham Police Department; her father, Donnie, was a longtime officer with the department. But although he'd inspired her to enter police work, he wasn't around during the fall of 2004. As a member of the U.S. Army Reserves who supported Special Forces operations, Donnie Doherty was doing a tour of duty in Afghanistan.

Kerri Doherty had applied to the cadet program after graduating high school in 2003. Though she wasn't completely sure about becoming a police officer, she'd wanted to give it a try just the same. She liked the variety in the work. Some days she took calls for service, the calls that came in on the police department's business line from people who needed police assistance of a non-emergency type, mostly people calling to report lost cell phones or lodge a complaint about their neighbors. Cadets took down notes by hand from those calls and then typed up reports. Other days, Doherty was charged with running checks for outstanding warrants or keeping track of people who were on probation. Occasionally, she was asked to fingerprint a prisoner or, if no female officer was on duty, do a body search of a female prisoner brought to the station for holding.

Doherty had been working full time, forty hours a week, for almost a year and had started taking night classes at nearby Middlesex Community College. The schedule was grueling, and although she liked her job, she was also considering going to law school.

But her future plans were not on her mind when she was answering calls that came into the police department's business line in the early afternoon of Tuesday, September 7, 2004. Although the line was not an emergency line, calls were still recorded. So far that day, she had taken calls for shoplifting, petty theft, and a car accident. When the phone rang again, just before 2 p.m., she answered as she had been trained to do.

"Waltham Police cadet Doherty, this line is recorded."

"OK, are you available to help me?" an official-sounding woman's voice asked on the other end.

"Yes," Doherty said, her pen poised.

"This is Lynn Nuti calling from Newton-Wellesley Hospital," the woman began. "We'd like to report a possible poisoning with ethylene glycol."

Doherty was surprised that this call hadn't gone to the 911 call center, especially because it was from a hospital. She repeated the words to herself as she started to write—*possible poisoning*. She knew her superiors would want complete notes.

"OK," Doherty said, indicating that she was ready for more information.

Nuti continued, "Due to, the patient did not have a history of, um, depression. Any concerns regarding injuring themselves were not communicated. Life support is going to be discontinued at this time, and it is a high probability that the patient will not survive."

Doherty was becoming a little frazzled. This was not the typical false-fire-alarm-going-off call she normally got on this phone line. She concentrated on writing down every little detail that Lynn Nuti passed on.

"OK, all right, let me," Doherty said as she tried to write and process what to do next.

Nuti continued, "We're going to call the ME. We're going to encourage the ME to take this case." Then she gave the cadet the victim's name. "The last name is Keown, K-E-O-W-N. The first name is Julie."

Doherty kept writing. "Do you have a date of birth?"

"Date of birth is 5-16-1973."

Doherty then asked Nuti for a contact number, because although calls to the emergency 911 line were traceable, those to the business line were not, and Nuti rattled off the number to the hospital.

"I'm going to send an officer to you," Doherty told her, before realizing that the hospital was actually in the neighboring city, not Waltham. "Actually, you didn't call Newton Police, did you?"

Nuti explained that she had called Waltham because Julie Keown lived there.

"All right, can you just hold on one second?" Doherty asked. "I just want to make sure we would send someone or if because you're in Newton, we would have a Newton officer go up there. Let me just double-check, OK?"

Doherty put the call on hold while she asked a supervising officer if they would respond. She quickly got back on the phone with Nuti to get directions for the officers who would be sent on the call.

"If they could meet me, I don't want the policemen in the unit where the family is, we can meet down here," Nuti said. "The family, I think, also had called the police, just so you're aware."

Doherty hadn't heard anything about the family making a report, but, then again, it wasn't the type of report she would normally be taking down.

"I'm located in the medical affairs office on the second floor, and I'm right across from medical records," Nuti told her.

Doherty wrote down the directions.

"OK, all right, we'll send someone over there right now."

Doherty hung up the phone and wrote the words "Julie Keown was poisoned with ethylene glycol."

She had no way of knowing that at that same time, Officer Richard Chiacchio was sitting in the sergeant's office of the police department's operations center taking the same report in person from Jack and Nancy Oldag, Julie Keown's parents.

The Oldags were in a state of shock as they sat before Chiacchio and told him that their healthy, thirty-one-year-old daughter was fighting for her life after being poisoned. They couldn't fathom how or where Julie could've ingested ethylene glycol, which they had been told was the main ingredient in antifreeze. Julie had been sick for several months with what she believed might have been related to a newly diagnosed kidney disease, but things had taken a turn for the worse over the previous weekend. Doctors in Massachusetts had determined that Julie was suffering from a mild form of kidney disease called focal segmental glomerulosclerosis, which accounted for test results that showed elevated protein levels and blood in her urine during prior doctors' visits in the late 1990s. The preexisting condition, which Julie had been unaware of until the summer of 2004, did not however account for the much more serious level of kidney decline seen when Julie went to the hospital on both August 20, 2004, and September 4, 2004. After getting a call from their son-in-law, James, with news that Julie had been admitted to the hospital and was on a respirator, the Oldags had quickly flown to Boston from their soybean farm in Plattsburg, Missouri, just outside Kansas City.

During a layover in Chicago, they had called James to check in on Julie, and he'd told them that she'd suffered a seizure and was unresponsive. By the time the couple called James from a cab on the way to the hospital in Boston, doctors had decided that Julie was the victim of ethylene glycol poisoning.

Jack Oldag was at a loss for how his daughter could have gotten antifreeze into her system. Julie, the Oldags told Chiacchio, had been an intensive care nurse until two years before. Since then, she had been working from home for Cerner, a hospital software design company, based in Kansas City. Their daughter and son-in-law had moved in January to Waltham, outside of Boston, because James was attending Harvard University.

Jack had asked James where the antifreeze could have come from. James didn't have an answer, but he did tell his father-in-law that over the weekend Julie had gone missing and he couldn't find her in the house. When he'd gone outside to check the yard, he'd seen Julie walking back to the house. He'd asked her where she had been, and she told him she'd gone for a walk because it made her feel better.

The Oldags just wanted to find out what had happened to Julie. They would later acknowledge that they were worried that the police in the large city would not take their daughter's case seriously. They wondered if the police in Waltham would really care what happened to a simple farm girl from Missouri.

CHAPTER 4

Plattsburg, Missouri, was a small midwestern farming community just thirty-five miles north of Kansas City geographically, but worlds away culturally. With its narrow dirt roads, single main-street business district, and mile after mile of farmland, Plattsburg was a true small town with small-town values, the type of town where people didn't need to lock their doors at night and neighbors helped each other without a second thought. And why shouldn't they—with just over two thousand residents in the town, no doubt most of them knew their neighbors, if not personally, then through friends or family.

But though Plattsburg was by no means a large town, its population had more than quadrupled since 1967. Nevertheless, the town had retained its rural, wholesome feeling with annual events like the Shatto Milk Company Parade and Ice Cream social each summer, and the Clinton County Fair, where the county's young people took part in 4-H competitions with sheep, goats, pigs, dairy cattle, and beef. One weekly newspaper, the *Clinton County Leader*, covered the entire county.

Julie Irene Oldag had grown up in this safe, friendly community on her family's farm off Southwest Middle Road, a bumpy gravel road so narrow that two cars must take care when passing, though the chances of meeting another car there were slim. About halfway down the road, past a small plant nursery, an old metal mailbox with a hand-painted rainbow marked the Oldag family farm. A modest yellow ranch-style farmhouse with neatly trimmed green hedges out front sat at the top of a small hill overlooking expansive fields on all sides. Behind the house, a silver silo stood next to a red barn. The closest neighbor, as well as the closest paved road, was several miles away.

The Oldags planted crops of soybeans and hard corn on the fields in front of and behind their farm every year. Like other children who grew up on a farm, Julie and her younger brother, Chad, learned to help out from a young age.

Julie's naturally caring personality and desire to help others led her to pursue a career in nursing when she was accepted to William Jewell College, a private Baptist college in nearby Liberty, Missouri. She was a good student with an obvious passion for becoming a nurse. "She wanted to be a nurse," said Dr. Nelda Godfrey, a professor. "For some people, school comes very easily; she worked very hard while she was here."

She also found time for socializing, and it was on the campus of the small private college that Julie Oldag was set up on a blind date with a fellow student named James Keown. Julie's naturally down-to-earth nature was the perfect complement to James's outgoing, sometimes overly ambitious personality, which was at times as lively as his brilliant red hair. Although James was prone to having his head in the clouds with his lofty ambitions for a career as a talk-radio personality, Julie was there to keep him grounded. James did pursue a radio career at both the college radio station and at a Kansas City, Missouri, radio station where he landed a job while he was still a student.

After college, the two married, and Julie got a job at Liberty Hospital, where she worked as an intensive care nurse. Julie's supervisor, Kathy Taylor, was impressed by the young nurse's happy and positive attitude. Julie earned a reputation as a good nurse whom the other nurses and doctors loved working with. Given a problem with a patient, Julie was always first to try to find a solution to get away from, over, or around the issue to help the patient. People just wanted to be around the bright nurse, whose energetic manner was almost infectious.

Although she left her first love for her job at the Cerner Corporation, it was obvious to those who knew Julie that nursing was her true passion. Even after she worked a full fifty-plus-hour workweek at Cerner, she would then turn around and work a twelve-hour shift in the ICU at nearby Liberty Hospital over the weekends. When friends asked her why she still worked at the hospital, Julie was quick to respond that it was what she loved to do. She never said anything about the money. It was always about how she loved being a nurse.

Julie was dedicated to her career, but she was equally dedicated to her family and friends. Though her plan to become pregnant and start her own family had not happened yet, Julie had her nephew, her brother Chad's little boy, Dalton, to lavish attention on, and friends could count on her to send out the latest photos of the little boy with a comment about how adorable and sweet he was on a regular basis. And she was always willing to drop whatever she was doing to help out a friend, or even just lend an ear.

One of Julie's closest friends, Christina Liles, once called while Julie was making a batch of her trademark homemade apple pies, including making and rolling out her own piecrust. Christina had gone through a rough relationship and often talked it out with Julie, but she didn't want to interrupt her friend's baking project. And it was quite a project, as Christina learned that Julie wasn't just making one pie at a time but spending the entire day making pies to freeze.

"Why are you making so many?" Christina asked.

"I just like to do that," Julie replied, adding that she always liked to have a pie on hand to thaw out if needed. But despite the fact that she was in the middle of rolling out the crusts, Julie stopped everything to talk to her friend that day.

People who met Julie for the first time were always struck by her open, warm smile and easygoing personality and sense of humor. They often felt an instant friendship with the pretty brunette. For Christina, who felt so close to Julie that she'd asked her to be her matron of honor at her wedding after only knowing her a short while, Julie was that type of friend you might find only once in a lifetime, that person who would always be there for you.

It was Julie who'd suggested that Christina should book the small chapel on the campus of William Jewell College for her wedding ceremony, and Christina felt it was the ideal location. On Christina's wedding day, in early December, Julie, along with Christina's daughter Kaitlyn, helped the bride put on the finishing touches before walking down the aisle. During the ceremony, while Julie stood by her friend, Julie's husband, James, read from the familiar verse of Corinthians:

Love is patient, love is kind. It does not envy, it does not boast, it is not proud.
It is not rude, it is not self-seeking, it is not easily angered, it keeps no record of wrongs.
Love does not delight in evil but rejoices with the truth.
It always protects, always trusts, always hopes, always perseveres.

To those at the ceremony, it seemed apparent that James and Julie shared these same sentiments about each other. For Christina, who was marrying a man she deeply loved and respected, having her dear friend Julie by her side was just the icing on the cake to a perfect day. After the ceremony, Christina and her new husband drove to their intimate reception in James's shiny new Jaguar.

Christina and Julie's friendship continued to thrive. When Christina became pregnant, Julie planned her baby shower. The shower was eight weeks from Christina's due date, but as she sat down to dinner that night, Christina felt her water break. The baby was coming.

Without any relatives in the immediate area, Christina called Julie, who lived right around the corner. At the hospital, Christina's labor was moving along at a rapid pace, too rapid for pain relief, and Julie calmly wiped her friend's head with a cool washcloth as the labor pains came.

"It's going to be OK," Julie told her as she held Christina's hand.

Less than two hours later, with her friend Julie watching, Christina's daughter was born. James took photos of the tiny baby as Julie and Christina held her.

Friends could also count on Julie to share the latest news about James and how proud she was of his new marketing career. That successful career meant that James was often not able to make gatherings that Julie instead attended with friends like Christina. Whenever someone asked about James, Julie was quick to explain that he had a great job in marketing with the Learning Exchange, a Kansas City, Missouri–based nonprofit organization that worked to promote innovation and reform in education through several specialized programs they developed for students. James was part of an initiative to expand the company's online presence and often put in long hours at the office. He often worked at night, he told his wife, because he entertained clients who might be interested in using or donating to the Learning Exchange's programs. Despite those long hours, though, James was a thoughtful and caring husband who often surprised Julie with long weekends away. During one of those long weekends, the couple went to look at land he wanted to buy for his wife in Missouri, so that they would be able to return to their Midwest roots after he finished his studies at Harvard.

During the few times that James accompanied Julie to events, he always impressed people with his accommodating and charming personality. Christina and her husband found themselves thinking what a nice guy James was as they watched him make drinks for their guests. James was clearly a very social person and doted upon his wife, who he called "Jules."

To Christina and her husband, it was obvious that James loved his wife unconditionally, and she in turn adored him.

CHAPTER 5

Lynn Nuti sat behind her desk on the second floor of Newton-Wellesley Hospital. She had short dark hair, and Detective Jon Bailey estimated her to be in her midforties. The nameplate on her desk identified her as the risk manager for the hospital.

Bailey and his partner that afternoon, Detective Stephen Taranto, had never worked together before on a case, but they had been friends for years. Though Bailey was newly assigned to the detectives division, Taranto was a veteran investigator who had been on the Waltham police force since 1985. After finishing his service with the U.S. Air Force, he'd started as a part-time police officer in West Newbury, Massachusetts, before getting a full-time position in Waltham.

The two investigators took seats in front of Nuti's desk while she filled them in on a patient named Julie Keown.

"I need to get her husband's permission before I can

give you more specifics," Nuti explained, but she was able to give them the basics. Julie Keown had been brought to the hospital three days earlier, on Saturday, September 4, at 9:11 p.m. A blood sample drawn by a nurse from Julie as she lay in the emergency room had tested positive for ethylene glycol.

Bailey had never heard of ethylene glycol and asked Nuti about it.

"It's found in brake fluid," Nuti said, before continuing, "but most commonly in antifreeze."

Antifreeze?

Bailey immediately found himself puzzling over how someone would get antifreeze into her body.

Nuti went on to explain that 30 ccs of the substance would prove deadly. A smaller dose of the poison would make someone act like she was in a drunken stupor. It would also cause kidney damage, which corresponded with Julie's symptoms. Nuti apologized that she couldn't give them any more real specifics until James Keown signed off on a release.

While they waited, Bailey pondered the sketchy details they had so far. They knew that Julie had the poison in her system. Could it have been a suicide attempt? Could the couple have gone out to dinner somewhere and ingested the poison accidentally? He asked Lynn Nuti about the husband.

"He's here and he's fine," Nuti told them.

Just after 3 p.m., James Keown signed off on a release giving Nuti permission to brief the detectives on Julie's doctor reports and notes. He also indicated that he wanted to speak with the detectives himself, when they were finished with Nuti.

Free to speak, Nuti told the detectives that James Keown had brought his thirty-one-year-old wife into the emergency room Saturday night in a wheelchair. She had

slurred speech and her balance was off. On an earlier
trip to the hospital, two weeks prior, doctors had found
that Julie's potassium levels were very elevated. Nuti
explained to the detectives that the high potassium was
an indicator of kidney failure. Julie was dealing with the
newly diagnosed kidney disease, but her symptoms were
extremely critical at this point and not consistent with any
mild side effects that disease might cause. Julie's blood
pressure was also elevated, at 237 over 132, and her pulse
was 120. She could not move her arms or legs and was
only able to nod her head yes or no in answer to the emergency room nurse's questions. Julie had indicated that
"No," she was not numb, and "No," she did not have a
headache, nor was she nauseated.

Emergency room personnel gave Julie a dose of Narcan,
a drug often given to people who overdose on opiates
such as heroin. Narcan works by counteracting life-
threatening depression of the central nervous system and
respiratory system. Julie was also given 10 mg of Labet-
alol to stabilize her blood pressure and bicarbonate of
soda because an initial toxicology screen showed that she
had metabolic acidosis. The bicarbonate would work to
help reduce the acid in her stomach.

Julie's condition was such that she was intubated to
help her breath. She was given Ativan to help her muscles
relax.

The responding emergency room doctor noted that
Julie seemed unresponsive to pain. James told them that
his wife had been treated on September 2 for nausea and
was undergoing treatment for renal deficiency.

James said Julie had not consumed any alcohol or
smoked cigarettes. She did not use any drugs. She had no
psychiatric history.

Detective Bailey found himself thinking that suicide
seemed unlikely.

Lynn Nuti pulled another report from a folder on her desk. Dr. Brian Minsk had been treating Julie for the past two months for nausea and vomiting. At that time, Julie was not dizzy or unsteady on her feet, as she'd been when she'd come to the emergency room three days ago. Minsk found that Julie had a condition known as esophagitis, an inflammation of the esophagus that is usually caused by gastroesophageal reflux disease. He placed her on steroids because of the autoimmune disease and referred her to a kidney doctor.

"Is there anything else, anything in nature, that could cause the same symptoms as ethylene glycol poisoning?" Bailey asked Nuti.

She shook her head no. He had the feeling she'd already followed up on that possibility on her own.

Bailey was baffled. This was just plain bizarre. How would someone unintentionally ingest antifreeze? It didn't make any sense. He found himself wondering about Julie's husband, James Keown, who he knew he'd need to speak with next.

CHAPTER 6

Although Julie was known as down-to-earth and satisfied with her life, James always seemed to want more—a
better job, a bigger title, a more expensive car.

Since the time he was a small child, everyone knew
that James, or JP as he called himself at work, had big
dreams and big aspirations for his life as a talk-radio personality. He had been voted "Most Likely to Succeed" in
his 1992 graduating class at Jefferson City High School
in Missouri, and it surprised no one when he showed up at
their ten-year reunion driving a top-of-the-line Mercedes,
back from Chicago, where—as he casually told his former classmates—he was now the voice of ESPN Radio.
He had moved to the job in the Chicago radio market
after starting his career at the small talk-radio station in
his hometown of Jefferson City and then moving up to a
larger station in Kansas City, Missouri, after college.

Some, like his lifelong friend Betsy Dudenhoeffer,

already settled with her husband, Mark, and several children, were a bit envious when they saw how much of a success JP had become.

But then, she wasn't surprised. Since the first day she'd met him, in Mrs. Jones's kindergarten class, James had had big dreams. Even back then, he'd dressed for success, usually with a neat bow tie and button-down shirt. Everyone seemed to just know that James was going places.

He always seemed to act older than his age, which Betsy attributed to his having grown up living with a father who was a major force in state politics. Jim Keown, James's father—a well-known and respected lobbyist in Jefferson City, the state capital—passed away when James was a young man, leaving James's mother, Betty, to raise James and his siblings. James was one of five Keown siblings, but he had the closest relationship with his little sister Shawna, who was more than ten years younger. He had very limited contact with his three older siblings, two of whom lived outside of Missouri.

Although James's showing up in junior high with a briefcase and copy of the *New York Times* every day seemed natural to those who knew his family background, his actions didn't fit in with the rest of his classmates.

James wasn't necessarily popular in the traditional sense. His red hair and freckled skin gave him a somewhat nerdy appearance. At one point during high school, he even experimented with using makeup to conceal the freckles. He pursued an interest in debate and drama, setting him apart from the jocks on the football team. He was active in numerous clubs and groups, including Spanish Club, Student Council, the Chess Club, History Club, Model United Nations, and the Harvard Model Congress Team. He was also involved with a club that taught high school students the basics for running their own businesses.

But his lack of athletics aside, James was always the life of the party. Whenever a group gathered, James could be found in the center, talking, engaging those around him, almost like a younger version of the politicians he encountered when he went to the statehouse with his father. He had the ability to fit into whatever social situation he was in at the time.

That gift of gab and ambition impressed radioman Warren Krech when James first marched into the KLIK radio station in Jefferson City at the age of twelve. He may have been young, but James was full of confidence as he told Krech he wanted a job at the station. Krech hired the young man, launching his radio career.

In 1993, Mike McCartney had just been named interim program director at the KCMO radio station in Kansas City when James walked into the station looking to get hired for a weekend DJ position on the station's FM oldies station.

"You couldn't help [but like him] when you first met the guy," McCartney recalled. "He had a real passion for radio; you could just kind of tell he had it all together."

Hiring James for the weekend spot was a no-brainer for McCartney, and James soon began to fill other spots when another DJ was sick or needed the day off. "He'd work whenever you wanted him to; he'd be there in a minute," McCartney said. "He was real dependable."

The station, which Missouri native Harry Truman had once owned a share in, had a long-standing reputation for providing news talk radio and local traffic on their AM station, while their FM station was a well-known oldies music station. James, who went by the on-air name JP O'Neil, also did some work for the campus radio station at William Jewell College, in Liberty, where he was going to school. The college, in a suburb on the northeast side of Kansas City, was about a fifteen-minute drive from the station. JP had also worked for a station in Jefferson City, he told McCartney.

McCartney was pleased with his new hire and genuinely liked JP, who had an enthusiasm for radio that was almost infectious. *This is the kind of guy who's going to go places*, McCartney thought at the time.

But James's radio voice was horrible. When he first started out in Kansas City, he had what those in the radio business would call a "Ron Radio Voice," which was a stereotypical radio voice, almost like he was trying too hard to come up with the right sound. His voice was nasal, a little high—he just didn't have the natural radio voice, and he tried to compensate. But JP's other qualities made up for the lack of a perfect radio voice. Those other qualities included a top-notch knowledge of the radio business and his connections to the who's who in Missouri, which McCartney found amazing for someone who was maybe eighteen years old at the time.

"You don't see those kind of people come along that often," he said.

As a result, the management at the station picked up JP and kept an eye on him. At first, he was working as a DJ for the FM station, announcing songs and commercials.

While he was working there, another area radio-station group bought the station. When the new owners came on, they brought veteran Mike Elder on as the program director. He was the program director of the two AM stations, KCMO and KMBZ.

A few months later, Elder went to McCartney to talk about JP. "I really like this kid, this JP, and I need a guy to kind of serve as my secondhand man to help me run both of the AM radio stations."

It was a full-time job, and Elder asked McCartney about the potential of hiring JP. "I'm asking you if I can just steal him from you."

McCartney told him, "Look, this kid is too bright to keep around here as a DJ."

JP did not hesitate to take the job with Elder, even though he was still in college. He felt the opportunity was too good to pass up, so he put his college degree on hold to pursue his radio dream.

"He was thinking, would he get better than this, even if he graduated?" McCartney recalled.

Eventually, Mike Elder left the station to go to Minneapolis and then Chicago. At the time, there was a lot of consolidation in the radio world, with larger companies coming in to take over smaller stations. The station that Elder was working for bought another station, which became a sports station. McCartney and the others at the Kansas City station heard through the grapevine that James was going to Chicago to be a program director, which rankled a lot of them.

"For a lot of us who had been in the business a long time, it didn't sound right," McCartney said. For one thing, Chicago was a big market for radio, and JP didn't have that much experience. McCartney had worked his way up in the business and worked very hard. He had a good head for radio, and he couldn't even get promoted to program director, so he found it odd that JP was getting such a big job. To be a program director by twenty-four, you would have to be a real shining star. But for those who doubted the story, others thought perhaps it was possible—after all, JP was very talented and he'd worked with Elder before.

But maybe JP needed that bigger job to support his lifestyle, McCartney thought, as he recalled the fancy BMW that JP had gone out and purchased soon after getting the assistant director job under Mike Elder. He'd wondered how JP, who was making a salary of maybe $40,000 a year, could afford such a nice car. But he also knew that JP's father, the influential lobbyist, had left his son something of an inheritance when he'd passed away.

Regardless, about a year after he went to Chicago, James returned to Kansas City and took another radio job with KCMO, which had been bought out again and become Susquehanna Radio. James hadn't changed a bit, especially when it came to his love of the finer things. He was the first in line to test-drive the new two-seat BMWs at a local dealership in Kansas City when the dealership invited the local radio and TV stations in to see the cars. James just had to get his hands on the vehicle, McCartney recalled, and he had people taking pictures of him posing in the car. It was clear from the photos that James's appetite for being viewed as a big shot was growing. The photo of James in the fancy car was just another example of how he wanted to portray himself to those around him as a much greater financial success than he actually was.

CHAPTER 7

As far as Detective Jon Bailey was concerned, Kevin Rankins looked like he could've still been in high school. Rankins was technically a hospital intern, but he looked years younger than someone who had completed medical school. Fresh-faced, with short dark hair and a trim physique, he reminded Bailey of TV doctor prodigy Doogie Howser. Rankins had arrived in Nuti's office and the detectives decided to speak with him before they met with James Keown.

Rankins told Bailey and Stephen Taranto that he had a bad feeling about Julie Keown's illness. He found the nature of the case and the actions of James Keown suspicious. Though he was just an intern, it was Rankins who had first approached Nuti earlier that day.

Rankins had met Julie on the afternoon of August 20, 2004, along with her husband, James. Julie's speech had been slurred, and she was a little dizzy. James had been extremely cordial and had even gone overboard to offer Rankins information about his wife's condition.

Rankins noticed that James answered about 80 percent of the questions on Julie's behalf. Rankins's training kicked into gear; he thought back to the warning signs he had been taught to look for, and he started to wonder if Julie was the victim of domestic violence.

"I'm just so tired," Julie lamented to Rankins as he talked to her.

Rankins had felt an instant camaraderie with Julie, who told him she was a nurse. He checked in on her daily for the next three days. She always asked him about her lab tests, and Rankins found himself explaining the results to her. Julie was very concerned about getting healthy again. With her desire to get well and her medical knowledge, she was a truly engaged patient. James was equally engaged, and he sat by her bedside like any loyal husband would do in the same situation.

But Rankins still couldn't shake the feeling of unease he'd had when Julie first came into the hospital. Although he didn't think James was necessarily a bad guy, he also knew that hospital protocol meant he had to ask the question. So one day, when James was out of the room, Rankins approached Julie about the issue.

"Julie, I don't mean to make you uncomfortable, but I'm kind of required to ask you this," he began. "Do you feel safe at home?"

Julie looked shocked and assured him she felt very safe.

James walked back in the room at that moment, and Julie turned to him. "Kevin just asked me if you beat me," she said, laughing.

James laughed, too, and Rankins laughed with them,

but inside he had an uneasy feeling. He didn't like the way that James had avoided responding to the question.

Rankins continued to check in on Julie, who always wanted to know what was going on. Had her condition changed? Had she improved? Did they have any idea of what was causing her illness?

James also spoke to Rankins alone a few times, and he seemed at a loss for what could be wrong with his wife, telling the young doctor that in their eleven years together, his wife had only been sick three times.

Eventually, Julie's condition stabilized, and she was discharged from the hospital under the care of a kidney specialist. Rankins called Julie a week later to find out how she was doing. James answered the phone.

"Oh, hey, Kevin, Julie's in the shower, but I'm glad you called," James said. "She's doing OK." He then passed the phone to his wife, who told the doctor that no, she still wasn't feeling very well. Rankins suggested that she call her primary-care doctor to have some new blood work done.

Julie e-mailed Rankins later to let him know she had followed up with her regular doctor.

Rankins was relieved. But then, on the morning of September 5, less than a week later, he again saw James in the hospital.

He asked James what was going on and if Julie was OK. James told him that on Friday, September 3, his wife had seemed fine. She'd gone for a walk or two outside, and they went out to dinner that evening.

"We had a great day," James told him.

But on Saturday morning, Julie was tired and stayed in bed all morning. She felt dizzy every time she tried to get up. Around noon, she got out of bed, and James went to buy doughnuts at the local Shaw's Supermarket.

The store was right around the corner from their apartment. A few hours later, Julie said she wanted a Sprite, and James went back to the supermarket to get her some. A few hours later, Julie had to use the bathroom but told James she wasn't sure she could walk.

Rankins's brow furrowed in worry, but he didn't have long to think about what he had just been told. His pager went off. A code blue, which meant someone was having a heart attack. And it was in Julie's room. James watched as Rankins ran toward Julie's room, but he did not follow him.

After Julie's condition was stabilized, Rankins went right back to James, who was still sitting outside in the hallway. James was crying. He looked up at the doctor.

"Is she still alive?"

Rankins nodded his head yes. He sat with James for three hours, leaving occasionally to check on Julie's condition. Although she had been stabilized, Julie's kidneys were shutting down. She was in a coma and the outlook was grim for any kind of recovery. Rankins thought it was odd that James was not pushing him for details about Julie's prognosis. James seemed content to chitchat and talk about sports. Every once in a while, his eyes would tear up, and once he asked to borrow Rankins's cell phone. He told Rankins he wanted to call family and friends and had left his own cell phone at home.

Rankins eventually left James around two that afternoon, but he saw him again at nine that night, in Julie's room. James was eating a sandwich. Rankins knew that the latest tests on Julie had shown that she had ethylene glycol poisoning. James knew the results as well. But like earlier in the day, he did not push Rankins for details or ask questions.

Kevin Rankins was starting to feel uneasy.

On Monday morning, September 6, Rankins returned

to check on Julie Keown again. This time, James was joined by Julie's parents, Jack and Nancy Oldag, and Julie's best friend, Heather LeBlanc. James went over to Rankins right away and hugged him. He seemed overwhelmingly thankful and glad to see him.

The Oldags and Heather LeBlanc immediately began asking Rankins questions about ethylene glycol poisoning. How had Julie gotten the poison in her body? What did it mean for her prognosis? Was she going to die? Nancy Oldag wanted to know if there were any household chemicals or products that might contain ethylene glycol, but Rankins explained that there were not.

James stood back, never asking any questions that morning. He only spoke up to tell the group that Julie had barely drunk any of the Sprite he'd gone out to get her on Saturday.

"I drank most of it," he said.

The next morning, Rankins met up with James again at the hospital. Again, James embraced him in a crushing hug and then introduced him to a friend, Ted Willmore, an emergency room doctor.

"You're amazing," James told Rankins that morning. All day, James repeated this to the group gathered at the hospital, which left Rankins feeling uncomfortable with the attention and thinking it was a bit over the top.

Later that day, James approached Rankins in the hallway. "So, what is the hospital's role in determining cause of death?" he asked the intern.

Rankins was a bit taken aback by the question, especially because Julie was still alive.

"We can provide an autopsy," he told James.

James appeared to think about the answer before posing his next question. "If the hospital calls this an accidental death, is that the end of it?"

Rankins was bothered by the question. "I don't know; we don't know what's caused this."

James looked into Rankins's eyes, pleading, "I'm asking you because you're somebody I trust."

Rankins wasn't so sure the trust went both ways.

CHAPTER 8

Nancy Oldag held a tissue in her hand, but she wasn't crying. Her voice was low and soft, and she drew out her words in a way that seemed almost foreign to Detective Jon Bailey, who was used to the fast-paced way people talked, and lived, in Boston. But it wasn't just her accent that puzzled Bailey; it was her demeanor.

Her only daughter was lying in a coma upstairs, barely clinging to life, but Nancy Oldag was stoic. Bailey found himself thinking it must be a cultural difference and perhaps just the way people from the Midwest reacted. The farmer's wife certainly looked like stoicism came natural to her, with her plain manner and appearance. Nancy didn't wear any makeup, and the only jewelry she had on was her wedding ring.

As she sat before detectives Jon Bailey and Stephen Taranto in a conference room, Nancy played with the tissue. She rolled it out, pulled it, and rolled it out again. Bailey wondered if that simple repetitive movement was perhaps what was allowing her to remain so calm as the two detectives asked her how she thought her daughter could have ingested the ethylene glycol.

"I have my thoughts as to how she got that in her system," Nancy said, but did not elaborate, as if she was not going to share those thoughts unless forced to by the two detectives.

Bailey and Taranto didn't push her, though, and Nancy continued in her slow way to tell the two what she knew about Julie's illness. Her daughter's doctor, Dr. Miguel Divo, had indicated that it appeared Julie had been receiving small doses of the poison for somewhere between one and two months, evidenced by the history of her symptoms. Julie had then received one big dose, what would become the fatal dose, on Saturday, based on lab tests that detected the level of poison in her body.

Nancy Oldag had last seen her daughter just two weeks prior, shortly after she'd been discharged from the hospital the last time. Nancy and her husband, Jack, had flown out to the East Coast from their Missouri farm after learning that Julie had kidney disease. They were told then that Julie would eventually need a kidney transplant. During that trip, the Oldags had also done some sightseeing with their daughter and son-in-law. James drove them by Harvard University and pointed out the building where he attended classes. Later, they stopped at the co-op bookstore, where he bought shirts for the couple that said "My Son Attends Harvard."

Julie told her mother that her kidneys might have had an allergic reaction to the protonic medicine she had been prescribed for nausea. Julie had been getting sick and actually had an episode at home earlier that summer before her parents' visit. She woke James up, and he brought her to the hospital, where she found out she would have to have dialysis because her kidneys were scarred. Though doctors had diagnosed her with the preexisting kidney disease, the symptoms were worse than expected based on her diagnosis. When she lived in Missouri, Julie never got sick, her mother told the detectives.

When she last saw her daughter, back in August, Nancy Oldag told them, Julie had seemed tired and had a low-grade fever. Her blood pressure was elevated, and Julie was concerned about what impact a transplant and dialysis would have on her plans to get pregnant. Her doctor told her that if she did get pregnant, it would be classified as a high-risk pregnancy.

The detectives asked Nancy about the relationship between James and Julie. The couple, Nancy said, was very supportive and respectful of each other. Julie was worried that she might not be able to have children and would not be able to hold down her job because of her illness.

"Did your daughter have any problems with any enemies out here?" Detective Bailey asked, on the off chance they might find another avenue to pursue in the investigation.

"No," Nancy said, shaking her head, adding that both James and Julie worked out of their home, so they hadn't gotten to know very many people in Massachusetts. They'd only been in the state since January, and James was not only attending classes at Harvard, but also still working for the Learning Exchange. The company had allowed him to keep his job because he convinced them that his studies at Harvard would help him perform his marketing job even better. Nancy did not know of any friends he had met during his classes there.

Julie had been to visit her family in Missouri in June.

She hadn't looked good then either. There had been dark rings under her eyes when she arrived. But she'd started to feel better by the end of the visit and had told her mother that it was the fresh air.

But when Julie returned to Boston, she started feeling sick again. James also felt under the weather, and Julie told her mother they had the flu.

As the detectives were about to wrap up their questioning, Nancy told them that there was something else she felt they should know. James and Julie quarreled because James could not hold down a job. In fact, Nancy said, he seemed to change jobs every couple of years. The latest move, which brought them to Waltham, had not been Julie's idea. Julie, her mother said, did not want to move to Boston.

Detective Bailey could sense that Nancy didn't approve of James's tendency to change jobs so frequently. She said that he'd had a job in radio when he and Julie were first married, then went on to build websites. In Chicago, he worked for ESPN, but he quit that job; then he worked for Susquehanna Radio in Kansas City, but his job was eliminated.

He appeared to have finally gotten out of radio for good when he took his current marketing job at the Learning Exchange, but recently Julie had found out that James had an interview with WRKO in Boston. It wasn't so much that Julie didn't like him working in radio, but when he was in radio, he switched jobs often, and she wanted her husband to hold down a steady job.

At 7:40 p.m., Jack Oldag, fifty-eight, sat down with the detectives. Like his wife, he was very matter-of-fact, stoic, but they could tell he was upset. Unlike his wife, he had more to say about how his daughter could have gotten poisoned.

Although sweet tasting, drinking antifreeze was an extremely painful and drawn-out way to kill oneself. As a nurse, Julie would have had access to a host of medications that could have provided a much less painless, and faster, way to commit suicide, he said.

"I'd bet my last dollar, Julie would not [knowingly] drink it. If she had a personal problem, she'd go after it; she's an ICU nurse, and she'd devise a more positive way to do it," he said. "My son-in-law hasn't given me any reason that he'd do it, but he's the only one I can think of."

James Keown didn't let his wife out of his sight, Jack Oldag said, but he didn't know of any problems between them. "I don't think money's a problem; she's putting fifteen hundred a month into savings," he said. "They moved to Boston because James got a scholarship to Harvard."

Jack Oldag did not know of any domestic violence or problems between his daughter and her husband. Their relationship, he said, was "good" and the only odd thing was that James had seemed to be going out of his way to be overly nice to Julie lately.

The detectives asked about Julie's trip home in June. Jack explained that his daughter's complexion had not looked normal and had had a sickly, dark appearance. Her face seemed "puffy," which also gave the look of someone who was not well.

Jack affirmed his wife's statement that Julie rarely got sick. The only thing he could remember was a urinary tract infection about ten years before.

There was something that was bothering him, though, Jack said. One of the doctors taking care of his daughter, an Austrian man, had told the Oldags that James had called the hospital at 11 a.m. Saturday about Julie's worsening condition. The doctor told James to bring her to the hospital immediately. The part that didn't fit, Jack said, was that he knew Julie hadn't been brought to the hospital until that night.

"If my daughter didn't do this to herself, statistically, it had to be my son-in-law," Jack told the detectives.

Detective Bailey was starting to have the same sense, but he knew it was just a hunch at this point.

The other thing, Jack said, was that James had told them that Julie had gone out for a walk on Saturday night. He told the Oldags that he had scolded Julie for leaving the house without telling him.

James thought there was the possibility that somebody had cleaned out a radiator and put the old antifreeze in a soda bottle. He also suggested to the Oldags that because Julie was taking the prescription drug prednisone, which made her spaced out and not completely coherent, she might have actually picked up a bottle of discarded antifreeze while out on her walk and taken a sip. James's theory about how his wife had ingested the sweet-tasting poison was far-fetched to say the least, but everyone was clutching at straws at this point.

James had called the Oldags at about 11 p.m. central time to tell them that he'd taken Julie to the hospital and she was on a breathing tube. Sunday morning, James called them again. This time, Julie was unconscious.

By 7 p.m. Sunday, the Oldags were landing at Logan International Airport in Boston. James had offered to pick them up.

What kind of husband volunteers to leave his critically ill wife at a time like that to go to the airport? Bailey wondered. Why hadn't he just told them to take a cab?

The detectives also spoke with Julie's brother, Chad Oldag, an auto mechanic, who told them he was familiar with ethylene glycol. There was no way someone would ingest the stuff willingly, Chad told them.

"If you get it in your mouth, you spit it out," he said.

Chad had spoken with his sister the Wednesday prior to see how she was doing. She was concerned about the dialysis and how it would impact her ability to have children. He hadn't seen her during her last trip home in June.

Chad didn't know of any problems between the couple. As for James's claim that Julie had disappeared on a walk alone that Saturday, Chad didn't buy it. "I don't believe that; I don't believe that happened," he said, adding that it was not his sister's style to leave without telling someone where she was going.

At 8:30 p.m., Nancy Oldag walked back into the conference room. The detectives followed up on some lingering questions they had after speaking with Jack Oldag. They focused on the account of Julie going out for a walk on Saturday.

James had told Nancy that it was after dark on Saturday, and he hadn't known where Julie was. He claimed that he went looking for her, but when he came back to the front of the house, he'd spotted her walking back down the street. When he asked Julie where she'd been, she'd told him she wanted to take a walk because it made her bowels better.

Nancy had spoken with James three times that Saturday. During the first call, he told Nancy that Julie was in bed and not feeling well. Detective Bailey found himself wondering if Julie was making herself ill, and he considered following up on the controversial disorder known as Munchausen syndrome, where a patient seeks out unnecessary medical help in order to get attention. But when Nancy told him about her next conversation with James, Bailey changed his mind. Around noontime,

James called Nancy again to tell her that Julie was really tired and in bed sleeping. James wanted to take her to the hospital, but Julie refused, saying if she went then she would have to stay in the hospital for the rest of the weekend, Nancy recalled. Bailey ruled out Munchausen syndrome because in this case it appeared that Julie was content to stay at home.

Nancy was worried but felt her daughter was in good hands.

"Thanks for taking such good care of my daughter," she'd told James before she hung up the phone.

The third phone call to the Oldags came in at about 11 p.m. their time. James had taken Julie to the hospital, where she was having blood tests done. She was dizzy and couldn't talk. Her body was limp. She'd been carrying on a conversation on the way to the hospital, James told them, but he hadn't been able to make out what she was saying.

"Could Julie have ingested this on her own?" Bailey asked Nancy.

"No, Julie had plenty of medications; she was a nurse," Julie's mother said, adding that if her daughter had wanted to commit suicide, "why didn't she just overdose on medication?"

Bailey knew he had to ask the last question, but it was not an easy one. He took a breath. "Who could have given her the ethylene glycol?"

Nancy Oldag did not hesitate in her response. "They were with each other all the time. If it was anyone, it would have been James."

As he watched her, Bailey felt that to Nancy, as to Jack, this was the only explanation for what had happened to her daughter that made any sense, even if it was unbelievable.

There was something else that was bothering her

about James, Nancy told the two detectives. He'd told his mother-in-law that it would be OK to bury Julie in Missouri, because he probably wasn't going to stay in Boston long term.

But at the time, Julie was still alive.

CHAPTER 9

After almost a quarter century of police work, Waltham Police sergeant Brian Lambert always went into an interview with an open mind. But at the same time, he had developed the ability to gauge whether someone was telling him the truth within the first fifteen minutes of the interview.

After fifteen minutes with James Keown, Lambert knew something was not right. It wasn't necessarily *what* James told Lambert and state police sergeant Ed Forster, but *how* he told them.

Julie, James's wife, was dying upstairs in the hospital, but Lambert didn't get the sense that James was sincerely upset about his wife's prognosis. Lambert, who had been married for more than twenty years, thought about how he would've acted in the same situation.

I'd be sick to my stomach and throwing up, he thought, as he listened to James just talk and talk and talk.

Man, the guy could talk. Lambert got the impression that James was the type of guy who could convince people to believe whatever he was saying, like a professional salesman.

Like Detective Jon Bailey, Sergeant Lambert was from a law enforcement family. His father was a career police officer, and his brother and sister were also police officers. And like Bailey, Lambert hadn't always been sure he wanted to follow in his father's footsteps with police work. He'd spent a number of years working at the local Polaroid factory in material handling. But eventually, he signed up for the police entrance exam, passed, and was hired in Waltham. Though he entered police work later in life than some, he was glad he did, especially after learning that a lot of the guys he worked with at Polaroid lost their pensions.

Lambert thought of himself as an aggressive investigator, an approach that may have come from his years of working the department's special motorcycle-gang unit. Before becoming a detective, Lambert had worked on the streets in the rougher areas of Waltham. He responded to bar fights and biker brawls, some more memorable than others. Like the time one recently paroled biker returned to Waltham, and the other gang members rented a hall to throw him a welcome-home party—but although the parolee may have been welcomed home, a number of his cronies were arrested and taken to jail after their rowdy behavior during the party resulted in the police being called to break up the melee.

Lambert's assignment to report to the Newton-Wellesley Hospital that afternoon seemed much more mundane compared to his days with the gang unit, but he was glad to learn that he would be working with state police sergeant Ed Forster. The two knew each other from several previous cases and worked well together. They had once spent eighteen months successfully investigating the murder of a jewelry-store owner in Waltham who'd been murdered by three men who attempted to hold up the store. After more than a year, they were able to get enough evidence to charge the killers.

The two investigators spent about forty-five minutes speaking with James Keown at the hospital on the afternoon of Tuesday, September 7, 2004. Lambert was initially surprised that James had even agreed to leave his wife's side to speak with them.

If that was my wife, I wouldn't have come down, he thought.

Lambert had never dealt with an interview subject like James before. In addition to his seemingly normal demeanor during an unimaginable time, James was able to recite very specific information about his wife's condition. He knew exact dates, times, doctors' names, and the names and amounts of prescriptions she was taking. The level of detail on the prescriptions was so exact that Lambert wondered how James could remember them off the top of his head; he wasn't sure the person taking the medications would remember details that were so minute and specific, let alone the patient's spouse.

How does this guy know all this stuff? And how does he stay so composed?

At one point, James had looked like he might break down and cry, but just as quickly, he'd composed himself and gone on talking. Lambert got the sense that the tears were an act.

James went through the background on Julie's illness, when her symptoms came on, when she first went to the hospital, and what had led to her most recent hospitalization. As the three talked about ethylene glycol poisoning, James volunteered that he had given his father-in-law, Jack Oldag, all of his antifreeze before he and Julie moved to Massachusetts. Lambert thought this was a strange piece of information for James to offer, but then the entire interview had seemed a little off to the seasoned investigator.

As Lambert and Forster prepared to wrap up the interview, there was a lull in the conversation as they sat at the table before James looked up at them.

"Do you have any specific questions of me, officer?"

Lambert and Forster asked James if he would give permission for them to look inside the duplex the couple shared on School Street. They planned to look around to see if there was anything in the residence that could be tied to Julie's poisoning.

"My wife's upstairs, and I can't go now," James responded.

They asked if there was someone whom James could send in his place, and he suggested his good friend Ted Willmore, who had arrived in Boston after learning about Julie's condition. James was informed of his right to refuse the search by the two investigators, but he willingly signed a form giving his consent for the police to search the duplex. By signing the form, James also gave his permission for the police to take anything from the residence that might be helpful in the investigation into Julie's poisoning.

When James asked if he could go get a drink of water, Lambert and Forster took a break from the interview, which was almost over anyway. They met up with Jon Bailey and Lieutenant Jim Connolly, of the Massachusetts State Police, in the hallway. The four investigators knew they were in for a long night; the early hours of an investigation are often the most critical time for collecting key evidence in a case, and everyone present knew that. Protocol in Massachusetts dictated that the state police had jurisdiction in any cases of untimely deaths. While

Julie was still alive, it was not expected that she would survive. Two state police officers from the special investigative unit of the Middlesex County District Attorney's Office had already arrived at the hospital: Ed Forster, who had been interviewing James with Brian Lambert, and supervisor Jim Connolly. Connolly, a tall man, at six feet three, and given to wearing dark suits, had more than twenty years of experience with the state police and was respected among the region's law enforcement officers as an extremely experienced investigator. Although known for being laid-back, and at times quiet, Connolly didn't miss a thing. When he said something, other investigators knew to listen, because he was usually right.

By law in Massachusetts, all deaths or incidents in which a death is likely, even unattended deaths that are not murders, fall under the jurisdiction of the local district attorney's office. Each district attorney's office has its own specially assigned Massachusetts State Police Detective Unit, which is assigned to investigate cases involving death along with the local police department. Connolly was the head of the district attorney's internal detective unit, and he, along with the Waltham police, would investigate but provide all facts to a prosecutor assigned to the case. Based on those facts, the district attorney's office would then make the decision of whether to prosecute. Throughout the investigation, the detectives would work closely with the prosecutors assigned to the case, even if no charges had been filed, to ensure that any legal matters were appropriately dealt with, such as search warrants or subpoenas.

As they waited for James to return, the four investigators compared notes. Lambert and Forster thought that James's account of his wife's illness was a bit too rehearsed. They wondered if perhaps this was a suicide. Bailey disagreed. He had a feeling that something was just not right with the situation, that James wasn't acting how a husband would typically act when his wife was fighting for her life.

Lambert and Forster also relayed to the other two that James had told them he'd gone to a CVS Pharmacy to ask about potential medication interactions for the prescriptions Julie was on.

"That would be easy to verify; they have surveillance video," Bailey responded. "Which CVS did he go to?" There were three CVS stores in Waltham.

"I don't know; I'll have to ask him," Lambert responded.

"There's one right down the street from him," Bailey said. "That would be the logical one."

Just then, James walked up to the group, a glass of water in his hand. He stopped, looked at the police, and immediately began apologizing for not asking if anyone else had wanted a drink.

"Oh, how rude of me," he said. "Can I get you guys something to drink?"

Bailey listened in disbelief and again found himself with a bad feeling about James Keown. Once James was out of earshot, he turned to Steve Taranto.

"Steve, I'm telling you, this guy did it."

CHAPTER 10

The duplex that James and Julie Keown rented was on the south side of Waltham's city limits, where the houses were old and close together, though their unit was brand new and had three levels. It was just off the main road behind the Three Fortunes Chinese restaurant, a small yellow-brick building that was a favorite take-out spot for locals.

Ted Willmore, a professional-looking young man with glasses and red hair, met Sergeant Brian Lambert and several other detectives at the door.

Ted had known James and Julie since college. His wife, Leila, was one of Julie's best friends, and the Willmores had considered themselves very close friends of the Keowns for the past decade. Ted had immediately flown to Boston when he heard how sick Julie was. Ted, an emergency room doctor, fully understood how serious ethylene glycol poisoning was for Julie. When he mentioned to the investigators that he was a doctor, Sergeant Lambert asked him about ethylene glycol poisoning, and Ted explained that a person would have to ingest a lot of the poison to die. He offered to log on to a physicians network using either James's or Julie's computer to find out more information for the investigators.

Lambert looked up and did a double take as he saw James Keown walking across the room.

What is he doing here? Lambert again found himself thinking that if it had been his wife lying near death in the hospital, he would never have left her side. James had told them at the hospital that he could not leave, but now suddenly he was at the duplex. It didn't make sense to Lambert, especially because Ted Willmore was already there to let the investigators inside.

What's wrong with this guy?

He didn't linger on James as he and Ted walked up to the third floor of the duplex, where the couple had a home office. After a minute of trying to log on to the computer, Ted turned to Lambert.

"This isn't working," he said.

The two started looking at the computers and noticed there were no towers or hard drives under the monitors. There were two workstations, and neither had a tower containing the hard drive; neither worked. Wires were hanging down from the back of the monitors. Lambert found this very odd, especially because both James and Julie worked from home.

Meanwhile, the other investigators on the scene were collecting potential evidence. They seized several items, including an empty Sprite bottle they found in a barrel on the deck behind the residence. Waltham police officer Lucas Hernandez took photos of the inside of the duplex, including the bedroom. The duplex was in good condition. The inside was tastefully furnished, neat, tidy, and lived in.

Ed Forster approached James during the search and asked about searching the Ford Expedition he drove. James agreed and initialed a sentence added onto the consent form indicating that it was OK for the officers to search his vehicle.

Forster found a couple of eyedroppers in the back of the Expedition that James said were for the couple's cat. James's explanation seemed believable to Forster at the time, and the investigator did not take the eyedroppers as evidence. In the early stage of the search and investigation, the investigators were focused on finding anything that looked like antifreeze or ethylene glycol, and the eyedropper did not appear to be consistent with that, or related to Julie's poisoning. At the time, Detective Bailey was the only investigator who was suspicious of James.

It was late, well past 11 p.m., when Jon Bailey and Steve Taranto also arrived at James and Julie's duplex after being told that Ted Willmore was interested in speaking with them. Ted met the two detectives at the door. Though he was serious in his role as a physician, Ted had a youthful, fun side, usually seen when he organized roasts for other hospital employees or wrote comedic songs for special events. But he was all business that night. Ted seemed eager to speak with the two detectives and agreed to go to the police station with them for an interview.

As the three discussed the plan, James suddenly walked up beside Ted.

"I don't understand how this could happen," James said, shaking his head. Bailey noticed there seemed to be no emotion with the statement. It was the first time he'd seen James outside of the hospital setting. Again, James, though subdued, did not seem overly upset about his wife's condition. And again Bailey found himself wondering why James would voluntarily leave Julie's side for something that didn't require his presence when she was in critical condition.

The thought stayed in the back of his mind as Bailey and Taranto went to the police station with Ted Willmore. Once seated in a conference room at the police station, Ted told the detectives that he and his wife had recently taken a trip with the Keowns, along with another couple, Mike and Stephanie Webb. The three couples had gone together to Sunset Beach, North Carolina, back in August, though they had to cut the vacation short because a hurricane was forecast to hit the area where they were staying. During one conversation with her old girlfriends, Julie had commented that she was so excited they had all married well and gone on to have successful lives and careers.

Julie was ill at the time and occasionally napped during the trip, but she seemed to have a normal appetite, Ted told them. Bailey observed the medical slant of Ted's observations as he took notes. It was clear that as a doctor, Ted was trying to look for signs and symptoms in Julie that might help explain her condition.

The detectives asked Ted what he knew about Julie's sickness. Ted had already spoken with a toxicologist he knew, and he knew that it would take 30 ccs of the ethylene glycol to cause kidney failure. As for how someone could ingest the substance, Ted said there were only three ways: suicide, accident, or homicide. There were no other ways to ingest the poison.

James had called Ted on Sunday, September 5, and the young doctor had arrived in Boston at 1:30 Monday afternoon. Even after their move to Boston, the Willmores stayed in regular contact with James and Julie, often speaking by phone. When they'd lived in Missouri, they usually got together for dinner or to visit about once a month. During these get-togethers and throughout the course of their friendship, Ted always felt that James and Julie had a normal relationship. James was a devoted husband and a very friendly guy.

Ted said he had no suspicions about James, but he did mention that he suspected money was tight for the Keowns. While in North Carolina, James had told Ted that he was looking for a new job. He wanted to start his own company, but he needed some capital to start it up. And before the trip, James had been supposed to mail Ted a check for seven hundred dollars to cover their portion of the stay. But Ted never received the check. When they got together, James told Ted that he had mailed the check, but he wrote him another one, for five hundred and forty dollars. That check did not clear the bank. Ultimately, though, Ted had decided to let the matter go because of Julie's medical issues and her friendship with his wife. As a doctor, he could afford to pay a little more.

It was late before Jon Bailey made it home that night. When he finally climbed in bed, he could not sleep. He tossed and turned as he lay next to his wife, Doreen, trying to process everything he had learned. On one hand, he felt Julie Keown's case was definitely going to become a murder case. There was no doubt she was going to die.

Any suggestions that she had ingested the poison on purpose bothered Bailey. She was a nurse, with access to all sorts of medications. If anyone knew how painful ethylene glycol poisoning would be, it was her.

Could it have been an accident? But he ruled out accidental ingestion when he came back to Dr. Miguel Divo's belief that she had been ingesting the poison for at least one month.

Bailey also puzzled over the fact that the state police

had not found any antifreeze in or around the Keowns' apartment. So where could Julie have gotten the poison?

It had to be a murder. But who would have wanted her dead? Despite James Keown's lack of visible emotion, everyone said he was a nice guy. There was no history of domestic violence. He did not fit the profile of a killer. He was probably in shock, Bailey thought, and his lack of emotion could be his own way of dealing with the situation.

He knew that everyone involved would remain a suspect until he could rule them out. But if it wasn't James Keown who was poisoning his wife, Bailey wondered, who else could it be?

CHAPTER 11

Detective Jon Bailey had no doubt that his first case in his new job was going to become his first murder investigation.

There was, however, doubt among some of the other investigators during those initial days. Even if this was a murder, how would they ever be able to prove that someone had intentionally made Julie drink antifreeze? With no family or friends in the Waltham area, she was the only witness to her condition, other than her husband, James. And James claimed to have seen nothing; he was as baffled as the investigators as to how his healthy, vibrant wife had been poisoned.

Still, Bailey couldn't shake the feeling that James was involved somehow, and as he followed up on leads on the second day of the investigation, September 8, 2004, he put in a call to both the Kansas City and Liberty, Missouri, police departments to find out if there was any reported

history of domestic violence between the Keowns. There
wasn't, though Bailey also knew that wasn't completely
uncommon in domestic-violence cases. Victims often
kept their situation to themselves for fear of repercussions
or guilt over staying in the situation. Still, the likelihood
was that there was nothing off in James and Julie's relationship. After all, everyone whom Bailey and the other
investigators had spoken to so far had described a loving
and considerate relationship between the young couple.

Bailey became the primary investigator for Waltham
police on the case, while Lieutenant Jim Connolly assumed the lead role for the Massachusetts State Police.
Connolly had called Bailey that morning with news that
Julie would be taken off life support that day. And despite
the fact that his wife would take her last breath by the end
of the day, James had found time to call state policeman
Ed Forster to tell the investigator that he'd remembered
Julie talking about whether it hurt when you die. As a
result, she had purchased 250 milliliters of chloroform
in May over the Internet. He was not sure if she'd ever
received the chloroform, but he felt that the investigators
should know. Forster passed the odd information along
to Jim Connolly. Later that day, James again left the hospital to meet Connolly at the Waltham duplex and give
Connolly two laptops that Julie had used.

Julie Keown passed away less than two hours later.

Several hours after that, James called Julie's best friend,
Heather LeBlanc, on her cell phone. Heather and her
husband, Ray, had left the hospital after Julie had been
taken off life support at 1 p.m. During the phone call,
James told Heather that he'd heard her and Julie joking
about suicide on the phone recently. Heather became
angry at the strange accusation, and she told James that
suicide was *not* something the two of them ever talked
about. There was no way that Julie had committed suicide,

Heather told James in no uncertain terms. James backed off and suggested that the conversation must have been between Julie and Leila Willmore, Ted's wife.

Several other investigators followed down leads during that second day, September 8, 2004. Sergeant Brian Lambert and Detective Lucas Hernandez, of the Waltham Police Department, conducted a check of the Keowns' neighborhood that afternoon. They canvassed the area and spoke with the seven residents in the immediate area. None of the residents had really even had a conversation with the couple. They recognized them from a distance as neighbors, but other than that, none had any knowledge of the couple or their relationship. Deborah Singleton, one of the neighbors, watched as the detectives canvassed the neighborhood and realized that something must be wrong. She didn't know the couple well but had said hello a few times and had always found James to be very friendly, personable, and bubbly. She assumed that he attended Harvard because of a large bumper sticker on his SUV that had the university's emblem on it.

The couple's landlord, Greg Stocklan, who lived in the other side of the duplex, told Lambert and Hernandez that he had not noticed anything suspicious about the couple. The only thing that had struck Stocklan as odd was that he was never invited into the duplex after James and Julie moved in. There were occasions when he had gone to their door and had conversations with them on the front porch area, but they'd never asked him to come inside.

———————————

Bailey and Connolly decided to back away from contacting Julie's parents or husband until after her funeral. And before Julie could be returned to Missouri to be laid to rest, the medical examiner needed to complete the autopsy.

Dr. Faryl Sandler conducted an autopsy on Julie on September 9, 2004. She found that Julie had suffered from kidney failure as a result of the toxin, ethylene glycol, which was an acute and chronic poisoning. There was scar tissue present on her kidneys and no indication of cancer in any of her medical records. Sandler's conclusions were based on both the autopsy she conducted as well as doctors' notes and police reports. Julie's doctors had initially thought that she might have been suffering from autoimmune disease and had put her on steroids as a result. The medical examiner said she did not feel the ethylene glycol poisoning was self-induced, as it would have been too painful to continue for such an extended period of time.

Although ethylene glycol has been recognized as a poison for half a century, cases of accidental ingestion remain all too common among both children and pets. American Association of Poison Control Centers statistics state that approximately 1,400 children accidentally ingest antifreeze each year, and the Veterinary School at Washington State University compiled statistics that estimated that ten thousand dogs and cats are poisoned each year by antifreeze.

Diagnosing those cases is often challenging, as the symptoms associated with ethylene glycol poisoning, such as nausea, vomiting, and central nervous system depression, are similar to the symptoms for a number of other poisonings and illnesses. In the case of accidental ingestion, a person might not be aware that he or she ingested the poison and thus not mention the possibility to his or her doctor. Treatment is effective in combating ethylene glycol poisoning, but the challenges in diagnosing cases may result in a delay in initiating that treatment, as was the case with Julie Keown.

Several countries have already adopted the use of a

denatonium benzoate additive, known as a bittering agent, to make the normally sweet-tasting antifreeze taste bitter, with hopes of reducing cases of accidental ingestion. Japan, Australia, and the United Kingdom have made it a requirement to add a bittering agent to antifreeze, as have the states of Oregon, California, New Mexico, Arizona, and Maine. The investigators had been told by those who knew Julie that she would not willingly drink the substance, not necessarily because of the sweet taste but because as a nurse she knew how slow and painful a way it was to die. As a nurse, she was aware of much-less-painful drugs to take if she was truly suicidal.

Bailey and Connolly found that a condition that mimicked ethylene glycol poisoning had been at the center of the 1989 murder case against Patty Stallings. Stallings's three-month-old son was having trouble breathing and was vomiting uncontrollably when he was taken to the local emergency room. The treating doctor diagnosed the infant with ethylene glycol poisoning and he was placed into a foster home, where he became critically ill and died. Stallings was convicted of first-degree murder though she vehemently denied that she had killed her son. While in prison, she gave birth to a second son, who began displaying the same symptoms as the infant who'd died. Through testing, the second child was found to have methylmalonate in his blood and urine and a condition called methylmalonic academia. Symptoms and conditions of the genetic metabolic disorder mimic that of ethylene glycol poisoning. Stallings was convicted in the death of her first son in 1991 and sentenced to life in prison without the chance of parole. But later that year, with a new lawyer, Stallings got a new trial, and her new lawyer presented evidence the jury didn't hear at the first trial, including expert testimony that her son had died from methylmalonic academia. That diagnosis, combined with testimony that showed the initial doctors who examined the child had failed to properly diagnose him and just assumed his ailments were caused by ethylene glycol, resulted in the prosecution's decision to drop all charges against Stallings. Her criminal record was later cleared.

The two Massachusetts investigators mentioned the case to one of the prosecutors who was consulting on the case, who also had a medical background. The prosecutor said that the condition was only seen in young children, and Julie's age ruled it out as a possibility. There was also one difference between the disorder and ethylene glycol poisoning—in instances of poisoning, crystals formed in the person's body, which had been the case with Julie.

Bailey and Connolly found only a handful of cases of murder using ethylene glycol. Poison in general was pretty uncommon—according to the Federal Bureau of Investigation, only 63 of the reported 70,140 murders reported from 2000 to 2004 involved poison. The only murder weapon used less frequently was explosives.

They did, however, find that ethylene glycol had been used to poison a spouse in at least one previous murder case. Wisconsin resident Mark Jensen was charged in 2002 with having poisoned his wife, Julie, with antifreeze in 1998. Prosecutors said that Jensen had been having an affair and had poisoned his wife to be with his lover, while defense suggested that Julie Jensen had intentionally killed herself by drinking antifreeze. Jensen was found guilty in February of 2008 of the murder.

Although some of the investigators initially wondered if Julie Keown could have committed suicide, the manner of poisoning made that seem unlikely. Julie had apparently been ingesting small amounts of ethylene glycol for some time. Doctors believed she'd ingested what became the fatal dose over the Labor Day weekend. Once she consumed the poison, it was quickly absorbed from her gastrointestinal tract into her bloodstream. Within minutes to hours after she swallowed the fatal dose, Julie might have become inebriated or euphoric, similar to someone who is drunk, which was very out of character for the wholesome midwestern girl, who rarely, if ever, drank alcohol. As the poison moved through her body, Julie may have vomited or become nauseated.

Her body then went into metabolic acidosis and suffered central nervous system depression as the poison was metabolized. The amount of ethylene glycol she ingested before her death, however, was great enough to cause her to lapse into a coma. It was a painfully slow, excruciating way for someone to die, and Bailey couldn't believe that anyone would intentionally ingest something so toxic. Bailey was convinced that someone other than Julie, likely James, was responsible for her death.

That feeling didn't translate to proof, though, and Bailey got to work confirming details from the interviews he had already conducted. One of the first rules of investigations was that all details had to be independently verified. With the Keowns having no friends or family in the immediate area to question, Bailey started with the person who'd had the most contact with the couple—their landlord.

Greg Stocklan had purchased the duplex on School Street as an investment property. He moved into one side of the house with his brother and rented out the other side. James and Julie's lease on the property was good until June of 2005. The rent was two thousand dollars per month, but when they moved in, they were required to put down four thousand dollars, for the first and last months' rent. Stocklan was concerned that the couple didn't make enough money to cover the initial deposit, but James told him not to worry. The company he worked for in Missouri, the Learning Exchange, was going to pay his rent as part of his compensation package. James was the vice president of strategic ventures, he explained to Stocklan, but would be working remotely while he attended Harvard University. He provided the new land-lord with a letter from the Learning Exchange confirm-ing that the company would in fact be paying his rent. A notary from the company had signed and notarized the lease agreement.

The problem was, Stocklan told Bailey, James had *not* been paying the rent, and Stocklan was growing more and more frustrated. The rent check that James sent on July 1, 2004, had bounced. The next check he submitted, on July 10, also bounced. James was extremely apologetic as he told Stocklan that he was having a problem with his bank in Kansas City. James eventually gave Stocklan a personal check that cleared for the July rent. In August, three separate rent checks to Stocklan bounced; finally, the fourth, a cashier's check, cleared.

But the rent problems didn't end there. Just the week before, James had confided to Stocklan that he and Julie were having financial problems. He asked if Stocklan would allow them to use their last month's rent deposit toward the rent for September. Stocklan knew that Julie was having some serious health problems and felt sorry for her, so he allowed it. James gave no explanation for why his company was no longer paying his rent for him.

Detective Bailey's mind was turning as he looked at the letter and the notary stamp. The name on the stamp was JoLynn Bethke. After learning of the rent problems, Bailey found himself wondering about the nature of the relationship between Bethke and James. Was she cover-ing for him for some reason? Were they having a relation-ship? Something was off about that notary stamp, but he wouldn't learn exactly what for another two months.

Bailey was also pondering the results of a subsequent search done on September 8 by investigators inside James and Julie's duplex. Investigators had found themselves looking at a large supply of Gatorade bottles. There were ten large bottles of the blue and orange flavors of the sports drink. The funny thing was that Julie didn't even like Gatorade.

CHAPTER 12

Christina Liles had a bad feeling. She had been trying to call Julie for days, with no answer. She left messages for James as well but received no answer on his phone either. Christina and her husband, Dave, were more than worried by the time she finally got James on the phone.

"I've been trying to reach you," James said immediately when he picked up.

"That's not true," Christina told him, knowing that her caller ID showed no incoming phone calls from James's or Julie's phone numbers.

James went on to tell her that Julie had passed away several days before.

"I'm sorry to say we've lost her," James said.

Christina was devastated to learn of Julie's death but also furious at James for having kept her in the dark about it.

"I can't believe it took you a couple of days to call me," Christina said through her tears. "What happened?"

James calmly explained that Julie had slipped into a coma and died.

"No, no, no," Christina said, as she listened in disbelief to the news that her closest friend was gone forever. A voice in her head seemed to tell her this wasn't the real story. As the voice persisted, Christina had the strangest feeling that it was Julie's voice in her head telling her, *No, no, this is not what happened*.

She started to think back to some of the things she knew about James and Julie's relationship. The things that never seemed to quite make sense to her or her husband—the expensive cars both James and Julie drove, the nice house they were able to afford, the upscale riverfront loft and expensive hotels they stayed in during visits back to Kansas City after they moved to Boston. And then there was the story that James told her husband, Dave, about his position with the Learning Exchange. James explained to Dave that he was a government employee with the Learning Exchange, which was part of Homeland Security. As a result he didn't have to go through the government hiring process. He was simply grandfathered into the job. Dave was a government employee himself and always found this explanation from James a bit off to say the least. In actuality, the Learning Exchange was a nonprofit educational company that developed educational programs for students in the Kansas City area. James's job was to market the nonprofit and had nothing to do with Homeland Security.

When Christina tried to call James back a few days after the conversation about Julie's death, his phone was disconnected. The uneasy feeling she had was still there. Something just seemed off to Christina, so much so that the next day, on her way to work, she picked up her cell phone and called the Waltham Police Department, where she was connected to Jon Bailey.

Bailey had a hard time understanding Christina at first through her sobs. She sounded like someone who was absolutely devastated and grief stricken by Julie's passing.

As she tried to speak, Christina told Jon Bailey that she just had a very bad feeling about what really led to Julie's death.

"There's no way Julie did this," she said between sobs.

She explained that Julie had been working from her home since she and James had moved to Waltham. She knew that Julie didn't go anywhere without James or have any friends in the area. And she knew that Julie did not do this to herself.

Christina and Julie had kept in touch through e-mail and phone calls after the move, though it seemed that Christina was often the one to initiate contact. On August 30, Christina had even asked Julie if someone could be poisoning her. Julie had responded that wasn't possible because she and James ate the same food and he was perfectly healthy. Julie told Christina she was scared about her condition and didn't know what was going on. Christina later asked James if Julie had been tested for poison and James told her no, which was untrue—her blood had already been tested and found to contain ethylene glycol before she died.

Julie told Christina that she had a kidney defect and it had caused her creatinine levels to decline and made her dizzy quite often.

"I feel like I'm going to fall over," Julie had said one day, adding that James was so good to her. He'd picked her up when she had a spell in the bathroom and took care of her. He'd rubbed her hair and encouraged her to drink fluids to get better.

"When this is all over with and I'm better, we're going

to have a baby," Julie told her friend during one of their conversations.

There were other things about James that bothered Christina, she told the detective, like the time Julie had called her with shocking news about James.

"You're not going to believe what happened to James," Julie told Christina in January of 2004.

James had been working late at the Learning Exchange and when he went to leave, he saw a man in the parking lot with a crowbar, Julie recounted. The man told James he was having car trouble and asked for help. When James went to help him, the guy beat him up and stole his wallet.

"Oh my gosh!" Christina exclaimed.

She knew that the Learning Exchange wasn't in the best area of town, but she was still surprised by the story, especially when she thought back to her wedding. James had been on crutches then, too, and another time he'd gotten hurt when he fell out of the attic. When she told her husband the story later that day, the couple remarked how odd it was that James was always getting injured.

Christina Liles told Detective Bailey that she'd never believed James had been attacked. She thought he'd made it up to encourage Julie to move to Boston. Despite Julie's reluctance to move, Christina said she did not know of any significant problems in the marriage. Before they moved to Waltham, James and Julie had lived in a comfortable split-level home in a nice suburb of Kansas City. They had a Jaguar and a Ford Expedition and seemed to be doing well. Christina and Dave often wondered how the couple, who made about the same income as they did, managed to afford the two expensive cars. The Jaguar was something James had purchased with some inheritance he received, Julie had once confided to her friend. But James told Dave that the car had actually been given

to him by a dealership, Aristocrat Motors, in exchange
for having designed a website for them.

Another time, Julie told Christina about a lawsuit James
had against a company he used to work for. The company
refused to pay James for company items he'd purchased on
his personal credit card.

Christina had found the whole story odd, as she did
a number of things about James, but she'd kept them to
herself at the time. But now, with her friend dead, and a
nagging voice in her head telling her something wasn't
right about it, Christina decided to do some checking up
on James. When she looked in the local court records, she
found a credit-card company suing him for $8,521.41, and
she also found that the Jaguar car dealership, in Merriam,
Kansas, was trying to repossess the car.

Bailey wrote down this information for his file—yet
more instances of James bending the truth about his
financial situation.

Christina also told the detective that after Julie and
James moved to Boston, Julie grew distant. Julie e-mailed
Christina on several occasions when they were planning
to return to Kansas City for a visit, but she seldom met up
with Christina and Dave. Although Christina had offered
to give them the guest room at their house, Julie explained
that they had stayed with a friend of James's who owned a
photo studio and had a loft down by the river. The trendy
lofts were out of Christina and Dave's price range, and
they found themselves wondering out loud about the
lifestyle the couple was living. Where were they getting
enough money to keep up with the lifestyle they led?

Christina and Dave did get together with James and
Julie for dinner on one of their trips back to Kansas
City. During that dinner, Christina noticed that Julie did
not look well. She had gained some weight and looked

bloated. She was letting her dark hair grow out and had gotten a perm. James was also changing his look and letting his hair grow longer than Christina had seen it in the past.

Christina seemed determined to find answers in Julie's death, and she was deeply, deeply distressed about her loss, but at first blush, Detective Jon Bailey was a little suspicious of her phone call. He wondered if she was a friend of James's trying to get information for him about the investigation. He hadn't shared any information with James, which was standard procedure in an investigation like this, and he didn't share any information with Christina Liles.

Still, when he got off the phone with her, he put out a call to the Kansas City police to inquire about the attack outside the Learning Exchange. It never hurt to follow up, regardless of how credible he thought Christina was at that time.

When he heard their answer, he made a mental note not to discount Christina Liles just yet.

CHAPTER 13

There was a palpable feeling of disbelief inside the Immanuel Lutheran Church in Kansas City on the afternoon of September 15, 2004.

No one could believe that Julie was really gone. She had been so young, so full of life, with so many things to look forward to, such as her desire to have children. No one could understand how a vital young woman like Julie had become so ill, so unexpectedly, and simply slipped away. Pictures of Julie's smiling face adorned a room to the side of the chapel in the church where the mourners gathered before the service. A number of Julie's coworkers from Cerner greeted each other in the room and whispered softly among themselves what they knew of her death. Julie's friend Lana Koon-Anderson stood with a fellow Cerner worker, Regan Barron, before the funeral.

"I heard it was ethylene glycol," Regan whispered to Lana.

Lana didn't immediately register what ethylene glycol was, but she knew it was bad. She didn't linger on the news as she saw James. She had never met James before, but she still vividly recalled the loving way Julie had described him on their work trip to Richmond. Lana's heart went out to him as he came over to thank her for coming.

"Thank you so much; Julie just loved her Cerner people," James said as he hugged her.

James looked like he had been crying, and Lana felt incredibly sorry for him. She heard him talking to others, saying things like, "Julie would be so happy that you would remember her that way."

Like Julie, the service was simple and sweet, right down to the memory card given to mourners with the familiar words of the Twenty-third Psalm printed on the plain card.

Pastor Brian Moss described Julie as loving, sweet, and caring, a woman known for her dedication to her family and friends.

The church was full to overflowing, with some people standing in the back during the simple service. James's mother, Betty, and sister Shawna were the only relatives from the Keown side of the family at the service, which was punctuated by soft sobs and sniffling as the minister talked about Julie's short life and her impact on so many people.

As the funeral drew to a close, Lana watched as the casket with Julie's body was wheeled down the aisle of the church. She just couldn't believe that Julie was really inside that box, that she was really gone so suddenly.

Lana didn't drive to the burial, which was a bit of a way from the city. But when she got home that night, she told her husband, Mark, about the ethylene glycol in Julie's system.

"That's antifreeze," said Mark, who did not even hesitate as he told her, "she was murdered."

"No way," Lana said.

"Yeah," Mark said.

"Oh God," Lana said, and she shuddered at what her husband's words meant. She thought back to James hugging her earlier that day, and somehow she just felt he was involved.

———————————

Christina Liles still had a bad taste in her mouth about James's failure to call her for days after Julie passed away. Christina and Dave spotted James almost as soon as they walked into the public viewing reception held the day before the funeral service. He'd seen Christina, but he quickly looked away, and she walked over to him.

"Hi, how are you guys doing?" James asked.

"James, I'm so sorry," Christina said, tears welling up in her eyes.

He responded with a quick "Thanks" and walked away. *That was weird*, Christina thought. She watched as James walked around greeting people and shaking hands, more like he was at a frat party than at a wake for his wife.

The next day, after the funeral service, the pallbearers began to move the casket down the aisle, and James stood to walk behind his wife. He had a big smile on his face as he walked, stopping to shake the hands of the mourners on his way out. Christina felt sick as she realized that James looked almost relieved.

As she got into the car with her husband, Christina turned to him.

"Dave, you would have had to pull me off the floor—I would have been crying. That man was not sad at all."

By the time the mourners reached the grave site, Christina knew that the feeling in her gut was more than just a feeling. She thought about her realization as she hugged James after the burial. *I know he did this*, Christina thought. It was the worst feeling she'd ever had in her life.

CHAPTER 14

Although Christina Liles suspected James was somehow responsible for Julie's death, she did not let him know how she felt. After the funeral, James called Christina to talk. He was planning to move back to the Kansas City area, but he wasn't sure when. He told her that he would be sure to contact her after he got situated.

Christina found it strange that James wanted to move back to Kansas City so soon after Julie's death, especially when, during a previous conversation, he had told her that he planned to stay in Boston to finish his studies at Harvard. Christina asked James if it was OK with the police in Massachusetts for him to move back to Missouri. It was, he said.

Christina felt like James was trying to determine her feelings toward him. It seemed to her that he was trying to find allies as the investigation into Julie's death moved forward. The police, he told Christina, had been really nasty about Julie when they'd questioned him, saying things like, "She must have been a real bitch to live with," and then accusing him of murdering her. He said that they repeatedly asked him, "You killed your wife, didn't you?"

James went on to tell Christina that he didn't have much confidence in the police who were investigating the case. He had found out that there was a lot of corruption among the police in Middlesex County, Massachusetts, and that two policemen were being sent to jail for corruption. The medical examiner was no better, he confided to Christina, and had been accused of not conducting thorough autopsies. Speaking of autopsies, he said, he actually had to ask the hospital to do an autopsy on Julie, as they weren't going to do one.

James felt like the hospital should have found the ethylene glycol in Julie's system during the first episode she'd had two weeks prior to her death. His confidence was so low with regard to the medical examiner that James said he wanted to hire his own private medical examiner to do an autopsy. As part of his efforts in that area, James said, he had hired his own attorney.

James walked Christina through the last weeks of Julie's life. He said he'd cooked dinner for her the night that she had her second bad episode. She'd seemed fine and even went for a walk while he was cooking dinner. It was the first time that Julie had felt up to having dinner since her first hospital admission. She finally felt well enough to eat.

Christina asked James when he would find out the results of the autopsy, and he explained that he'd been told it would take about twenty weeks. Christina did not know if this was the truth or just something James made up.

Christina was still looking for answers in Julie's death and asked James if her friend had been depressed at all.

"No," he began, then paused and added, "now that I'm thinking about it, maybe she was."

"James, why do you think she was depressed?" Christina asked. Julie had seemed fine to her during a phone call after the first hospital admission, and had even been talking about trying to get pregnant. She seemed happier.

James said that he suspected that Julie was depressed because of a conversation he'd had with Ted's wife, Leila Willmore. He said that Leila told him that Julie seemed depressed to her and that the Thursday before Labor Day weekend, Julie had been extremely upset during a phone call. Julie reportedly told Leila, "If God is going to let this happen to me, then fuck God."

"That's unlike Julie," Christina responded, thinking that she had never heard her friend talk like that.

But the police had confided to James that Leila did not tell them about Julie's depression during their interview with her. The police told James that he and Leila gave conflicting statements.

Christina just didn't buy James's claim that Julie was depressed.

"James, don't you think Julie would have left a note? Sent one to her parents or told me she was depressed?"

James didn't think that Julie would have sent a note to any of her friends or family but certainly would have left one for him, but she had not.

"Why would Julie do that to herself?" Christina asked, as it seemed that James was suggesting that Julie was suicidal.

The answer was simple, James told her. Julie didn't want to burden anyone because of her kidney failure, and she was afraid she had something worse wrong, like cancer. That, coupled with the fact that Julie was upset that she wasn't going to be able to get pregnant, must have been too much for her to bear, James told Christina.

James encouraged his wife, he explained, telling her that they could get a second opinion about her ability to get pregnant.

Christina tried to console James during the conversation. She told him she knew he needed time to grieve and that he wasn't able to do that with the unresolved issues surrounding Julie's death. She didn't want him to become suspicious and stop talking to her. She made certain not to tell James about her contact with the police in Massachusetts. But as James poured his heart out to Christina, she sat on the other end of the phone, taking detailed notes of the conversation, which she later sent in an e-mail to Detective Jon Bailey.

During the phone call, Christina made a point of telling James that she thought the funeral service for Julie had been very nice, and that she was buried in a very nice spot. James explained that he hadn't picked the burial location; Jack and Nancy Oldag had selected it. He did think the location of the funeral was ironic, though, he told Christina. At one point he and Julie had driven by that funeral home when they still lived in Kansas City, and they'd remarked that it would be a nice place to have their funerals. This was beyond the realm of anything that Christina had ever heard from someone her age. What healthy person in her thirties even thinks about that kind of thing? Weren't most people their age thinking about their next vacation or their weekend plans, not their funerals?

CHAPTER 15

Part of Detective Jon Bailey's routine as he settled into a rhythm with the investigation became taking almost daily phone calls from Jack and Nancy Oldag. Though it was always Nancy who made the call, Jack was usually on the line as well.

"Yeah, Jon, Jack here," he'd begin as he brought up something he thought might be relevant. One day Jack recalled that James had given him two bottles of anti-freeze before he and Julie left for Boston. James had told him at the time that he didn't need them anymore, which was odd because the Boston-area winters were far more frigid than those in Missouri.

Nancy pointed out that Julie had a yellow legal pad she carried around with her when she got sick. She used it to write down questions about her illness. Nancy wondered why she would go to that trouble if she was taking the poison voluntarily. It didn't make sense.

Although she'd had some reservations about the move, Julie seemed happy in Waltham, Nancy recalled. The move had turned out better than she'd expected, and she said that she and James were saving fifteen hundred dollars per month. Nancy found this odd because it later turned out that James hadn't had enough money to pay for the funeral. The Oldags had learned that an anonymous friend of Julie's had covered the cost.

Nancy was on to something, but Bailey kept quiet. He knew that James and Julie hadn't been saving any money but were, in fact, deeply in debt. In addition to the bounced rent checks, their bank accounts had negative balances in them. They also had twenty thousand dollars in credit-card bills. That kind of massive debt didn't make a lot of sense for a couple who both had good jobs, and Bailey wondered where the Keowns were spending their money.

Nancy told Bailey about a top-of-the-line Jaguar that James used to drive but that he had gotten rid of after the move to Waltham. The car was given to him in lieu of payment by a dealership outside of Kansas City after he developed a website for the dealership. After he got the car, it was always breaking down, Nancy said, and eventually the dealership just bought it back from him. Nancy felt like something wasn't right about the story James told about that car, but she couldn't pin it down.

During one of their phone conversations, Nancy said, Julie had also confided to her mother that James was applying for a job with a local radio station. Although James had once promised Julie he would not return to radio, Julie was happy about his decision to do so, because she didn't think his job with the Learning Exchange was going well. Jack spoke up then, telling the detective that he didn't think that James was still with the Learning Exchange anymore anyway, because the company hadn't sent any flowers to Julie's funeral.

"We're not giving up, but this may take a long time," Bailey told Nancy and Jack more than once when they called. He wasn't about to give up on the case, and when the frustration became too much to stand, he looked at a picture of Julie that he kept on his desk. He knew the Oldags felt the case wasn't going to go anywhere because Julie was not from Waltham and they were not in the area. Sometimes Bailey felt like that was why they called every day. Some of what the Oldags told Bailey was not relevant to the case, but he didn't know how to tell Julie's parents that the information would not help. His heart went out to them, but the longer he sat on the phone with them every day, the longer it would be before he could follow up on other leads.

With Julie's funeral behind them, the Oldags were searching for answers about their daughter's death. And so was Jon Bailey. Although he and Lieutenant Jim Connolly had found a number of things that didn't make sense or add up, they didn't know why or what they meant. James's behavior was still peculiar to Bailey. On September 24, James had given investigators a nail polish cosmetic kit. He told them it was unusual because Julie did not even use nail polish, and he thought it might be a clue or be relevant to the investigation.

James was not technically considered a suspect, however, though he seemed to feel he was under suspicion. He was no longer cooperating with police and had hired a lawyer after his most recent meeting with Massachusetts State Police sergeant Owen Boyle. The details of that meeting were not made public but investigators felt they were significant to the case.

The police weren't the only ones to whom James had stopped talking. Nancy Oldag was starting to think that James's lawyer had told him not to speak to his in-laws anymore so as not to incriminate himself. Nancy had noticed that James had become more withdrawn, and he was not returning her phone calls. She called him twice one day to ask him to send one of Julie's scrapbooks to her. He had not returned either call. Nancy felt this was not just a coincidence; James was hiding something.

The change in James's personality wasn't the only thing raising Nancy's suspicion of her son-in-law, she told Bailey one day. She kept thinking about a cat that James and Julie had when they lived in Kansas City. The cat, Mickey, had gotten sick abruptly the year before and been put to sleep. Detective Bailey put in a call to the cat's veterinarian and learned that the seven-year-old cat had stopped eating, had been vomiting, and had been inactive. Mickey had signs of liver failure, which was common in cats, the vet explained, but the cat was ultimately put to sleep. James and Julie did not want an autopsy on the cat, who was cremated at the veterinary clinic.

This was nothing he could ever use in the case, but Bailey felt in his gut that Mickey had been a test run by James in using antifreeze as a poison. Bailey thought the sudden and unexplained illness, organ failure, and death in both the cat and Julie were similar enough that both had been caused by ethylene glycol poisoning. But although he felt like the cat's death was a clue, it wasn't anything that would help from an investigative standpoint.

Bailey went back to his file to find something with investigative value. He and Lieutenant Jim Connolly began verifying everything they had been told that far in the investigation, starting with James's account of going to the CVS Pharmacy the weekend before his wife's death to ask a pharmacist about possible drug interactions. Detective Stephen Taranto requested the surveillance tapes from the CVS on Harvard Street in Waltham, which was the pharmacy James said he'd gone to. Bailey found the choice of location a bit odd, because there was another

CVS right up the street from the couple's duplex, while the one on Harvard Street was a good ten-minute drive away.

James told police that he'd gone to the store around 1:15 p.m., so Bailey viewed the tapes from 11 a.m. until 2 p.m. It took forever, but there was no sign of James in any of the tapes from the front-door camera. Bailey decided to give James the benefit of the doubt and also viewed the tapes from the pharmacy-area camera for the same time period. Again, there was no sign of James. Bailey hadn't expected to see him. Viewing the lengthy surveillance videos simply confirmed his hunch.

Taranto also requested the surveillance video from Shaw's Supermarket, where James said he'd gone to get Sprite for Julie that last weekend. Unfortunately, the videotape had already been recorded over per the store's policy, and Bailey knew there would be nothing used in court from this area of the investigation.

Police weren't getting any solid evidence in the case, and although numerous people had brought up lies that James had told them, no one had anything worse than that to say about him. Everyone had thought he was a nice guy and a great husband who'd really dedicated himself to caring for Julie when she became sick. If he'd poisoned her, why would he be taking so much care of her in helping her to get better? Numerous people told Bailey and Connolly they were focusing on the wrong man. If you had seen them together, you would never think this, more than one person told Bailey. You just don't know James, they said.

But some of those descriptions of James and Julie as a happy couple raised the red flag of a domestic-violence situation for Bailey. James had complete control over Julie's schedule. He never let her out of his sight. One of Julie's friends referred to Julie leaving the house as "breaking loose."

Despite some inconsistencies in James's version of events, and a growing number of instances where he was obviously lying about things, the investigation stalled. Although these things cast doubt on James's credibility, they weren't evidence that would lead to an arrest. As he got deeper into the case, Bailey often thought about Julie. She was fast becoming the focus of his life. Although he would never meet her, he felt like he was starting to know her. Everyone who'd known Julie spoke of her friendly nature and willingness to do anything for friends and family. Bailey felt just terrible whenever he imagined how she must have suffered before her death. It was a horrible, horrible way to go.

To Bailey, it was obvious that Julie Keown had wanted to get better. He had Julie's own words to prove it. Julie had spent the last months of her life e-mailing friends about her condition, often with updates and theories about what might be making her ill. Many of those friends were fellow nurses whom Julie sought out for their opinions and suggestions as she went through a battery of tests she hoped would lead to an answer about her mysterious illness.

Bailey pored over the details in the e-mails, which he had received copies of from Julie's friends, such as Joyce Bouyear. Joyce was a nurse Julie had known from her previous position at Liberty Hospital, and Julie knew that Joyce was also living with a different form of a kidney disease.

"I was just wondering if you had any words of wisdom about how to really live with this," Julie wrote to Joyce on August 30, 2004. "Any words of wisdom would be greatly appreciated."

Joyce e-mailed Julie back right away, telling her that she had been able to live with her kidney disease for close to twenty years by managing her diet and working with her doctor.

"You didn't share much about your disease, but I'm saying hang in there," Joyce wrote back to Julie. "It is scary but learn all you can and find a doctor that will work with you. I'll pray for you and Jim and if you want I'll add you to our church prayers list. Miracles do happen!!! I'm here."

Later the same day, Julie wrote back to Joyce, thanking her for her support and giving her more specific details about the tests she'd had done so far and those that were still to come. She said they still didn't have a prognosis for her, and admitted that "I am basically overwhelmed right now. I can only read so much before I get to tears. . . . I feel very tired and am having problems with my GI tract. I don't know if it is all related or not. Last Friday morning I woke up with slurred speech and unable to purposefully control my legs and arms. I thought I was stroking only it wasn't one side more than another."

Julie also told Joyce about how her kidney trouble was affecting her chance of getting pregnant. "My nephrologists said with fifty-five percent renal function, she said I can try, but it would be high risk. So am I just asking for problems for trying. We actually had been trying the last couple of months. Now, I need to see a high-risk OB. I guess I am starting to ramble. Joyce, thanks for listening to me. My world has truly been rocked. You are just a phenomenal person. I will listen to any advice you can give."

Julie e-mailed Christina Liles the same day to tell her about her illness, and she related the same strange stroke-like symptoms she'd been having.

"Life hasn't been going so swell. Been in the hospital last week. It looks like I have some form of kidney failure. . . . Got to the hospital and my electrolytes were way, way off balance. Finally got me stable and now I am home. I don't think they are sure what is really wrong with me, so for now it's monitoring labs and more tests."

In a later e-mail, she added that the doctors in Boston did not think what she was going through was cancer, and said, "I know I tested negative for ANA, lupus and HIV. The current thought is that my kidneys had an allergic reaction from taking Prilosec which I started taking about two weeks ago. . . . But the CAT scan of my kidneys shows chronic renal failure that I had no idea about. The nephrologists says that this happens a lot and usually they never really know the cause." She mentioned the chances that she'd eventually need a kidney transplant and admitted, "I am exhausted. I just want to know what is wrong. Once I get the MRI and MRA's done and a little more lab work done, I am going to get a copy of my chart and send it to some doctors for second opinions."

The next day, Tuesday, August 31, Christina sent a quick e-mail to Julie from her office at the Sisters of Charity of Leavenworth Health System in Lenexa, Kansas, asking if she felt any better.

Julie responded less than an hour later.

"Not really. I am having a lot of problems sleeping and problems with dizziness last night. I am going to my primary-care physician today around noon. Thanks for asking."

Julie and Christina e-mailed several more times that day with news from her doctor's appointment and the results from her testing.

That night Christina and her husband, Dave, talked about Julie's condition. Dave wondered if Julie was taking any birth control or diet pills. Dave suspected that if Julie had stopped taking birth control pills in order to get pregnant, it might have thrown her adrenal glands "out of whack" and caused the renal failure. Christina passed her husband's suspicions on to Julie in an e-mail the next day.

Julie thanked the couple but said that she'd only taken "birth control for one month when I was 18, otherwise, that was it, and I have never taken diet pills, so I guess that couldn't be it either. I wish it was, so I would know. . . . I had been taking fish oil a while back with my daily vitamin. We were wondering maybe if that might have caused something. We haven't told the nephrologists that yet. Don't know if there is something with that. Although, with all the things I have read, that is supposed to help your kidneys. Who knows? Hope today is treating you well."

That would be the last e-mail Christina Liles ever received from her dear friend Julie.

As his frustration over the lack of progress in the case took hold, Bailey went back over what he'd learned so far. He and Connolly found themselves going over the same interviews and papers again and again, hoping to find something they might have overlooked the first time. Bailey was searching for meaning or the missing piece in the puzzle; there had to be something, some motive. Yet the only thing that seemed to indicate a possible motive were the couple's money problems.

On October 21, 2004, investigators received a call from the human resources department at Liberty Hospital in Missouri. They wanted to let police know that James had contacted them to find out about Julie's retirement benefits. They were sending out a letter about possible options for the life insurance. James was the beneficiary of a $250,000 life insurance policy on Julie, and he wanted to know if the policy would be paid out to him upon his wife's death.

Now this, Bailey thought, could be a motive. But why go to all of that trouble to murder someone for a $250,000 payout? Couldn't James have just gotten a loan or, if it was that bad, a divorce from Julie? It didn't add up, especially because both James and Julie seemed to have good careers, with established companies that paid them well. Even so, Bailey was intrigued, and he knew he'd have to take a closer look. And he wasn't prepared for the information he would soon learn about James.

CHAPTER 16

As the CEO and president of the Learning Exchange, Tammy Blossom wasn't involved in initial interviews of those applying for positions with the Kansas City, Missouri, nonprofit educational company, whose offices were located within the campus of the Penn Valley College (though not a part of the college). First-round interviews were done by Joe Constantino, a company vice president who handled human resources. By the time Blossom was brought in to interview James Keown for a marketing position with the company in May of 2002, James had already been recommended for the job.

Still, the final decision would not be made without her approval.

Blossom was a midwestern native, in her midthirties at the time, and had achieved a high level of success in her career. When she returned to the Midwest for the position at the educational consulting and reform organization,

Blossom left a position in New York City as the CEO and president of the Community Change Consortium, where she'd worked with President Bill Clinton and General Colin Powell to help launch America's Promise.

Tammy Blossom was an experienced, respected, and capable leader, dedicated to advancing the Learning Exchange. In 2002, she was working on a plan to add a consulting arm to the educational reform services offered through the nonprofit. To start up the consulting arm, the company had decided to launch an interactive website and needed someone to work on developing that site as well as a business plan to market the consulting component of the Learning Exchange.

The first thing Blossom noticed as she walked into the conference room was James's appearance. He was dressed to the hilt in a suit that must have cost close to one thousand dollars and shoes that easily cost five hundred dollars. He was poised, well groomed, and articulate, all ideal qualities, she thought, for someone who would be interacting with clients in the new position.

James was phenomenal at selling himself to Blossom and the others at the company. He spent almost fifteen minutes giving a very enthusiastic, and in-depth, expla-nation of the work he had been doing in Chicago for ESPN. Though James had actually had a minor job at the radio station, he embellished his experience to fit exactly with the job requirements for the web-based market-ing position at the Learning Exchange. While at ESPN, James told Blossom, he'd been responsible for the devel-opment and launch of the websites that went with the opening of the ESPN Zone restaurants. The interactive sites promoted the ESPN Zone restaurant and sports-bar chain that was opening around the country, including in Chicago. In actuality, he had been an assistant, similar to the role he played to Mike Elder in Kansas City.

James's apparent credentials and experience with the ESPN websites were almost the identical skills needed for the person who would help launch the Learning Exchange interactive site. James easily discussed how he had led the ESPN project, with specific details that impressed Blossom and the others in the interview, including a working knowledge of the exact software program the Learning Exchange was using.

To those in the interview, James seemed like the ideal candidate for the new position. Not only did he have an extremely powerful résumé and the ability to speak well with a group and explain the complex concepts associated with the interactive website, but he was charismatic. He was also likable, well dressed, professional, and experienced.

Despite all of this, Tammy Blossom and the company's HR director did find themselves questioning why someone with James's expansive experience, which he claimed included jobs with six-figure salaries, would want to work for a nonprofit for a lot less money.

James grew serious as he explained to Blossom how the terrorist attacks of September 11, 2001, had changed his life. After the attacks, James and Julie had decided they wanted to move home to the Kansas City area to be near family and friends. He wanted to change the direction of his life and work in a meaningful job at a nonprofit organization because he wanted to give back. Giving back was personal to him, he told them, because of his own upbringing. His father had been a lobbyist when James was young, but he had a very serious alcohol problem, and that background made James want to help others. Money no longer mattered to him, James said, as much as the chance to offer his skills, talents, and time for a worthy cause. James seemed sincere, though not everyone in the room felt so sure. After he left, the team members discussed whether they should hire him for the position.

"There's something I can't put my finger on that's kind of like smoke and mirrors about JP," Elaine Bieberly, the company's marketing director, told Blossom. "But still, I'm going to recommend him for the job because I think we really need to step out of the box here."

The others were all unanimous in their decision to hire James, who told them he preferred to be called JP, for the job. Blossom felt that the company had found a real gem.

JP Keown arrived for his first day of work at the Learning Exchange driving a top-of-the-line Jaguar, which he thought nothing of easing into a parking spot in front of the office reserved for clients. The car was magnificent and went along with the image JP had presented during his interviews, with his expensive suits and shoes. When asked about the expensive car, JP easily explained that he'd made a very good income when he worked for ESPN in Chicago and could afford it.

Employees were supposed to park across the street from the office in a parking garage. JP, however, was not happy about leaving his pricey ride anywhere near the garage. The Learning Exchange was in an area of Kansas City called Midtown, which was known for its high crime rate. He went to Elaine Bieberly, his supervisor, with his concerns almost immediately. Bieberly took JP's request to park in front to Blossom, who turned it down, pointing out that the spots were reserved for clients and needed to stay open for those clients. Despite having been denied, JP continued to park in the spots reserved for clients and was routinely reminded to move his car.

Though this behavior irked Tammy Blossom, it didn't stop JP from sidling up to the company CEO. He seemed to have a phenomenal talent for becoming close to the most powerful person in the company, just as he had with Mike Elder at KCMO years before. It began very casually, with JP just moseying on by Blossom's office and starting up conversations. Often he handed her a chart or memo about a plan he had for marketing, with an explanation that he knew he was supposed to go through his immediate supervisor but that he thought Blossom would like to get a look at his idea. She was impressed by JP, who was quickly known by everyone in the company for being very bright and somewhat debonair.

Elaine Bieberly, on the other hand, was not as impressed by the copper-headed charmer as Blossom and others were. She approached Blossom several times with concerns that JP was not producing the type of work he was supposed to be churning out. The more Bieberly questioned JP, the more JP dropped hints to Blossom about reorganizing the marketing department. His subtle suggestions about Elaine Bieberly became more focused as time went on. Bieberly had a "tired" approach to marketing that didn't mesh with what JP saw as his more progressive approach. Having worked at ESPN, James told the CEO, he had a better, more modern skill set for marketing, and Bieberly was standing in the way of real progress. In fact, she was just an example of how the company had one too many unnecessary people in upper management. By streamlining the company, and getting rid of Bieberly's position, it would save the Learning Exchange money, JP argued.

Eventually, Elaine Bieberly had enough. She was tired of JP's condescending attitude toward her and his constant suggestions to Tammy Blossom. She turned in her resignation from the company.

With Bieberly gone, JP easily slid into a lead role in the marketing department. This also gave him a more direct line to Tammy Blossom, whom he began regularly asking for a promotion. Every month to three months, JP handed Blossom a recommendation he had written that detailed why she should make him a vice president. Every time, Blossom turned him down. At one point, JP told her that he wouldn't even request a raise in his salary if she gave him the title. She still said no, to which JP was visibly upset and frustrated. He seemed determined to change her mind and always returned with another request for the title.

Frankly, Tammy Blossom always found these requests a little strange; she didn't understand why the title was so important to him. She explained that any kind of promotion would be made as a result of his demonstrated abilities and achievement of goals within the company. Within a short time, Blossom was starting to question those abilities; JP's knack for writing extravagant masterpieces on why he should be promoted were far superior products to the actual work he accomplished at the Learning Exchange.

As he assumed the leadership role in the marketing department, JP began a weekly practice of taking the staff members he worked with out for drinks. He called it a team-building exercise, which he said would build camaraderie in the marketing department. Most of the staff were attractive young women just a year or two out of college. They were immediately impressed by JP's generosity on these outings because he almost always paid for their multiple drinks, usually pulling out a credit card to do so. Back at work, the young girls often whispered about JP and how they thought he must make a huge salary. How else would a young, married man be able to pick up the tab every single Thursday night?

Every Friday morning, JP would wander into Blossom's office to give her an update on how his weekly night out with the employees had gone. The events were going so well, he told her, that he suggested the company pay for them. Blossom quickly shot that idea down, pointing out that the Learning Exchange was not going to pay for alcohol out of its budget.

As the Thursday night outings continued, Blossom started to get a little uncomfortable with the idea. At one point she brought her concerns up among the senior management team members. It wasn't that she thought there was anything inappropriate going on, and although Blossom didn't see anything wrong with the employees going out a few times a year to bond, every week seemed excessive. In the back of her mind, she also wondered how JP could afford to pick up the bill every week. She knew what the Learning Exchange was paying him, but she also knew that he was under close watch with regard to his finances by his wife, Julie. He repeatedly told Blossom about the close eye that Julie kept on their finances.

"Julie has me on such a tight budget," he often told her. "She manages all the money in our house."

Apparently, Julie had spreadsheet after spreadsheet, detailing their expenses and how much money they were saving. During one of these conversations, JP told his boss that Julie's hold on their money was just killing him. Friends of the couple knew that Julie was far more conservative with money than James, who thought nothing of spending money and wanted to have the best of everything even when it was beyond his means.

The couple seemed otherwise happy, however, and JP always spoke of Julie in high regard, though he never brought her on the Thursday night outings with his coworkers.

Tammy Blossom had only seen the couple out together socially twice, but she was struck by their closeness. On those two outings, both benefits that Blossom had extra tickets for, JP always sat with his arm around his wife. They were happy, and Julie was always smiling, almost bubbly, as she talked with Blossom about JP. Julie had raised a strange concern about her husband, though.

"James keeps falling down the steps at home and hitting his head," Julie had confided, before explaining that she thought James had a problem with his equilibrium. Blossom found herself thinking how sincere Julie was in her concern for James and his well-being.

James found out early on in his job at the Learning Exchange that Tammy Blossom had an Ivy League education. She'd earned her MBA from Columbia when she was working in New York City, and James often asked her what it was like getting her master's degree.

Blossom sensed that getting a master's degree was important to JP, given how he seemed to bring the topic up repeatedly. So she wasn't totally surprised when James showed up in her office one day with a proposal that would allow him to advance his education. "I know that you believe strongly in this level of education," he told her before explaining what he wanted to do.

Based on the type of work that James was doing for the company, he felt he could work remotely while earning his master's degree. He wanted to go to Harvard University, he told Blossom, adding that it would look good for the company to say that one of their employees was at Harvard.

James had the idea to use his studies at Harvard to enhance the work he was doing for the Learning Exchange but tailoring his studies to the type of projects he was working on. Still, James was not sure what type of master's degree would be the best for his career. He sought Blossom's opinion on this, and the two spent many hours discussing whether he should focus on public affairs, marketing, or business administration in his studies. Blossom knew firsthand how much work it was to complete a master's degree, but she told James that if he could prove that it would benefit the Learning Exchange and his work there, she would consider his proposal.

And he still had to apply, and be accepted, to Harvard before she could really make a decision.

In the late fall of 2003, James stopped by to see Blossom with an update. Not only had he been accepted to the prestigious MBA program at Harvard, but he'd been awarded a full scholarship to attend and was considered a "senior scholar" because the university was so impressed with his academic ability. Blossom had not heard of the term, but James had not given her any reason not to believe him.

Tammy Blossom agreed to JP's request to telecommute from Harvard, but she told him that to finalize their agreement, she would need a letter from the admissions office confirming his acceptance. Within days, a letter from the admissions office at Harvard was on her desk, along with a list of courses that JP would take and the type of work that he would be doing in those courses to benefit the Learning Exchange.

She finalized the terms of the agreement with James in December of 2003, including buying him a new company cell phone that would allow them to stay in touch in the least expensive manner. The phone, which was one of the first nationwide cell-phone plans, allowed unlimited minutes between cell phones from the same company. All James needed to do was to find somewhere to live near Harvard and plan his move to the East Coast. Though James had told his landlord in Massachusetts that the company was picking up the tab for his rent, there was no such agreement made with Blossom.

But by January 2004, JP had still not left Kansas City, which concerned Blossom, who knew that the spring semester was starting. She approached him and asked why he hadn't yet left for Boston. The answer was easy, he responded, pointing out that because he was in a special scholarship program, he did not have to be on campus at the start of the semester. That didn't sit right with Blossom. It wasn't how Ivy League schools operated, and she questioned James several more times.

After one of these rounds of questions, James called in sick to work for three days. Blossom cringed when JP returned to work. His face, head, and arms were covered in scabs. They looked like a really bad case of hives. It was so bad that James had shaved his head. She took one look at him and sent him home to recover. She didn't know what he had, but whatever it was, she didn't want him in the office.

When he returned to work about a week later, JP confided to Blossom that he might have multiple sclerosis. To Blossom, it had looked more like an allergic reaction; hives were not a symptom she had ever heard mentioned with multiple sclerosis. James went on to explain that he was going to miss some more work while he underwent tests for multiple sclerosis. He was back at work the next week, scab free, looking almost normal again. James never mentioned the results from his testing for multiple sclerosis, and Blossom didn't have time to ask him, since he left for Harvard very soon after that. Any questions she had were pushed to the back of her mind as he moved to the East Coast, began classes, and continued to work remotely from his new home office in Waltham.

Tammy Blossom heard from JP regularly after his move to Waltham, but a phone call she received from him at home one evening disturbed her. It was almost 10 p.m. when Blossom's home phone rang. It was JP. He was really upset, he said, about Tracie Burrow and her treatment of him. Burrow, the chief financial officer for the Learning Exchange, was really on his tail. She was giving him a hard time about his expense reports when there was no need. She wouldn't let up on him, and he had enough. She needed to go.

"I think you should fire Tracie," he told Blossom.

Blossom was shocked and quickly told him she would do no such thing.

"Don't you ever call me at home again," Blossom said, and she hung up the phone as her husband asked who had called them so late.

JP's charm was wearing thin not only with Blossom, but the rest of the executives at the Learning Exchange. He wasn't producing the work he was supposed to on deadline. His supervisors were growing frustrated and often nagged him to turn in past-due assignments. Still, when it came down to the wire, and they were about to really crack down on him, JP always pulled through. Miraculously, the memo or report would show up, although it wouldn't be as well executed as the company's decision makers had hoped. But before they could dwell on the substandard written product, they would again be wowed by JP's compelling oral presentation that went along with the project. Although he was living in Waltham while attending Harvard, James did make trips back to Missouri for important meetings at the company.

Tammy Blossom began to notice how much of the best work seemed to come from the young women who worked under JP—the same young women whom he had taken out for happy hour every Thursday night. James seemed to have an uncanny ability to bring out the best in the employees underneath him.

Blossom and the others were growing particularly frustrated with the lack of progress on the interactive website James had been hired to create. Whenever they asked about the status of the site, James was quick to respond that he was working on it. He may have been, but he never had anything to show for all of his work. Tammy Blossom and Tracie Burrow were losing patience and demanded that James put together a presentation on the site. They had been writing checks for months to the web design and development company, Interactive Methods, which James had contracted with for the actual design work, and wanted to see something in return. James continued to put them off while assuring them he would put something together very soon.

It wasn't soon enough for CFO Tracie Burrow. She wanted answers. She began by looking up the address for Interactive Methods and decided to pay the company a visit one afternoon. James was halfway across the country in Massachusetts and not providing adequate answers about the site. She was determined to find out what was going on. She stopped in to tell Blossom her plan before she left.

Blossom was still at the office when Burrow called her. Blossom would never believe where she was, Burrow said. She was standing inside a UPS store where the company was supposedly located. All she'd found was a post-office box where she had been sending the checks.

Blossom had a bad feeling, which only got worse when the Learning Exchange received a bill from Wetsu Creative for $9,100 for developing the same website that Interactive Methods had been hired to design. The Learning Exchange explained to Jason Jett, the head of Wetsu Creative, that they weren't paying the bill, and he needed to take the issue up with James Keown. When confronted by Blossom, James didn't have a straight answer or explanation. He claimed he had no idea what the invoices meant or why they were being sent to the Learning Exchange.

The executives at the Learning Exchange started to question whether there were other things James had not been completely truthful about. Blossom pulled a copy of his résumé and started to double-check the list of references JP had provided a year and a half before. When James had applied for the job, each reference had answered immediately and provided glowing recommendations for him. The funny thing was, now she couldn't get through to any of the numbers. They were all disconnected. Tammy started to wonder who those references really had been. James had several cell phones and a good radio voice. She wondered if it was possible that he'd acted as his own references.

Blossom again thought back to the uncomfortable feeling she'd had when James didn't leave for Harvard at the start of the semester. She knew a school of that caliber would not make exceptions for someone, regardless of his or her intellect. James's explanation that he was allowed to start late because of the program he was in had never rung true to her. She faxed the copy of James's acceptance letter to the director of admissions at Harvard. Even with her uneasiness, however, Blossom was unprepared for the phone call she received from the dean of the business school at Harvard.

Not only was James *not* a student at Harvard, the dean said, but the letter James had provided was a fraud. The dean insisted that she had not signed the letter. She had not sent the letter. She had never even heard of James Keown.

Blossom felt like she was peeling back the layers of an onion. It seemed that everything JP had told them was a lie, part of a facade.

It was obvious that the company was going to have to fire James, but first they needed to do a bit more digging into his background and actions while at the company. They started to research Interactive Methods, the company they had paid for the website. Again, they were not expecting what they found: according to the Missouri secretary of state's office, James Keown was listed as the owner of Interactive Methods. The Learning Exchange had been writing checks for a website that was never created, and James had been signing those checks, then depositing them to his own account.

Along with their company lawyer, CEO Tammy Blossom, CFO Tracie Burrow, and the other executives gathered around during a conference call to collectively fire James. James was adamant that he did not know what they were talking about. It wasn't true, he said; they must be mistaken.

"I can't believe what I'm hearing," he responded. "I have not done any of this."

James had one request for his former employers—could he have a friend come by the office to get his belongings? Blossom wasn't sure what he had in his office, so she went to take a look after they ended the phone call.

Her jaw dropped when she saw what was inside. The office looked like a mailroom. There were about fifteen stacks of mail, each two to three feet high, stacked along the walls around the room. What in the world was all of this mail doing here?

She went out to the front desk to ask the receptionist about the mail. Oh sure, the receptionist explained. JP had been having his personal mail sent to the office since about the second week that he worked at the Learning Exchange. He'd asked if it was OK to have the mail sent there because his mailbox at his house was getting broken into.

Tammy Blossom went back into the office and looked at the return addresses on the envelopes. None of them had been opened, though they mostly appeared to be bills, bank statements, and insurance information. Why wouldn't JP ever open the mail? What was going on here?

CHAPTER 17

November 8, 2004

After living outside Boston his whole life, Detective Jon Bailey was used to navigating city traffic. But navigating the narrow country roads from Kansas City to the Oldags' farm in Plattsburg, Missouri, was a different story entirely.

Jack Oldag had given Bailey and Lieutenant Jim Connolly directions to the farm using not street signs or numbers but landmarks, for example, to turn at a certain rock or large tree. The two investigators had landed in Kansas City, about forty-five minutes south of the Oldags' farm, and headed north on a two-lane highway, before exiting the highway for a narrow paved road. It was amazing to Bailey that the area could become so rural, so remote, within such a short drive from a major city. The countryside was dotted with rolling fields; old barns accented with metal windmills that looked antique, almost like something from *The Wizard of Oz*; and livestock. The pickup trucks that passed them on the road far outnumbered the passenger cars. There was no doubt that the two investigators were headed right into farm country.

The real purpose of the trip was to visit the Learning Exchange, where James Keown had worked, and to interview the couple's friends and acquaintances in Missouri. Bailey and Connolly were also stopping by at the Oldags' to reinforce to them that they were serious about their investigation and about finding out what had really happened to Julie.

The two investigators drove down the long driveway to the Oldags' yellow ranch-style farmhouse, taking in the vast fields that surrounded the farm on all sides, before parking and stepping out to greet Jack and Nancy Oldag. The couple was very matter-of-fact as they thanked the investigators for coming and for staying on the case. It was the same reaction they had expressed before, and Bailey was used to the couple's midwestern mannerisms by this point. Still, it was important for him to let them know they were serious about the investigation.

Bailey stood on the front porch of the modest farmhouse. The house was well maintained, in a beautiful location, but there was nothing extra, nothing extravagant about the place, which seemed to fit with the personality of both the Midwest and the Oldags themselves. Bailey was struck by the fact that there was nothing but open farmland on all sides. He wondered what would make someone like Julie leave such a beautiful place to move to a city like Waltham. Though he had lived in the city his whole life, Bailey knew that if he had been in Julie's situation, he never would have been able to leave the peaceful rolling fields and unspoiled landscape.

Bailey had spoken with the Oldags by phone countless times by this point, and every time, they seemed to be grasping to think of something, anything, that would help Bailey and Connolly in their investigation. The couple had remembered one more thing about James that they passed along to the detectives during the visit. Over the summer of 2003, James had used Jack's American Express card to order some airline tickets. He was supposed to reimburse his father-in-law for the charge. But several months later, when Jack asked when he might get the money paid back, Julie was furious at James. Her mother recalled that Julie turned to James and angrily reprimanded him: "You told me you already paid my father for those." Nancy stressed to Bailey just how upset her daughter seemed at the time. A short time after that conversation, James finally paid Jack for the tickets. Bailey took notes on the conversation, making a mental note that the incident was very similar to the one in August of 2004, when James had failed to repay Ted Willmore for the trip to North Carolina.

The two investigators left the Oldags, again giving them their word that they were following up on the case, and drove back to Kansas City and the Learning Exchange.

One person they definitely wanted to speak with was managing director JoLynn Bethke. Her notary stamp and signature had appeared on the lease James had given his Waltham landlord, when James told his landlord that the Learning Exchange would be paying his rent. Bailey was still wondering whether Bethke was somehow involved with James. When they were all seated, he asked her how it might be possible that her signature and stamp had been on the document. Bethke explained that she left her notary stamp in her desk drawer at work, so it was possible that James could have taken the stamp. And she had a suspicion how James may have gotten her signature. Bethke remembered a time during one of the weekly bar gatherings when James had asked people how they signed their names. He had everyone sign their names on napkins during what had seemed like a lighthearted moment. But it was possible that James had studied how Bethke signed her name and later forged her signature on the lease for Greg Stocklan.

Bailey was noticing a pattern of forgery on James's part, not only with the lease document, but the references he had provided to the Learning Exchange to get the job. CEO Tammy Blossom had since determined that they were fakes. The phone numbers she had called when he was hired had since been disconnected, with no other information available, and she suspected that James had disguised his voice to provide his own references.

Both Bethke and Blossom told the investigators they'd noticed that James seemed to lead a lifestyle way above his means. They pointed to the Jaguar, his habit of paying the tab at the weekly happy-hour outings, and his regular routine of buying lunch for the boss, despite her demurrals.

By the time Bailey and Connolly arrived at the Learning Exchange, the company executives and employees all knew that James had faked his admission to Harvard and been fired from the company. Many had taken to calling him "Mr. Smoke and Mirrors" for his ability to sell himself and his stories based on almost nothing. Tammy Blossom gave the investigators a timeline of James's employment at the company and when they'd started to realize something wasn't right with the invoices for the website design. She filled them in on the information she had obtained from Jason Jett at Wetsu Creative, whom the investigators planned to visit themselves the next day. Blossom also had a copy of the memo that James had submitted along with his course schedule at Harvard, where he was supposedly attending classes on Mondays from 3 to 5 p.m. and Tuesdays from 7 to 10 p.m.

"Classes worked out very well this semester," James wrote in the memo. He told Blossom he was taking Internet and Society: Technologies and Policies of Control at the Harvard Law School; Decisions, Games, and Negotiations (using mathematic principles in negotiations), also at Harvard; and an online course offered at Harvard called Preliminary Research.

Later, when he returned to Waltham, Bailey compared those class times with James's credit-card records from the same time periods. Although the investigators already knew that James Keown had never attended class at Harvard, the records proved to be a second means of confirmation. During times that he was supposed to be in class, James's credit card had been used in Kansas City and at a computer store near Harvard in Cambridge, Massachusetts. Bailey had no idea what James had been doing in Missouri during that time period. On February 19, 2004, James bought a gas storage container, a can of WD-40, and two beach chairs at a K-Mart store in Missouri. Bailey found himself wondering what James needed the items for and, again, why he was in Missouri.

The investigators also asked James's co-workers if they knew anything about James having been mugged outside of the office. Those who had heard James's version of the event were skeptical. He'd told his co-workers he had been jumped by two black guys and pistol-whipped. It sounded frightening, but what made people suspicious of the event was that James didn't seem to have any visible injuries. After speaking with Christina Liles, who had also been suspicious about the incident, Bailey had already learned that the Kansas City police didn't have any report about the mugging. But while they were in the area, he and Connolly decided to double-check with the Penn Valley College security officers, who covered the area around the Learning Exchange, which was located within the college campus. They spoke with the director of security at Penn Valley, but the only report he had from James was from December 2002, about a stolen leather jacket.

It was confirmation of more lies that James had told, but just being a liar didn't make someone a murderer. And why would he make up such an elaborate story about being mugged?

Perhaps the interviews they had planned for the following day with the Keowns' friends and acquaintances, including Jason Jett at Wetsu Creative, might shed some light on what led James to lie.

CHAPTER 18

Detective Jon Bailey and Lieutenant Jim Connolly started the next day just outside Kansas City at the home of Mike and Stephanie Webb. Stephanie stayed home with the couple's children, and the two investigators stepped around numerous toys before sitting down with Stephanie.

Stephanie explained that she'd first met Julie at William Jewell College in 1991 and was the one who'd introduced Julie to Leila Willmore. Stephanie was also present when James and Julie were set up on their first date during college. She had always thought that James and Julie had a good relationship. They didn't argue or disagree. Julie seemed to help James stay on track when he tended to get his head in the clouds, but there was never anything disturbing about the relationship.

Stephanie and Mike had stayed in touch with James and Julie after college and after the other couple's move to Waltham. The Webbs had been the third couple on the trip to North Carolina with the Willmores and the Keowns in August of 2004. During that trip, Julie told Stephanie she thought she might have an ulcer, but that the doctors were not really sure of her exact diagnosis. James had seemed genuinely concerned about Julie's condition and was very loving toward his wife during the trip. They didn't talk much about what James and Julie were doing in Boston, but James did mention that the cost of living was expensive in the Boston area. James also confided that things weren't going well with his job at the Learning Exchange and that he was thinking about getting back into the radio business.

Stephanie Webb was one of the few people whom the investigators spoke with who knew that James hadn't graduated from William Jewell College. He'd dropped out when he was offered the job at the radio station in Kansas City and had never finished his undergraduate degree.

After Julie's death, the Webbs occasionally heard from James. Stephanie spoke with James a few weeks before she met with the two Massachusetts investigators. At the time, he was in town for a job interview in Columbia, Missouri, which is just about one hundred miles east of Kansas City. Ted Willmore told Stephanie that Julie had died from ethylene glycol poisoning, and Stephanie stressed to the investigators that she didn't believe that Julie would have intentionally ingested antifreeze. But she didn't think that James was responsible for it either. She was hoping that it turned out that the poisoning was the result of a metabolic disorder that Ted had told her about, rather than the alternatives of suicide or murder.

Later that morning, Bailey and Connolly sat down with Stephanie's husband, Mike Webb, at his office. Mike was a vice president at a local bank, and he told the two detectives that he'd never really believed all of the stories James told. He felt James had a tendency to embellish his stories, or even outright lie, the reason for which was never clear. For example, on one occasion James told Mike that he went to the gambling boats with Ted Willmore, but Ted later told Mike he'd never been on the boats. And there was something that never really sat well with Mike about James saying he was going to Harvard; when they had been in college together at William Jewell, James wasn't a very good student. His GPA at the college was only a 1.9.

Mike knew that Julie had been experiencing health problems for several months, and he stated she was very sleepy when they were on vacation in North Carolina. After Julie's funeral service and burial, James and Mike had gone go-kart riding the same day. Mike had been there for James in the week leading up to the funeral, and he had even gone with James to the church to help make the burial arrangements for Julie. At one point during the drive to the church, James had turned to his old friend and said, "You know, the bitch of the situation is I lost my best friend, wife, partner, and the person I was going to spend the rest of my life with. I'm the only person who knows I didn't have anything to do with this."

The detectives next headed to an eBay shipping store called Deal Express to meet with Troy Rivas, another college friend of James and Julie's. Bailey and Connolly had not been aware of James's leaving Massachusetts, but they soon learned that he was actually back in Missouri at the time, and he was staying with Troy and his wife, Jennifer, while he looked for somewhere to live. James had told Troy that Julie had died from a rare kidney disease and that the doctors had found something in her bloodstream that should not have been there. He also told his friend that he wasn't sure how his wife had ingested the substance but that he was helping the police as much as he could in their investigation. James said that he'd turned all of the chemicals in their home over to the police in Massachusetts and had spoken with them for about four hours. He also told Troy that he really just needed a break from the police; he felt like they were looking at him like a suspect just because he was the husband. Troy mentioned to James that morning that the police had called him, and James responded that he expected that the police were still following up on the case, even though he hadn't heard from them in a while.

The one thing James never told Troy, however, was that he hadn't killed his wife.

Like Stephanie Webb, Troy was one of the few people who knew that James had not finished college at William Jewell. James claimed that he was at Harvard to first finish up his undergraduate degree, and then he'd work to obtain his graduate degree. He also told Troy that he planned to quit his job at the Learning Exchange because a radio station in Boston had offered him a job. But he hadn't ended up taking the radio job because Julie got sick.

Troy didn't feel like James was the same person after Julie's funeral. Lately, though, he'd seemed to be getting back to normal. He was talking about buying land near Julie's parents to be close to them, even though his mother, Betty, lived in his childhood home in Jefferson City, just two hours from Kansas City, and he had gone to an interview with a radio station in Columbia. James had even broached the subject of possibly starting a consulting business with Troy, who had once operated a company called Orion Digital.

As for the Jaguar, the story that James told Troy was that he'd purchased the car but the engine had major problems and needed to be rebuilt. As a result, James had sold it back to Aristocrat Motors.

As he took notes during the interview, Bailey wondered how James was able to keep all of his different stories straight. Earlier that same day, Bailey and Connolly had been to the luxury-car dealership. James had claimed to other friends that Aristocrat Motors had given him the Jaguar in exchange for designing their web page. The two detectives already knew that the car had been repossessed, but they wanted to follow up just the same. Arnie McMett, a manager at the dealership, confirmed that James had indeed purchased the Jaguar and that he'd had nothing to do with any website design project.

It seemed that James told a different version of events to every person he spoke with, not only about Julie's death, but his work plans and the Jaguar, even his move back to Missouri. There was one thing that was consistent in the interviews with James and Julie's friends, however—the feeling that James was always trying to keep up with the lifestyle of his more affluent friends.

Robert Patterson, another person who had known James since college, described him as "trying to keep up with the Joneses." When Robert bought a new big-screen TV, James immediately went out and bought a larger big-screen TV. But despite James's show of being the big man on campus, Robert's wife, Caren, considered James very immature, almost childlike in the way he depended on Julie to do everything for him. As for Harvard, the couple thought that James was going to a night-school program there, not graduate school.

Their next interview, with another friend of James's, made the investigators suspect that he not only lied to make himself look better, but also to gain financially. Jason Jett, who owned Wetsu Creative, had also known James since college and was the one who James used to design the website for the Learning Exchange. It was the same job that Jason was never paid for.

Jason felt the website job was strange from the beginning. James first approached his friend about the job during Jason's wedding, in May of 2002. James pulled him aside to ask if he'd be interested in designing the website. Jason had tried to brush him off—it was his wedding after all—and asked if they could talk about it another time. James persisted, asking for a ballpark figure of how much the design work might cost. Jason threw out a figure of about eight thousand dollars, which seemed to appease James at the time.

James eventually told Jason that he had been selected to design the website for the Learning Exchange, but after Jason asked James for a tour of the offices, so that he could get a sense of the organization before starting work, he found it a bit odd that the tour was after hours, when the offices were closed. Still, he went forward with designing the website and sent his bill for the job to James. This was the same bill that Jason would eventually submit directly to the Learning Exchange after his efforts to get paid through James failed.

Jason detailed his efforts to get paid for designing the Learning Exchange website. He sent invoices to James but never got a response. Over the spring and summer of 2004, he called a number of times about the unpaid invoices, but James never returned his calls. Jason did speak with Julie by phone several times as well, but he didn't want to involve her in the business dealings so simply asked her to have James call him. In August of 2004, he eventually got James on the phone. James admitted to him that he hadn't been completely truthful about the website and its billing, but he assured Jason he would make sure he was paid.

Jason didn't necessarily consider James a liar but more of a "storyteller" who liked to exaggerate details to enhance the story. And he did seem to live above his means. Back in college, they used to joke about James and his desire to live above his means. Even when James had no money, he always drove a Cadillac. At one point, Jason had suspected that James's tendency to spend more than he made was catching up with him. The two had been out together when Julie called James, crying and very upset. When Jason asked James what was wrong, he replied that "the lawyers" were calling and bothering her again. Jason suspected it was a collection company but never asked.

The two investigators asked Jason if he thought that James was capable of killing Julie. They were surprised when he said yes, and they followed up by asking what reason James would have to kill her.

The answer was simple: money.

Bailey and Connolly wrapped up their interviews of James and Julie's friends by visiting the home of Ted and Leila Willmore, in Columbia, but the Willmores were still completely baffled about how Julie could have ingested ethylene glycol and didn't have anything new to share.

––––––––––––

That night, the two investigators drove to the outskirts of Jefferson City for their last interview, hoping that they could find James's mother, Betty Keown, before they flew back to Boston in the morning. Her house, on Covey Lane, was dark when they drove up, but they could still tell the house was large, well maintained, and impressive. Perhaps James hadn't always aspired to live above his means; it appeared that James's mother lived very comfortably.

Bailey put in a call to Betty Keown from the driveway, unsure if they would find her at home, or still awake. She not only answered, but sounded completely at ease about speaking with them and invited the investigators to come in.

When Betty answered the door, however, Bailey was a bit taken aback. She greeted them like they were old friends, and her face was perfectly made up, but she was clad in only a pink bathrobe. Bailey knew it was late and she'd probably already been in bed, but he wondered why she hadn't gotten dressed after he'd phoned. He couldn't picture his own mother answering the door for two strangers at night in her bathrobe, yet Betty seemed completely unfazed by the hour, her dress, or their visit.

"Come in; can I offer you a drink?" she asked as she ushered the two men into her home.

On the inside, the house was just as impressive as it had been outside, and Bailey calculated that in the Waltham area, the same house would easily cost close to a million dollars.

"You have a beautiful home," he said and was stunned when she told them how much the house cost, far below what he expected to hear. She then led them on a tour of the spacious home, proudly pointing out numerous plaques and awards on the walls that her late husband had received as a lobbyist in the state.

Bailey's surprise at Betty's reaction to their visit only grew when her daughter Shawna called. "No, I'm just talking to the cops from Boston," Betty told her daughter, as if it was nothing out of the ordinary.

James and Julie had a good relationship, Betty told the detectives. She had been east to visit them in July, along with Shawna and Shawna's fiancé. Nothing seemed out of the ordinary about the trip. But she knew that Julie had been unwell since May or June, Betty told them, and had an existing kidney problem. Bailey made a note of her mention of the kidney problem. Betty could not remember where she'd heard about the kidney problem, but not from James, she said. Before Julie's illness, it had actually been James who seemed to have medical issues, his mother said. Notably, he had been jumped in the parking lot outside the Learning Exchange, she explained to the two investigators, and Betty went on to tell the detectives that two years earlier, he'd tripped over the cat and ended up with head injuries. He just seemed to have rotten luck.

Betty also said that her other daughter-in-law's sister or stepsister might have committed suicide with antifreeze in North Carolina. Bailey would later verify that there had been a distant relative of Betty's daughter-in-law who'd committed suicide with a household product, but the substance had been Drano, not antifreeze.

Betty had last spoken with Julie on September 3 in the evening. At the time, Julie had been playing cards with James.

According to Betty, James said he thought he was still being considered a suspect, and after his meeting with Sergeant Owen Boyle of the Massachusetts State Police, he decided he wanted to get an attorney. He couldn't return to Harvard that fall because classes had already started for that semester, so he returned to Missouri. But James was having a tough time with his finances since coming back, his mother explained. His money was "all tied up" in Kansas City, he'd told his mother, because a death certificate was still pending for Julie. As a result, all of his money was off-limits.

Bailey and Connolly knew that this was not the case, but they did not share their information about the couple's finances with Betty Keown. They did have one last question for her, though, which they expected would be tough for her to answer: did she think her son could have had anything to do with his wife's death?

"I can't say for sure that my son didn't do it, but I can't say that he did either," Betty said.

The statement didn't make sense to the investigators, who wrapped up their interview with Betty, somewhat puzzled by her response. What had Betty Keown really meant?

CHAPTER 19

Not long after James Keown arrived back in Missouri, his résumé landed at an executive head-hunting service, where it eventually caught the eye of Tim Trabon, a very successful Kansas City, Missouri, entrepreneur, who was looking for a talented marketing professional to take his latest business venture to the next level.

Trabon was impressed when he saw the résumé and thought to himself that he wanted to meet James, who seemed like he'd be a good addition to his growing business. Though as a child Trabon had dreamed of being a writer or adventurer, seeing more of the world than the flat farmland of the Midwest he had known since childhood, he had inherited a printing business when his father had passed away, when Trabon was just a sophomore in high school. For twelve years, Trabon worked night and day to build the company now known as one of the top printing companies in not only the Midwest, but the country.

Then one day, when he was twenty-eight years old, Trabon took a look at his life. What would he be doing if his father hadn't died when he did? Where would he have gone? *I'd be doing something adventurous, like being with Jacques Cousteau or something*, he thought to himself.

With the printing business going strong, Trabon left it in the capable hands of his head employees and went out to see the world. Through a series of amazing events, he *did* end up with Jacques Cousteau on his boat *Calypso*. For eleven years, Trabon traveled with the famed explorer while making trips back to Kansas City to keep his printing business going.

Now back in Kansas City, Trabon was ready to expand his business ventures. In addition to the printing business, he already raised beef cattle and quarter horses on a large ranch several hours outside the city, but he was looking for another business to grow. His early recognition of the value of information technology as a business enabler led him to start Trabon Solutions in 1998 with a partner and a small team of developers.

By the fall of 2004, the custom software company had developed a product for human resources management. Although the firm had been successful in implementing the software in a company setting, Trabon needed a marketing person to take it to the next level—someone who was not just a marketing genius, but also had an understanding of computer software and human resources management.

The position would require a top-notch employee, and when the résumé for James "JP" Keown landed in his e-mail inbox, Trabon immediately thought, "We've got to meet this guy."

JP sounded almost too good to be true. He stated on the top of the résumé that he was relocating to Kansas City, before listing his numerous attributes.

"Competitive, tenacious, organized, and results-oriented professional combining innovative marketing, sales, and programming skills to significantly enhance organizational growth," the résumé stated.

James listed his core strengths as "innovative marketing and sales leadership; senior-level relationship management; extensive technical knowledge and experience; focused entrepreneurial spirit; brand development and management and hands-on team player."

His current job was listed as director of sales, marketing, and new media for ABC/Disney Marketing Group in Boston. In that position, James stated that he oversaw marketing and sales for an innovative experienced marketing group, developed hundreds of high-profile events every year, and connected clients with the world's top entertainment brands. Prior to that job, he claimed to have spent 1998 through 2000 at ABC Radio in Chicago as director of operations and new media, overseeing the relaunch of a heritage AM radio station in the number-three market—managing programming and marketing staff and supervising both the Chicago Bulls and Chicago White Sox radio networks.

The impressive résumé didn't end there. While working for Entercom in Kansas City from 1993 through 1998, James had also allegedly helped lead the launch and operation of the station's first all-news radio station.

He concluded with his education, including his current work at Harvard University, where he stated that he was "specializing in cutting-edge HR principles such as Balanced Scorecard" and studying with the Berkman Center for Technology Law at Harvard.

The executive head-hunting firm contracted by Trabon had also seemed impressed by the professional connections James seemed to have.

"Attached is the second eval for JP. As I understand

it, the reference given is from one of the top executives with ABC. He has been in London solving some problems for ABC and was very prompt in responding to our request via e-mail. I'm starting to get the sense that JP really has some 'contacts,' former Governor of MO and top execs at ABC, *not bad*," Eric Walters, a senior technical recruiter, wrote in an e-mail to Trabon and one of his partners, Greg Deitch.

The e-mail also included the comments from the supposed ABC executive, who began with a somewhat flip statement: "Greetings from foggy old London."

The reference went on: "Sorry this has taken me so long to get this back to you. JP mentioned that you were under a bit of a deadline. Attached, you will find the completed form. As you have probably already discovered, JP is an excellent candidate. He is one of those individuals you meet that can excel in almost anything, but especially sales and marketing. You will find my gushing compliments in the form. You are very fortunate to be working with him. If there are any horrible typing errors, I blame it on jetlag."

Soon Trabon and his partners sat down for an interview with JP, who was self-assured and seemed completely at ease with the executives. Trabon was impressed with JP's depth of knowledge in human resources management and software. JP explained to Trabon that he wanted to move back to Kansas City because his wife had recently passed away and he had family in the area.

Trabon felt sad about JP's situation, but it was his résumé, knowledge, and enthusiasm for the position that impressed him. So much so, in fact, that he not only hired JP but agreed to pay his moving expenses from Boston to Kansas City. The invoice from Seibs Allied Moving stated that the exact delivery address in Kansas City was not yet determined. The total bill for the boxes, packing, and moving came to $9,376.91, which was paid by Trabon as part of the compensation package agreed to with James. Though he had been staying with Troy Rivas, James soon moved to an expensive loft he rented in Kansas City after getting the job with Trabon.

"I thought he would just be a stellar contributor to our company," Trabon later recalled.

Trabon's partner Dave Kelley felt the same way after meeting the outgoing redhead. "He seemed very bright and intelligent and capable," Kelley said. "That's exactly what we were looking for."

Trabon didn't spend a lot of time working one-on-one with JP, but he was getting reports about how well he was doing marketing the software. During meetings with the company partners, JP had all sorts of ideas about how to branch out and approach companies that might be interested in the software. And he seemed to know everyone and have connections everywhere. JP had appointments with people he knew at General Electric, Disney, and other major companies. Though none of them materialized into a sale, Trabon was impressed by JP's efforts and felt that he had made a good hire.

JP seemed to have high hopes for his success at the company, too, and almost immediately went out and bought a new BMW and told his co-workers that he put down a deposit on a loft-style apartment in a very desirable and trendy area of Kansas City. A partner at Trabon Solutions had recently purchased a unit there, and some wondered how JP could afford the place.

That's pretty optimistic for someone working on commission, Trabon thought as he saw JP drive around in the sporty car and heard him talk about his riverfront loft. But he didn't know much about JP's background or financial situation, so he brushed it off as a man who was trying to make a fresh start after the death of his wife.

Soon, however, despite JP's ideas and enthusiasm, some

started to wonder if there was anything more to the new employee.

"Whenever I would walk by his office, he would always be looking out the door, like he wasn't working, or maybe he was a little paranoid and watching out for himself," Kelley later recalled.

Trabon found himself wondering how JP had gotten into Harvard. Sure, he was smart, but he just didn't seem to have that intellectual polish that he would've expected from a student of an Ivy League college. Trabon didn't consider himself an elitist by any means, but during his travels with Cousteau, he had met all sorts of people from all sorts of backgrounds. Something about JP's education just didn't seem legit.

Still, Trabon tried not to judge people, and he felt he should try to get to know his new hire a little better. One afternoon, he called JP to come into his office.

"I know this is none of my business and if you don't feel comfortable talking about it, I understand, but I'm curious about what happened to your wife," Trabon said.

JP responded in a very matter-of-fact manner that his wife had a rare kidney malfunction, became seriously ill, and was hospitalized for a time. It seemed she was going to get better, but shortly after returning home, she was taken back to the hospital and died. Trabon was struck by the composure the young man displayed as he talked about his wife's recent unexpected death.

After JP left, Trabon had a nagging feeling about the conversation. Something just wasn't sitting right with him about JP's level of composure. Julie Keown had only died two months before.

People deal with traumatic situations in all different ways; some don't show their feelings, or talk about them, but JP had told Trabon all about his wife's death, with no sign of stress or sadness.

Tim Trabon was one of the last people still in the office a few weeks later when his phone rang just after 5 p.m. A woman he knew, though not well, was on the other end of the line.

"The person you have working for you now isn't who he claims to be," she told Trabon of JP. "I'm really afraid to say any more; that's really all you need to know," she said.

Trabon's first thought was that the two must have a personal history and this was nothing more than a case of sour grapes. What was her motivation? He didn't know. It could just be a case of a jilted lover or a business deal gone wrong.

But he didn't simply dismiss the caller's statements; he decided to do a quick Google search on his new hire. A marketing-company press release came up on the search results, with JP Keown listed as the contact person.

The company had not been listed on JP's impressive résumé.

That's strange, Trabon thought. He picked up the phone, called the company, and asked for the owner.

The man on the other end of the phone seemed pleasant and willing to talk as Trabon began, "I believe I've got someone working for me who may have worked for you in the past."

"Sure, what's his name?" The man's attitude changed abruptly when Trabon mentioned JP's name. "I can't talk about that," he responded, almost too quickly.

"Did he work for you?" Trabon asked.

He again told Trabon he could not talk about JP. Trabon was starting to get a bad feeling in his gut.

What was going on here?

"Listen, I've got him working for me right now; is there something I need to know?" Trabon asked.

"You should call this number," he told Trabon as he rattled off a phone number.

Trabon dialed the number and got an answering machine—it was the voice mail for Detective Jon Bailey of the Waltham Police Department.

Holy shit, Trabon thought. *What is going on?*

It was late. He didn't know if Bailey was gone for the day. He knew he couldn't sit there and wait for Bailey to call him back. Was there someone in his company who was a danger to his employees?

He called back the man who had given him Bailey's phone number.

"Something's going on here," he said to the man. "I've got employees here. I don't need an incident."

The man still wouldn't say much.

"I really can't talk about a whole lot, but he's under suspicion for a pretty bad crime. The detectives from Massachusetts are watching him."

As he hung up the phone, Trabon's mind starting turning—JP's wife had died while they were living in Massachusetts. Could he have a murderer working right beside him?

Detective Bailey returned Trabon's call the next day. Trabon explained that he had JP working at his company.

"You do," Bailey responded, giving away nothing. "What do you know about him?"

"He worked at Disney," Trabon said.

"Oh, he told you that," Bailey responded, again revealing nothing, but Trabon got the sense there was much, much more than what Bailey was saying.

Bailey explained that he couldn't discuss JP because of an ongoing investigation, but Trabon started to read between the lines.

He told Bailey he was going to fire James.

"Don't fire him on my account," Bailey insisted.

"I'm not; I'm firing him because he lied on his résumé," Trabon responded.

Trabon had the distinct sense that JP was under suspicion for murdering his wife. What else could it be? He called a meeting with his partners and briefed them on what he had learned. The other men were in disbelief. This had to be a case of mistaken identity, they told Trabon. JP was the ideal employee, a great guy, not the type of person who would ever be tied to something as sinister as killing his wife.

"Trust me on this one; I've been up all night," Trabon said, resigned to the fact that he had someone in his company who was a potential murderer.

And he knew he had to fire him. But with little information from Bailey about the case, he didn't know what to expect. Trabon wasn't taking any chances, so he called a security firm he had dealt with in the past. He explained the situation.

"I'm going to fire this guy. I have no idea what to anticipate from him. I don't know if he's dangerous. Can you have a guy come in here?"

With a security guard stationed in the office, Trabon walked into JP's office the next day. He got right to the point.

"I'm letting you go," he told him.

JP appeared genuinely shocked as he asked Trabon why.

"Because most of what you told me is not true," he said.

"I don't understand," JP responded.

"You very well understand; you've fabricated a lot of information," Trabon told him, and he ordered JP to leave the building.

JP's jaw dropped, and for just a minute Trabon wondered if maybe he was wrong about him. Maybe he wasn't a murderer. But he wasn't taking any chances. Even if he wasn't a murderer, he was a liar—the entire résumé he'd used to get the job at Trabon Solutions had been false.

As JP got up to leave, Trabon noticed there were no personal photographs on his desk to pack up, no photos of Julie, no personal mementos other than a portable stereo to play music or listen to the radio, which he picked up as he walked out of the office.

Sitting on the desk when he left was the brand-new laptop computer the company had purchased when he started the job.

Well, at least that wasn't a total loss, Trabon thought. Dave Kelley, one of the partners, needed a new laptop. Rather than buy another new one, he'd just give Dave the one they'd bought for JP.

Kelley took JP's laptop home with him that night to set it up. As he turned on the laptop, he refreshed the list of wireless networks. A network called "Keyser Soze" came up on the screen as JP's home network or the name he chose for his personal network.

That's a strange name, he thought, and decided to Google it. The top result for Keyser Soze was as a character in the movie *The Usual Suspects*, which won an Oscar for best screenplay.

He spent the next forty-five minutes reading everything he could about Keyser Soze on the Internet. *This is significant*, he thought, with an uneasy feeling in his gut as he realized the meaning behind the name and how it related to James.

Kelley ran out at 11 p.m. to his local video store to rent *The Usual Suspects*. Within the first fifteen minutes of the movie, the feeling in his stomach had gone from unease to something much worse.

In the movie, Kevin Spacey (who won a best supporting actor Oscar for his role) plays Roger "Verbal" Kint, a disabled con man who chose the wrong victim when he

scammed fifty thousand dollars belonging to an under-
world crime boss named Keyser Soze. Because of the
debt, Kint is among a group of criminals in the movie
recruited by Soze as part of an elaborate plot to hijack a
boat and get revenge on Soze's rivals.

The movie centers on Kint recounting the story of the
deadly job for a police detective. Kint appears terrified of
Keyser Soze, and he stresses the crime boss's power and
ruthlessness throughout the interrogation. At one point,
Kint tells the detective, "You think you can catch Keyser
Soze? You think a guy like that comes this close to getting caught and sticks his head out? If he comes up for
anything, it will be to get rid of me. After that . . . my
guess is you'll never hear from him again."

At the end of the movie, Kint is released from police
custody and begins limping away. As he walks, he loses
the limp, and his disabled hand miraculously straightens
out and moves. At the same moment, inside the police station, a fax arrives with an artist's sketch of Keyser Soze.

It is Kint.

But by that point, Kint has been picked up by a car and
disappeared from sight, never to be seen again.

———————————

When Dave Kelley walked into Tim Trabon's office
early the next morning holding the laptop, Trabon knew
something was wrong. Kelley's hair almost seemed to
be standing on end as he told Trabon they should have
their technical people go over the computer because there
might be information the police would be interested in.

"You've got to show this to the cops; it might say something about who he was," Kelley said, and he told Trabon
who "Keyser Soze" was.

Trabon put in another call to Detective Bailey, who
immediately went out and rented the film himself. He,

too, had goose bumps as he watched and realized what James's choice of Keyser Soze for the name of his home computer network could mean.

If James Keown thought he was Keyser Soze, perhaps he thought he was going to be able to slip away without anyone knowing what he had done—climb into a car and escape with no one any wiser about what had happened to his wife. Jon Bailey knew he could not let that happen.

CHAPTER 20

Detective Reed Buente never set out to be a cop. His father had been a pharmacist in his hometown of Warrensburg, Missouri, a small community about fifty miles east of Kansas City. Reed was the youngest of his siblings and considered the last hope to take over his father's business. And although he soon realized he did not enjoy the math and science that went along with his father's job, the small-town pharmacy eventually led him to police work.

He got to know all of the police officers as they came in to get their prescriptions filled and soon found himself working in his hometown police department. In 1982, he took a job with the Kansas City, Missouri, Police Department, and four years later he became a detective, where his first assignment was in the homicide division. He went on to work on a specialized gang unit within

the department and eventually moved on to the Career
Criminal Squad, which is where he was in late 2004. The
squad was made up of local and federal agencies, and in
addition to targeting violent and repeat offenders, members sometimes assisted outside agencies.

The call Buente received from Hugh Fowler, a friend
of his from the Missouri State Highway Patrol, with a
request to help some investigators from Massachusetts
sounded pretty straightforward.

Fowler had gotten a call from a Lieutenant Jim Connolly in Massachusetts about getting help from the police
in Missouri with a search warrant in Kansas City. Connolly needed to obtain a search warrant for a business
called the Learning Exchange.

Buente was more than happy to help out.

Just after Christmas, Connolly put in a call to Buente
and filled him in on the case to date and what they
needed at the Learning Exchange—mostly any papers,
computers, or belongings left behind by James Keown.
He e-mailed Buente an affidavit in the case, which Buente
simply cut and pasted from the e-mail into an application
for a search warrant in Jackson County, Missouri.

The affidavit stated in part:

> Lt. Connolly states that he has probable cause to
> believe that the crimes of murder and use of a poison-
> ous substance, to wit: ethylene glycol have occurred
> and that evidence of those crimes will be found in
> the following items, which are currently located
> within the premises of a company called The Learn-
> ing Exchange . . . Lt. Connolly [was looking for] the
> following: electronic files and data within a Toshiba
> personal computer, Serial No. 81251803PU, and its
> peripherals, including CD's and diskettes; electronic

files and data within the hard drive of the personal computer work station used by Keown at the Learning Exchange as designated by Ms. JoLynn Bethke; electronic files and data within the server belonging to the Learning Exchange; and various paper documents.

In addition to the details of the investigation and need for the warrant, Connolly laid out some of the suspicions of the investigators. He pointed out that a *Court TV* special had aired the month before Julie Keown's illness began. The special was about Lynn Turner, who'd poisoned her husband with antifreeze. A medical expert, Dr. Brian Friset, was on the show talking about how antifreeze can be hidden in food to avoid detection. As for where or how James might have learned more about poisoning with antifreeze, investigators suspected he had used a computer. As a result, Connolly included a paragraph concerning computer information that might be relevant to the case in the warrant:

Any electronic file or paper document specifically pertaining to the Internet activity of Keown (including, but not limited to file menus, Internet navigation directories and logs, "cookies" sent from Internet sites, "cache" directories and files, temporary Internet directories and files, and electronic mail logs) which may identify, trace or record the fact, date, time, modification, alteration, transmission and/or receipt via the Internet (or other computer-to-computer transmission mode) of any computer files.

Buente knew that the standard process for obtaining a search warrant included filling in a template provided by the court system. After he filled out the warrant, and pasted in Connolly's information, Buente's sergeant reviewed the application. The application then went to the prosecuting attorney for the area for review before it went to the judge.

A Missouri judge approved the search warrant on January 18, 2005. The next day, Lieutenant Jim Connolly and Detective Jon Bailey arrived in Kansas City from Boston and met up in person with Buente.

Buente was struck by how professional the two Massachusetts investigators were. They certainly were well prepared and knew exactly what they were there to find. Buente also sensed that Bailey and Connolly knew their investigation was going to be a long, tedious process.

Buente drove as they headed out to the Learning Exchange offices, located inside a group of buildings on the Penn Valley College campus. They were met by managing director JoLynn Bethke and CEO Tammy Blossom, who led them to an office where all of the items James Keown had left behind were laid out on a table. Blossom explained to the detectives that she had moved the items out of James's old office because they'd needed the space for a new employee.

The investigators found the Toshiba laptop, five CDs, two mini CDs, and a magnifying glass along with all of the personal mail James had sent to the office. There was also a bag, an MP3 player, pieces of carpet, a notebook, and some odds and ends. No one had any idea why James had the carpet in his office. Tammy made it clear to the investigators that the Learning Exchange did not want any of James's belongings. As far as she was concerned, James had abandoned the property because he'd refused numerous requests from her to pick it up.

Blossom had sent a letter to James immediately after he was fired requesting that he return any intellectual property belonging to the company, such as logos, articles, and photos of the educational programs operated by the Learning Exchange and being run around the country. He was also asked to return a key to the building, and the company offered to pay for him to return it. She got no response until she followed up a month later with an e-mail she copied to the company's attorney, asking again for James to return the intellectual property. That time, James e-mailed her back and apologized for not returning the property but said he was busy because his wife, Julie, was in the hospital suffering from renal failure and that he would try to get the materials to Blossom as soon as possible. He never did. That was the last time Tammy Blossom or anyone at the Learning Exchange had heard from James. At the time, Blossom informed all of the company employees that because of the circumstances of James's termination, they should not speak to him, and any contact from him should be reported to her. She didn't have to worry, though, because James never contacted them again or made arrangements to pick up his belongings.

So when the police showed up with their search warrant almost six months later, Blossom was more than ready to hand over the pile of items that had been taking up space in the office.

Bailey and Connolly carried the laptop back with them by hand to Massachusetts, where it would be entered into evidence, while Buente packaged the CDs and magnifying glass, which were shipped via Federal Express. As a result of the search warrant, they also searched the computer server at the Learning Exchange for any evidence related to the case but found little of value. On the actual laptop, they found forged reference documents that James had used when the Learning Exchange hired him. These were in addition to the fake contracts for the website design and the bogus admission letter from Harvard.

Before they returned to Massachusetts, Bailey and
Connolly scheduled a few interviews with Julie Keown's
co-workers at the Cerner Corporation. The Cerner offices
sat on a hill overlooking Kansas City and had a very modern feel to them. Those who had known Julie were still
shocked at her sudden, and painful, death from ethylene
glycol poisoning. The detectives first sat down with Barb
Sheets, who told them she had worked with Julie in July
of 2004 on a proposal for work. Sheets considered Julie
a very accomplished nurse and good person. She didn't
know James, but Julie had confided that she was a little
frustrated with him at one point, telling the other woman
that she got after James because he needed to focus more,
especially with regard to their move to Boston earlier that
year. James, she told her, had a tendency to do things "off
the cuff."

Jill Lawson, an attractive blond woman, had first met
Julie in August of 2003 and had become friendly with
her in the months that followed. Jill knew that Julie was
having health problems and was told it was renal failure.
After the trip to North Carolina in August of 2004, Julie
told Jill that she felt as good as she had for a while.

Jill had spoken with James on September 5 about
Julie's worsening condition. At that time, James told her
that the doctors had found ethylene glycol in Julie's system and were assuming she was suicidal. Jill had felt a
bit disturbed by how calm, and almost cold, James had
sounded when he'd told her about Julie's prognosis.

Bailey made a note of Jill Lawson's statement regarding Julie feeling better, as it was the second time he had
heard about Julie's symptoms improving; the other time
was when Julie took the trip back to the family farm in
Plattsburg in the early summer of 2004. In both of those

instances, she got better when she was away from James or when she and James were not alone.

———————————

By this point, some of James and Julie's other friends had begun to question whether James was responsible for her death. Ted Willmore told investigators that James had made a statement about wearing his wedding ring until after the holidays and then he might start dating. James also confided to his friends that he was going to use Julie's life insurance policy money to build a house, buy a new BMW, and then start a scholarship in her name with whatever was left.

James's statements about spending Julie's life insurance money also gave investigators a little more to go on in terms of the financial motive angle, but they needed more concrete proof to move forward with any charges. For that, they looked to the computers and a computer forensic expert.

Massachusetts State Trooper David McSweeney had been with the state police since 1993 and worked out of the Norfolk County District Attorney's Office White Collar Crimes Division. His area of expertise was computer-related investigations, computer search and seizure, and the process of computer forensics.

McSweeney had a master's degree in criminal justice administration from Western New England College, but more significantly for the current investigation, he was trained in the use of the EnCase software. EnCase was the software of choice by law enforcement for computer forensic analysis. The software was used to access material in the computer from a user's Internet searches, and it could also access information inside the files of the computer, where the search terms provided are used.

On January 28, 2005, McSweeney received the Toshiba laptop from the Learning Exchange as well as two Dell laptops owned by the Cerner Corporation that Julie Keown had used for work.

The two Dell laptops had been reviewed in the early weeks of the investigation in September of 2004 by another computer forensic specialist, James Schwaab. Schwaab conducted a preliminary search using EnCase at the direction of one of the assistant district attorneys handling the case, Steve Hoffman. That initial search by Schwaab provided investigators with a timeline for Julie's last day at home, a timeline that conflicted with the one that James gave investigators. Julie had gotten up early that day and was on her computer most of the morning looking at dolls and doll clothes, which was a hobby she enjoyed. James had told investigators she was in bed and so sick she couldn't even speak to her parents on the phone.

Schwaab's search was a bit different in that it was the result of a consent search given by James Keown and not a search warrant.

When McSweeney was given those computers, along with the Toshiba, he was also given a list of search terms that Bailey and Connolly thought might be relevant to the investigation, such as *antifreeze*, *ethylene glycol*, and *poison*. Connolly also provided fifty key search words to McSweeney that were the result of suggestions from the prosecutors on the case as well as investigators.

McSweeney previewed the computers and made copies of the hard drives for his analysis. There were 218,000 files on the three computers, and in the end, the investigator flagged less than 1 percent of those files as something potentially related to the case.

McSweeney searched on or about the day that Julie

died in 2004 to see if there was any web search activity during that time on her work computer.

It turned out there was.

Julie Keown had been searching on the Internet for how to get better.

CHAPTER 21

Jefferson City might've been the capital of the state of Missouri, but to locals it was almost like the little sister of nearby Columbia, which had a larger and more thriving city scene. Most visitors were surprised to find a state capital more like a small town than the hub of the state's activities. For many who lived there, Jefferson City was just that—a small town, where people who were born there ended up staying their entire lives. Sure, they might go away to college, but many found themselves, despite vows to leave after high school, eventually back in Jefferson City. And although they may have bemoaned the lack of things to do, including only a small handful of restaurants and a tiny movie theater, Jefferson City was a good place to raise a family. The crime rate was low and the cost of living even lower. A brand-new three-bedroom apartment in Jefferson City might rent for $350.

Jefferson City was a place known for its conservative

nature and even more conservative politics. With two high schools in town, both the public high school and a private Catholic high school, Jefferson City had a reputation across the state for its football teams. During football season every fall, it seemed the city's political lifeblood, which dominated the news, was given a run for its money by the city's other passion—high school football.

In November of 2004, after being fired by Tim Trabon, James Keown left the expensive Kansas City loft he'd been living in and moved in with his mother, Betty, who was then employed as a cafeteria worker at one of the city's schools. Though the family had always been considered well-off by Jefferson City standards, some wondered if Betty's job meant that their wealth had run out. Betty Keown's house was in one of the more upscale neighborhoods in Jefferson City, a few miles down the road from the local country club. The house sat directly on the side of a large lake, and it had a dock that went into the lake, where Betty tied up a paddle boat in the summer. And just past the country club, on the side of the Capital Plaza Mall, was the KLIK station, where James first got his start in the radio business.

Some lifelong residents felt that the small-town atmosphere tended to lead to cliques, and like many small towns, people loved to find out about each other and often get involved with people's personal business when they were not welcome. At times it could feel like everyone knew everything about everybody in Jefferson City. But in the fall of 2004, no one knew anything about the real reason James Keown had returned to his Jefferson City roots. When James moved home, many who knew him but were unaware of the suspicious circumstances surrounding Julie's death saw the move as an understandable way for a young widower to get his life back together.

James returned to his hometown and sought out a job at the local radio station KLIK.

Those who knew James Keown in the radio world could not believe that the experienced "big market" radio personality was coming back to work at the local AM station. His former mentor Warren Krech, still working at the station, hadn't hesitated to give James a recommendation. Warren still thought of James as perhaps the most talented young person he had ever hired. James had been just twelve years old when he'd first walked into the KLIK station looking for a job.

For the local radio station, hiring James for a second time was almost too good to be true. The famous JP O'Neil—James Keown's on-air name—had returned to the station that launched his national radio career. Some people may have wondered why someone with JP's résumé, which included being the voice of ESPN Radio in Chicago and a top person in Kansas City radio, would return to the local station. But others saw JP's move, which came just months after the death of his wife, Julie, as a way for him to be close to his mother and his lifelong friends as he recovered from his grief. Either way, they were glad to have the legendary radio talk-show host back as part of their team.

News Director Dean Morgan hadn't seen James in about four years. Dean had been in Missouri media for a number of years and had first met James in the early 1990s, when James worked at another station, KWOS, also in Jefferson City. James's knowledge of the radio world and his ability to network had impressed Dean back then, and he remembered how those talents had landed James a job as the affiliate representative to the Kansas City Royals baseball team for one radio station. Dean knew that James had applied for the program director job at KLIK earlier in the fall, a job that eventually went to Brian Wilson. But then Wilson hired James to do the *Party Line* news talk show and report on local news events. Right away, Dean loved working with James.

"He seemed like the same James, happy-go-lucky, sociable, warm," Dean later recalled. "Even if he wasn't telling the story, you wanted to be around him."

But James wasn't without fault. He was very good at doing the news, but it depended on how interested he was in pursuing a story. Some stories got the attention they deserved to flesh them out, while others fell short but were passable. Still, from Dean's perspective, James was an absolute pleasure to work with.

James's daily *Party Line* show had been a tradition in the Missouri state capital since 1954. Although the show was always popular, that popularity grew when James hosted. He had plenty to talk about. For the first time in decades, the Republicans had the majority in the Missouri General Assembly, and their newly elected Republican governor, Matt Blunt, was busy making good on his campaign promises of reducing the state's one billion dollar budget deficit. For a political hound like James, with personal connections to many of the state's top politicians, the stories were endless and perfect fodder for the daily talk-radio show.

James picked up where he'd left off with the local radio scene, with both his on-air guests and sources that included top government officials in the city. He launched a regular segment with local prosecutor Bill Tackett, called *Tuesdays with Tackett*, and presented himself both on and off the air as someone who was "in the know." To his new co-workers in the radio world around Jefferson City, James Keown quickly became one of the gang. He was a regular guest at the weekly press corps meetings in nearby Columbia, where the area press gathered at McNally's Pub for drinks and shop talk each Tuesday.

He also picked right back up with his lifelong friends, like Betsy Dudenhoeffer, a pal since kindergarten. The two had not seen each other since their ten-year reunion from Jefferson City High School, in 2002, when James had arrived in the top-of-the-line Mercedes, oozing success and confidence as he told her about his job with ESPN Radio in Chicago. At the time, it had come as no surprise to her that James, who had been voted "Most Likely to Succeed" in high school, was doing so well.

"We all knew he was going places," she would later recall.

When he returned to the radio station, he and Betsy, who was working as an advertising representative at KLIK, caught up over lunch and quickly became as close as they had been during school, often going out for a glass of wine at the Native Stone or Summit Lake wineries or for after-work drinks with co-workers. Yet, despite their close friendship, James never talked to Betsy about his wife's death.

It's just too raw, and it's still too soon, Betsy assumed whenever she wondered why he hadn't brought Julie up in conversation.

She had never met his wife and was curious about her. When she'd asked James about his wife and where she was at their ten-year reunion, James gave a simple answer: Julie was sick. Betsy now wondered if that sickness had anything to do with Julie Keown's death.

McNally's Pub, in Columbia, Missouri, was a modest brown building with brick accents, a flat roof, and hunter green trim, a plain-looking place you might not notice if you weren't specifically going there, and the type of watering hole known for reasonably priced drinks and hearty pub food. It was located just outside the downtown business district of Columbia, across the street from the police department and around the corner from the *Columbia Daily Tribune*.

Its proximity to the newspaper made McNally's a convenient location for the official gathering spot for the area press. Every Tuesday, newspaper reporters, photographers, and the occasional journalism graduate student met in the bar to catch up and talk shop. It wasn't just the bar that was a gathering place for journalists, but the city. The University of Missouri at Columbia was known for having one of the best journalism programs in the country. The university was known by many as "Mizzou," and graduates of the prestigious journalism school were often referred to as the "Mizzou Mafia" in media circles because they were so prevalent in journalism.

Columbia was the type of place where many people lived and breathed journalism, priding themselves on being able to ferret out a story or lead. Still, none of the area press noticed anything unusual about James Keown when he started showing up at the Tuesday night press corps gathering just after Thanksgiving of 2004. He was jovial, boisterous, and friendly. His colleagues were sympathetic after James's brief explanation that he'd returned home to Missouri to be closer to his family after the recent loss of his wife. His tendency to push his way into the center of attention, however, didn't go over well among some of those already established in the area, who had already determined the pecking order among themselves.

James quickly became one of the regulars, like *Columbia Daily Tribune* columnist Tony Messenger, KLIK news director Dean Morgan, and Lene Johansen, a fresh-faced

James and Julie Keown at her friend Christina Liles's
wedding in December 2002.
Courtesy of David Liles

James and Julie met when they were both students at
William Jewell College, a private college in Liberty, Missouri.
Lara Bricker

Julie Keown was the matron of honor to her friend Christina Liles.
Courtesy of David Liles

Julie planned a baby shower for Christina in 2003
while still living in Missouri.
Courtesy of David Liles

Julie Keown's parents, Jack and Nancy Oldag.
The Boston Herald

Julie Keown grew up on this soybean farm in Plattsburgh, Missouri.
Lara Bricker

Waltham Police detective Jon Bailey devoted four years of work
to bringing James Keown to trial for murdering Julie.
Lara Bricker

James and Julie lived in this newly renovated duplex in Waltham,
Massachusetts, in 2004 so that James could allegedly
attend Harvard University.
Lara Bricker

James abandoned all of the furniture in his bedroom
when he left Massachusetts after Julie's death.
Courtesy of Waltham Police detective Jon Bailey

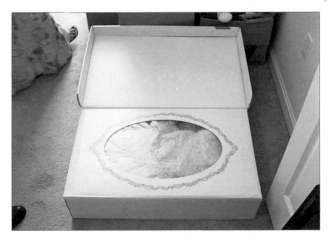

James even left his wife's wedding dress behind
when he fled the Waltham duplex.
Courtesy of Waltham Police detective Jon Bailey

Police found a half empty bottle of Gatorade in the refrigerator
at the Keowns' duplex during a search of the residence.
Courtesy of Waltham Police detective Jon Bailey

Police believed that James Keown used Gatorade to mask the flavor
of the antifreeze he used to poison his wife, Julie.
Courtesy of Waltham Police detective Jon Bailey

James Keown moved into his mother's waterfront home in an upscale neighborhood in Jefferson City, Missouri, after his wife's death.
Lara Bricker

James returned to the Jefferson City AM radio station KLIK, where he'd worked in high school, and got a job as a talk show host under the name "JP O'Neil."
Lara Bricker

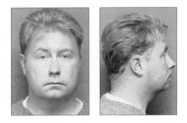

James Keown was officially booked and photographed at the Waltham Police Department after his arrest in Missouri in November 2005.
Courtesy of Waltham Police detective Jon Bailey

James Keown enters the Middlesex County Superior Court
during a hearing in his murder trial.
The Boston Herald

James Keown finally made it to Harvard; after his conviction
for murder in 2008, he was sent to the Massachusetts State
Prison in Shirley, located on Harvard Road.
Lara Bricker

brunette with a dimpled smile who was completing her graduate degree in journalism at the University of Missouri. Lene had been drawn to the university by its reputation three years after she emigrated from her native Norway. She was serious about her journalism and later moved to Washington, D.C., where she was a frequent television news commentator on topics related to science, policy, and free-market economics.

Lene watched as James tried to find his place among the group. Often dressed in pink button-down designer shirts, a fashion trend he said he'd picked up while at Harvard, James liked to tell stories. He talked about his connections with the executives at Clear Channel Communications. He talked about his connections with the governor of Missouri, Matt Blunt, whose sister James said he dated in high school. He told Lene that he had even been invited to the governor's mansion for family dinners when Blunt's father, Roy Blunt, was the governor. And he told war stories from his father's time as a lobbyist.

These stories earned James the name "Mr. Big Deal" among the area press. His charisma tended to commandeer the attention of everyone when he entered the room, and his flashy style was unusual among the local journalists.

Dean Morgan always attributed this to the fact that James had left the area and seen the world. To Dean it seemed that James had an air of sophistication gained from his experiences and time away from Jefferson City.

Ryan Smith, a Chicago native and the crime reporter for the *Jefferson City News Tribune*, didn't go often to the press corps happy hours. But during his brief interactions with James, he at first felt a sort of kinship with him as someone who knew there was more to the world than the relatively small area around Jefferson City and Columbia.

Over the university's winter break, Lene went home to visit her family in Norway. It was not long after she returned to school for the second semester that James asked if she wanted to get together outside of the press corps. James was easy to get along with, very flirtatious, and Lene saw no harm in going on a date with him. She felt she was a good judge of character, and nothing about James had raised any red flags for her.

James arrived to pick her up in an old van from the radio station with the KLIK letters painted on the side. Lene didn't find his transportation unusual for Missouri, as a number of the area press had unique cars, including a longtime photographer who drove an old El Camino and a former newsman turned landscaper who often drove his company work truck to social gatherings. James thought it was a great perk of his job that the station allowed him to drive the van, he told Lene as they headed out. He liked the fact that he didn't have to spend any of his own money on a car.

However, from Lene's observations, James wasn't exactly saving money. He was spending, all the time, and making a show of it in front of Lene and the other members of the press corps. He always had at least one thousand dollars in cash in his wallet, money he seemed to display during their outings in an almost nonchalant way. He always picked up the bill when they went out.

After a number of dates with James driving the KLIK van, he arrived one Saturday in a shiny new tan sedan. When Lene commented on his new car, James explained that he was upset to have been taking her out in the station's old van. He had gone out that morning to get the new car because he thought it was a nicer way to go out on a date. After she climbed into the car, Lene went with

James as he bought a radio receiver that would enable him to wirelessly connect his MP3 player to his car stereo. As was typical with James, he pulled out a large wad of cash to pay for the stereo equipment.

During a conversation early in the relationship, James's face had once grown serious. He said he was thinking of his wife, and he explained she had died from kidney disease. He had a look of profound sadness and grief on his face. Lene didn't press for any more details, knowing that people usually share such things as they need to. His sense of grief seemed genuine to her, and she felt she was helping a friend deal with what seemed like a very real sense of loss.

The radio station employees from KLIK and its sister station, KFRU, in nearby Columbia, didn't necessarily take part in the press corps at McNally's, which some viewed as for the print media. The radio station staff members often got together on their own for drinks and appetizers on the weekends or for game night during the week.

James easily moved back and forth between the two social circles. Matt LaCasse, the assistant news director for KFRU, first met James during a company party in January 2005. Matt, a twenty-six-year-old who'd grown up on a small farm in Iowa, always remembered what it felt like to be the new guy at work, and as a result, he always went out of his way to invite new people out with the group. James had immediately struck Matt as a friendly, outgoing guy, gregarious even, who was good at making people laugh. He could hold the attention of those around him, and Matt was drawn to him right away. James seemed like he would be a cool guy to hang out with.

Though the two radio stations were considered sister

stations, and Jefferson City was only about a thirty-minute drive from Columbia, there was a definite divide between the two cities. Columbia was often seen as the liberal college town neighbor to the more conservative Jefferson City, and some didn't make the trip.

After their initial meeting, Matt made a point to give James a call during the week to give him a heads-up about that weekend's plans. James was more than welcome to attend, Matt told him, and he usually did.

They frequented several of the college bars in Columbia, and although they were home by nine or ten on any weeknight outing, they often closed the bars down on the weekends. There were more times than not that Matt, James, and the rest of the group saw the lights of the bar come on, signaling the end of a long night of drinking.

Though the mood was light during the nights out, James and Matt did talk some about their backgrounds. James told him he was originally from Jefferson City and that he'd moved back after living in Boston. His wife had died, and he wanted to come home to start over. James wasn't specific about how his wife passed away other than that it had something to do with her kidneys.

Matt was used to the Midwest, where people took each other at face value. He had spent two years on the East Coast and didn't feel that the people there were sincere. They never looked you in the eye and didn't go out of their way to say hello or offer a smile. Though he acknowledged he may have been a little naive at times, Matt preferred the outgoing, friendly nature of people in the Midwest.

When James opened up about Julie's death, Matt saw no reason to question him. He thought of himself as a farm kid from Iowa and wasn't about to push James for specific details on a painful topic. He simply sat back and listened to James because he felt that was what his new friend needed, someone to talk to about his grief. That grief was palpable to Matt. James was somber as he spoke about Julie, who he always talked about in reverent terms to the young news director.

"She was the light of my life," he told Matt more than once.

"I lost my better half when I lost her," he said at other times.

"I can't believe she's really gone."

It was heartbreaking. During these conversations, Matt felt like James was trying to regroup and just wanted to get back into the swing of life. James seemed deeply saddened by his wife's death but was always up for going out and socializing, and Matt wasn't going to argue with that. After all, he was twenty-six, had a decent job, and wanted to have fun. James seemed like the perfect friend to have along for the ride.

CHAPTER 22

February 15, 2005

Detective Jon Bailey knew there was a piece, or pieces, still missing as the investigation into Julie Keown's death dragged on in early February 2005. They were following up on leads all the time, but nothing seemed to pan out. James Keown looked awfully suspicious, but at the same time, everyone said that James was a great guy, a supportive and loving husband, the last person who would ever poison his wife. Bailey needed something tangible, something that would be direct evidence—a girlfriend, a more obvious motive, something that would help the investigation move to the next step.

The results of the computer search offered more proof that Julie certainly didn't seem to have wanted to die. She'd spent a lot of time looking on the Internet for ways to get better, even have children. So, the early possibility that she could have been suicidal no longer seemed plausible.

Bailey knew by now that James was a liar and a very good one. He had followed up on the nearly ten thousand dollars that Tim Trabon had paid for James's moving expenses to Missouri for his job at Trabon Solutions. The bill from the Seibs Allied Moving Company was a fake. Police believed James had printed it out from his own computer. Based on information that Bailey would later receive from James's Waltham landlord, Greg Stocklan, James had never moved his belongings out of the duplex. His inspiration for the fake moving company's name could have been from Carrie Seibs, a real estate agent he knew in Missouri, or John Seibs, a Kansas City man James knew through a mutual friend. James had stayed with John Seibs in his downtown Kansas City loft on several trips back to Missouri with Julie when he was allegedly "on break" from Harvard. And then there was the question of what James did all those days when he was supposedly attending classes at Harvard. Bailey and Lieutenant Jim Connolly had put together a paper trail using James's ATM records from the months before Julie died. There was no question that he was in Harvard Square at the times he was supposed to be in classes. The ATM receipts showed that James went to a computer store in the area of Harvard Square, but there was only so much time a person could walk around a store, Bailey thought. What else had James been doing? Bailey was growing more frustrated with the case but was optimistic that if he kept looking he would find something, either the missing love interest or perhaps a very large credit-card purchase that would explain things. There had to be something.

By February of 2005, Jon Bailey was not the only one who was frustrated when he thought of James Keown. Greg Stocklan had been trying to get in touch with James for some time. He put in call after call to Betty Keown's home in Jefferson City, where he knew James was staying, but no one ever called him back.

Stocklan was starting to get worried about the duplex, which had been vacant since James had returned to Missouri in November. He also noticed mail overflowing from the mailbox and a pile of newspapers in a heap in the driveway.

It wasn't just the condition of the duplex that was bothering Stocklan but the fact that he hadn't been paid on time for the monthly $2,000 rent since the previous July. After Julie's death, Stocklan felt sorry for James and so he didn't push him on the back rent. On December 27, 2004, James sent a letter informing his landlord that he would be moving out in two weeks but would make good on the rent. Along with the letter, James sent a certified check for two thousand dollars for one month's rent and a second two-thousand-dollar check written from his mother's account. The payments cleared James through the end of December of 2004.

On February 15, 2005, as his frustration mounted, Stocklan put in a call to Detective Jon Bailey. He wanted to let Bailey know that he would begin the process to evict James on March 1. Based on the call from Stocklan, Bailey decided to go by the duplex and see what condition the place was in. From the bottom of the porch behind the house, he could see through a sliding door on the rear of the building, where he saw several boxes, sealed with packing tape. The boxes had the words Smart Move on the side.

Next to the kitchen counter, Bailey saw another box. This one had the words *James's Computer* written on the side in black marker. The box was sealed up with tape. Bailey thought back to the first night at the duplex, when James's doctor friend Ted Willmore and Detective Brian

Lambert had found the computers upstairs with no hard drives. He wondered if these could be the computers they had been looking for and, if so, what information might be stored on them.

But just seeing the box marked *Computer* was not enough to get a search warrant.

As the frigid temperatures common during a New England winter continued to drop that February, Stocklan became concerned that the pipes might freeze inside the unoccupied duplex. Under the terms of the lease agreement, Stocklan had the right as the landlord and property owner to go inside the apartment in case of emergency—such as his concern about something like the pipes freezing—or when it appeared the apartment had been abandoned by the tenant.

He spoke with his attorney first to make sure he was doing the right thing and based on that OK, Stocklan went into the duplex to check on things on February 28, 2005. The place was freezing. It was clear that both the heat and utilities inside had been disconnected. Whether it was on purpose or because James had stopped paying his bills was unclear. But either way, Stocklan knew he was right to be concerned about the pipes as soon as he felt the frigid air. He immediately called the utility companies and had the accounts transferred into his name so that he could get the heat turned back on.

Though his last correspondence from James, in December, had indicated that he would be moving out, the duplex was still full of James and Julie's belongings and furniture. It seemed that the only thing that James had taken with him when he left were the clothes on his back. The furniture, electronic equipment, and some computer equipment were all still in the apartment.

After he walked up to the third floor, Stocklan went and looked into a closet. Sitting on the shelf, in a plastic bag, was a green substance. It looked like marijuana. He put in a call to Detective Bailey, who immediately called Assistant District Attorney Lynn Rooney.

The suspicion of an illegal substance in the apartment, seen by the landlord, was enough to get a search warrant for the duplex.

On March 4, at 1:30 p.m., Bailey, Connolly, and a team of investigators entered the apartment. Just like Stocklan, Bailey was struck by the sense that James had simply abandoned the place. Dishes were still in the dishwasher. The trash was full. It was as if the person who'd lived there had simply up and vanished one day, leaving everything behind. The question was whether any of the things left behind would bring them any closer to solving the case.

In a third-floor closet, investigators found another computer, an IBM Thinkpad laptop computer, as well as a Samsung video camera and two computer hard drives. These were most likely the missing hard drives that investigators had wondered about that first night of the investigation. The computers and the video camera were all labeled and put in evidence bags.

On the second floor, they found twenty-five CDs in a cardboard box in the spare bedroom, eight Zip discs, and miscellaneous documents. In the basement, they found yet another computer, this one an Apple Macintosh Power PC G3, along with the monitor and sixteen CDs in a cardboard box.

After three hours, Bailey and Connolly had gone from the top to the bottom of the duplex. They were joined by Waltham police detectives Tim King, Bill MacEwen, and Brian Smith and a Massachusetts State Police trooper who helped them bag up everything that might be evidence for their case. At 4:30 p.m., they walked out, evidence in hand, wondering what of any value James might have left behind at the duplex.

Ironically, the plastic bag of green vegetative matter, which had enabled police to enter that day, was not marijuana. Lab tests were negative for both marijuana and ethylene glycol, and the identity of the substance remained a mystery. Could James have left it behind intentionally to throw off the investigators or to try to make them think that Julie had been using drugs? In his gut, Bailey felt like he had.

By the end of March, Greg Stocklan had reached the limit of his patience. On March 21, 2005, he sent an eviction notice to James at his mother's address in Jefferson City. James never responded. All of James's belongings were taken out of the duplex and placed in storage. Stocklan told James in the eviction letter that he would get his belongings back once his back rent was paid. If the money was not paid within ninety days, Stocklan would sell all of his belongings.

James never did pay the back rent. And Stocklan didn't sell the items. Instead, he gave most of them to charity or friends.

CHAPTER 23

Betsy Dudenhoeffer had gone out for drinks after work with some of the women from the radio station. As she walked across the parking lot outside the KLIK station to retrieve her car, she noticed a light was still on inside the station and saw James's car in the parking lot.

I wonder what he's still doing here, she thought, and she went inside to say hello. Perhaps it was the lack of inhibition after a few drinks, or perhaps it was just her naturally forward personality, but Betsy decided it was time to ask James about his wife's death. She found him in the editing studio preparing for the next day's show. She got right to the point.

"I guess your emotions are still pretty raw about Julie," she said. "How did she die, James? Do you mind if I ask?"

James stopped what he was doing and looked at Betsy.

"Well, she had stomach cancer," he said, looking down as he spoke.

"Did she live very long after she was diagnosed?"

"It was very quick," he said, his voice serious. "She was diagnosed about nine months before, and we were told she would be able to get better with radiation and chemotherapy. But it didn't work."

"Oh, James, I'm so sorry," Betsy said as she leaned closer to hear him. "Do you still keep in touch with her parents?"

James looked away from Betsy as he responded.

"No, her mom, she got pretty belligerent and blamed me for Julie's death."

Betsy's heart went out to her old friend. She felt so sad thinking about what he must be going through. But just like that, James changed the subject, and he confided that he was thinking about asking Monica Senecal, the morning radio host at their sister station, out on a date. He asked Betsy what she thought about Monica.

"She's cute. I like her," Betsy said.

James asked where he should take Monica if she said yes.

"I have no clue where you should take her, but it would have to be somewhere in Columbia because she won't want to date you if you take her out in Jefferson City—your only options here are a movie and dinner at Applebee's," Betsy joked.

As she drove home, Betsy found herself mulling over the conversation. *That was odd,* she thought. *He went from talking about his wife dying less than six months ago to asking another woman on a date.* She chalked it up to his way of dealing with his grief. Everyone handles grief differently, and maybe a date was what James needed to help him move forward.

Matt LaCasse had also sensed that James was lonely and looking for someone to be with, so he wasn't surprised when James asked Monica out. She agreed, though after a few casual dates, both decided they were not ready for a relationship.

During one of their dates, Monica asked James how Julie had died.

Cancer, he'd responded.

Though the relationship never went anywhere, James was still a regular among the radio group on social outings. The female employees, including Monica, saw James as a perfect gentleman. He always bought the group drinks and was the life of the party. A few times, James became too drunk to drive and slept in Monica's guest room. She was impressed that despite being drunk, and their brief romantic relationship, James never made any advances toward her. They enjoyed a friendly relationship during regular game nights even though Monica often beat James at the game Win, Lose or Draw. "How can you be better than me?" James asked Monica one night. "You spent forty thousand on an education and I have a Harvard education."

James did eventually pursue another woman at the station, and Matt sensed that he was more serious about her than he had been about Monica or Lene. But the woman did not return his interest and it went nowhere. James didn't seem broken up about the rejection, but Matt still got the feeling that James wanted to be with someone. He wanted to fill that hole in his life left when his wife died.

During this time, no one questioned James's account of Julie's death. That wasn't to say that there weren't a few whispers about Julie's death and speculation about the police investigation in Massachusetts. In the middle of winter in 2005, Dean Morgan was home recuperating from having his wisdom teeth out. Though he was out of work and admittedly a little foggy from the painkillers, Dean stayed in touch with the program director at another local station via e-mail. The program director e-mailed Dean back with news that KLIK had hired a new female coanchor and also questioned whether Dean knew that James was being investigated in his wife's death.

The news about James didn't quite register with Dean at the time, which he chalked up to the painkillers he was on. But when he returned to work and saw James again, he thought about what he had been told. To Dean it seemed like typical Jefferson City, a small town where everyone was in everyone else's business. No one could keep a secret in Jefferson City, but he wasn't convinced that there was any truth to what he had heard about James. Still, when they were out after work at a restaurant or bar, Dean sometimes thought about the rumor as he listened to James talk, especially when Julie came up in conversation. James's story to him never changed, though Dean would later learn that the story was different depending on who James told it to. James's mannerisms never changed. Dean told himself there was no way the rumors could be true. He knew James, and the James he knew could not have poisoned his wife.

Investigators in Massachusetts still thought differently and were waiting for the results of a forensic analysis of the computers seized from the Waltham duplex back in March. After the search, Bailey and Connolly took five items to State Trooper David McSweeney, including two hard drives that were not installed in computers when they found them, an IBM Thinkpad laptop, an Apple computer monitor, and an Apple Macintosh desktop computer. McSweeney previewed the contents of the computers to get a sense of whether there was anything of evidentiary value stored on them. He quickly ruled all of them out because any searches done on them had been done long before Julie Keown's sickness and death.

After all they went through to get the search warrant for the duplex, the resulting evidence turned out to be a dead end. Police still needed something more if the case was ever going to move to a grand jury for indictment.

CHAPTER 24

May 2005

As Jack Oldag walked out behind the machine shed on his farm, something shiny caught his eye. It was about four hundred feet in front of him in the area of the north fence. He couldn't tell what it was, so he started to walk across the field to get a closer look.

The field had most recently been planted with corn, though it had been planted with soybeans the year before that. It was early May and not time for the planting season to begin, though Jack had already plowed the field this spring.

Something else caught Jack's eye as he walked across the field—a yellow piece of plastic was just visible in the dirt. It was partially covered by dirt on top of a drainage tile line Jack had installed in the late fall of 2003. He couldn't tell what it was and went in for a closer look.

As he pulled the plastic out, Jack did a double take

when he realized what he had found—a Prestone anti-freeze bottle. Prestone was the most expensive type of antifreeze, and Jack never bought it unless it was the only kind available.

So where had the bottle come from?

He remembered seeing James walking out in this field after Julie's funeral. Could he really have been out there to dispose of evidence? Jack wondered. He felt this bottle could be important to the case and got a stick to mark the spot where he found it. He didn't want to touch the bottle again, because he knew it could become evidence. He used another stick to pick it up and bring it back to the machine shed.

As he looked at the bottle, still covered in dirt, Jack noticed that there was a large hole in the side. He suspected that it was made by anhydrous ammonia, which he had put on that field the previous spring.

Jack immediately called Detective Jon Bailey about his find.

"Yeah, Jon, it's Jack here," he began as he always did.

Jack sounded excited to Bailey as he explained that he thought the bottle had been manufactured in 2001 because of the label and design, which he had looked up on the Internet.

Bailey wasn't sure if it was something that would help the case or not. He wondered if it was related to James and Julie's cat that had died mysteriously, the cat he still felt had been a test run. It was hard to know if it would be relevant, but either way, Bailey knew he had to preserve the chain of evidence. He put in a call to Kansas City detective Reed Buente and asked him to go out to the Oldags' farm to pick up the bottle.

Reed lived in a small community a short drive from the Oldags, and he told Bailey he'd stop and pick up the bottle on his way home. Reed was used to the remote area and the distance between homes and farms. He noticed that the closest neighbor to the Oldags was several miles away from their house.

Jack and Nancy met Reed at the door and took him into the laundry room inside the home. The bottle was lying in a box on the floor, still covered in dirt. Reed's heart went out to the couple as he thought about what they were going through. As he picked up the box and prepared to leave, Reed told himself that if anyone was going to bring the Oldags justice for their daughter, it was Jon Bailey and Jim Connolly. Before he left, he photographed the area where Jack found the bottle.

Ultimately, the Prestone bottle was another dead end for investigators. But an e-mail that Bailey received a few weeks later proved to finally be the break he had been looking for.

The e-mail on May 17, 2005, was from Sam Shoemaker. Sam, a forty-five-year-old intensive care nurse who had worked with Julie Keown at Liberty Hospital, always assumed that the police were coming to talk to him. Sam had remained friends with Julie after she took the job at Cerner and then after she moved to Waltham. Because of their friendship, Sam had simply expected the police to contact him.

And so he'd waited.

Sam Shoemaker was by all accounts an extremely private person and had never been involved with something like this before. Still, as the months went by, he kept thinking about a conversation he had with James Keown the previous September. It was odd, or at least had seemed odd to him. The more he thought about it, the more it didn't add up, but Sam didn't tell anyone other than his wife what James had told him. And he told his wife that if anyone asked her what James had discussed with him, she should say she knew nothing.

Sam kept the information to himself for fear it would become twisted or spread around, but when he heard police had already been to Kansas City, and they had not talked to him, he started to wonder if he should contact them instead. Although he hadn't told anyone what he knew, Shoemaker had heard plenty of talk about the circumstances of Julie's death. Like a number of people who worked with Julie, Sam was beginning to think that there was a side to James that he had not known about.

When he decided to contact Jon Bailey on the morning of Tuesday, May 17, 2005, Sam really believed that he was simply giving police the same information they already had.

"The information I have is probably not new," Sam wrote in the e-mail that day. He had no way of knowing that the information he had would give investigators the break they needed to tie James directly to the poisoning.

Sam had been out of town for the Labor Day weekend holiday the year before. When he got home, there was a message from Ruth Poirer, a co-worker from Liberty Hospital, who explained that she had bad news about Julie Keown. He called Ruth at the hospital and learned that Julie was in a coma and not expected to live. She gave Sam a phone number to reach James in Boston, but as it was late, Sam decided to wait until the morning to call.

"She's probably brain dead," James told Sam when he called.

James didn't expect Julie to live past that day.

"What happened?" Sam asked James.

"Antifreeze poisoning," James replied.

"How could that happen?" Sam asked.

James told Sam that for the last several months, Julie

had been having kidney problems and that a kidney specialist she saw prescribed her prednisone. The drug made her act erratic and "goofy," James told him, like she was having a stroke or something. Her speech was slurred, and she often stumbled around. As a result, James said, he'd had to keep Julie locked in the house to make sure she didn't wander away. But, he told Sam, she must have escaped one day. James told Sam that he was not sure but that he thought that Julie had drunk the antifreeze from a Gatorade bottle that she found by a trash Dumpster.

"You have to be kidding," Sam responded.

"I found her sitting by the curb drinking from a Gatorade bottle," James told him.

James thought that the neighborhood was having a special recycle pickup and that someone must have left antifreeze in a Gatorade bottle to get picked up. He believed that Julie in her confused state of mind must have picked up the bottle and taken a drink. James sounded anxious to Sam as he told him that he wanted to go door-to-door in his neighborhood to find out if someone had put antifreeze out for the pickup.

James wanted to bring Julie back to Kansas City to see the doctor she knew from her time at Liberty Hospital, James Redington. Julie felt that Dr. Redington would have been able to figure out what was going on with her kidneys. Sam had no idea that Julie was having health problems. He tried to make small talk with James as the conversation wrapped up.

"How are you holding up?" Sam asked, before adding, "How are Julie's parents holding up?"

"We're all devastated," James said.

Before he hung up, Sam asked James to keep him updated on Julie's condition. A few days later, James left a message that Julie had passed away. He asked Sam to be a pallbearer at the funeral, an invitation that the fellow nurse gracefully declined.

After hearing the story about antifreeze poisoning, some red flags went up in Sam's mind. He had been an intensive care nurse for nineteen years, and although he didn't have much experience with antifreeze poisoning, he *had* been involved in one case in which a patient was suspected to have committed suicide by drinking antifreeze. After his conversation with James, Sam became very concerned about the references to Gatorade and the Gatorade bottle. James had been very specific that he thought Julie drank the antifreeze from a Gatorade bottle, which Sam thought was a strange container for used antifreeze. He thought an old milk jug, or even, say, an antifreeze bottle, would have been more likely; if someone was changing the antifreeze in his or her car, there would be a lot more liquid than could be held in just a Gatorade bottle. It didn't make sense.

A lot of things weren't adding up for Sam about the situation, including James's description of how Julie was acting on prednisone. In his almost two decades of nursing, Sam had never seen a patient on prednisone have the symptoms that James described with Julie. The symptoms were more consistent with antifreeze poisoning.

As he went over the details of the story, Sam thought back to a dinner conversation he had with James and Julie before they moved east. Over dinner, James recounted how their cat had recently gotten sick and died. James suspected the cat had accidentally ingested antifreeze somewhere. At the time, Sam didn't think much of the story. But as the details of Julie's death came out, he thought back to that conversation again.

Just as Bailey had wondered, when Nancy Oldag told him about the cat's death, Sam Shoemaker suspected that the cat's death might not have been an accident. Although the details of the cat's death weren't going to tie James to Julie's death, Sam Shoemaker's direct account from James of Julie drinking antifreeze from a Gatorade bottle just might. Bailey and Connolly did find it strange that none of the Gatorade they found in the couple's Waltham duplex was the specific yellow-green color so similar to both antifreeze and Gatorade. Bailey wondered if the presence of both blue and red Gatorade, and absence of the yellow-green drink, was another attempt by James to mislead investigators.

With what Sam Shoemaker had just e-mailed him, Bailey had a feeling that there was now enough evidence for Assistant District Attorney Lynn Rooney to get an indictment. He followed up with Julie's best friend, Heather LeBlanc, on June 14, 2005, to find out if she had ever heard James tell his wife to drink Gatorade.

She had.

"I was talking with Julie once, and James yelled out in the background to me, 'Tell Julie to drink her Gatorade,'" Heather told Bailey. "Then he started a conversation with Julie reminding her that the doctor (not sure which doctor, but possibly the kidney specialist) said that the Gatorade would help restore balance to her electrolytes. She told me that she knew what the doctor said, but she didn't like the taste of it. She thought that recently nothing tasted right anymore. She said this particular Gatorade was purple and she kept calling it Smurf Juice as the color reminded her of Smurfs, which I actually think are blue. Anyway, I tried to get her to drink a sip of the Gatorade and a sip of water. She didn't want to, so I suggested a glass of the Gatorade and then a glass of water. She didn't like that either, so we went off to the next topic of conversation, whatever that was. This happened sometime during the two weeks between when I saw her in August and when she died in September. We talked so often during that time that it's hard to pinpoint."

With one witness who had heard James urging his wife to drink Gatorade and a second who James had directly told that his wife drank Gatorade, Bailey knew he had a good case building. But he still continued following up on other leads as well, just as he had done since that first day at Newton-Wellesley Hospital. On June 21, 2005, Bailey, Connolly, and Assistant District Attorney Lynn Rooney went to the School Street duplex, still sitting abandoned by James Keown and still holding a number of his personal belongings. Although Greg Stocklan had given many of the items away to charity, the three investigators collected some of the remaining items as evidence. They included a Harvard banner, a Harvard coffee mug, a framed copy of *Kansas City Magazine*, James Keown's birth certificate and Social Security card, and an original deed for a parcel of land in the Meadows of North Brook in Kansas City. There were also several prescriptions for Julie still in the duplex including Protonix, sucralfate, prednisone, and Norvasc.

There was also a reminder of the couple's financial troubles—an original court summons in the case of *Jaguar Credit versus James Keown*; a case brought in an attempt to repossess his fancy Jaguar, the one he told everyone had been free and a gift from the dealership. Though they weren't direct evidence of murder, they lent weight to the theory that James might have been driven to kill his wife because of mounting financial problems.

CHAPTER 25

As police continued to build their case, James was busy among his social circle in Jefferson City. He often planned cookouts at his mother's house on the lake. Though Betsy Dudenhoeffer had been to the Keown family home many times, a number of the other employees of the station were awed by the location and home when James invited them over for a cookout.

"Everybody was like, 'Oh my God, your house is in Quail Valley,'" Betsy recalled.

James casually told his co-workers that he owned the house but let his mother, Betty, live with him, and in lieu of paying rent, she cleaned and cooked for him.

Betsy knew this was a lie but never said anything to James or the others. She assumed that James didn't want people to know that he lived with his mother. James had the need to be perceived as a successful high roller to those around him.

Matt LaCasse didn't attend the cookouts at the house, but he did come over once for a birthday party James hosted. On that occasion, most of the crowd from Columbia who'd made the trip to Jefferson City for the party ended up sleeping over because they had been drinking.

James's mother was nowhere to be seen.

As the summer went on, James and Matt spent more and more time together. Matt considered James one of his best friends, and they went out to the Columbia bars a lot that summer. If they weren't out at the bars, like Big 12 South or Johnny's Scenery, they were at someone's house watching a game or hanging out. They went to Kansas City to watch the Kansas City Royals and Cardinals play.

Betsy Dudenhoeffer was spending a lot of time with her childhood friend as well. He was intelligent, confident, and a blast to be around. A few times, he played Betsy a CD of himself on air at ESPN. He seemed proud of his job at the major network and would reminisce as they listened to the recording.

James planned a surprise party for Betsy's thirtieth birthday at Dominico's, a popular restaurant in town. As had become expected, James always picked up the tab, and this night was no different. Betsy was well aware of the large amounts of cash that were always in James's wallet, so she was not the least bit surprised by his offer to pay for the party—though she knew the money wasn't from working at KLIK.

One Monday when James arrived at the station and flashed a thick roll of cash, Betsy asked him how he had so much money all the time. James smiled and told Betsy of his success on the gambling boats. His mother liked to go on the boats, he said, so there were many weekends that he took Betty Keown for a trip to the casinos.

"What can I say? I always win," James told Betsy by way of explanation for his fistful of cash.

Betsy took him at face value, but later, after hearing about a situation with James at a bar in Columbia, she started to wonder. One night, one of the women from the radio station was being hit on at the bar by the man next to her. She wasn't interested and didn't look happy. James noticed and went over to ask her if she wanted him to take care of it.

Sure, she told him.

James walked away and made a phone call. About twenty minutes later, a man no one in the group knew came in and spoke briefly with James before going to sit next to the man who'd been harassing the woman. A while later, both men left the bar.

At the station the next day, James told the crew that the man who had been bothering their co-worker had been taken out into a field where he was beaten up and stripped naked.

Betsy found herself wondering about who or what James was involved with. She wondered if the large wads of cash he had in hand every Monday had anything to do with it.

She quickly brushed her questions aside, however, despite another strange occurrence. One day, Betsy and James went to lunch at Madison's Café, an Italian restaurant and lunch spot downtown. Betsy's husband, Mark, an investigator with the Missouri State Attorney's Office, happened to be having lunch with the Jefferson City Police chief Roger Schroeder when Betsy and James walked in, so they stopped to say hello on their way to a table.

Betsy thought nothing of the brief exchange until she got home that night and saw Mark's face. Her husband was serious as he told her he needed to speak with her about something. Chief Schroeder had asked Mark how his wife knew James, and Mark had replied that they'd grown up together. Schroeder mentioned that Betsy might want to cut back on the amount of time she spent with her childhood friend, confiding that there was speculation that James was under investigation for his wife's death.

Betsy was furious. Julie Keown died of stomach cancer, she retorted angrily to her husband.

Mark explained that he was just passing on what he'd been told.

Betsy immediately called her best friend, Jocelyn Knaebel, who worked in sales at the radio station, to tell her what she'd heard about James. The two women laughed as they decided that there was no truth to the story. They agreed that it was the most ridiculous thing either of them had heard in a while.

CHAPTER 26

September 8, 2005

It had been one year since Julie Irene Oldag Keown had passed away, many miles from the rolling farmland of Missouri where she had spent most of her life. Since his return to the Midwest after her death, James Keown had only shared brief anecdotes about Julie with his co-workers at the radio station.

News Director Dean Morgan noticed right away on the morning of September 8, 2005, that James seemed depressed. When Dean asked how James was doing, the normally talkative radio host mentioned that it was the one-year anniversary of his wife's death, and he just didn't feel like being at the station that day. James loved to be at work, so for him to say he wanted to be at home rather than at the station was notably unusual to Dean.

Matt LaCasse was working at the Columbia station when he got a call from James later that day.

"Hey, my mom and I went out to Julie's grave today and laid roses," he told Matt, before continuing, "I don't want to be alone tonight. I'd like to go out and hang out with some people."

"OK, that's fine," Matt responded.

It was during the week, but Matt managed to round up a few people from the station to meet at Legend's Sports Bar and Grill in Columbia. James was the first to arrive. Matt noticed right away that it looked like his friend had been crying. He seemed very depressed and genuinely sad.

And he was drinking—a lot. James quickly became hammered, what some might describe as a sloppy drunk. Matt attributed James's drinking to the first anniversary of his wife's death, but some of the others in the group questioned the behavior. Matt tried to be understanding, but the scene wasn't pretty. As the night went on, James started to ramble. He wasn't making much, if any, sense, as he leaned on the table and talked about Julie.

"I miss her; I wish she was still here," he said.

Matt felt horrible for his friend. No one seemed to know what to do or say as James went on about Julie.

"She was always my better half."

"She was just an angel."

"She was just so kindhearted. I loved her so much and still do."

Matt didn't know how to respond. One of the women from the station left, saying she just couldn't stand to watch James any longer.

Matt stuck by his friend throughout the night, painful as it was, telling himself that this was a man mourning the loss of his wife. Matt's apartment was right up the street from the bar, and he eventually managed to get James back there, where he passed out.

But it wasn't long after that drunken evening before another Julie was the topic of James and Matt's conversations. Football season was under way when James started talking about a woman he called "new Julie."

Her name was Julie Webber, and she and James had known each other in high school. They started dating, and James confided to Matt that he really liked spending time with her. There was no doubt in Matt's mind that James was interested in a long-term relationship with her; when James spoke about her, he was affectionate and happy, but still, to Matt it was not even close to the reverent way James spoke of his wife. Nonetheless, he was happy for his friend, who he sensed really wanted to be in a relationship. He even thought that James might eventually marry Julie Webber if things worked out.

There were a few morbid jokes around the station, which Matt characterized as "gallows humor," about the fact that James's new girlfriend had the same name as his wife. What if he did marry her, would she be Julie Keown as well? His co-workers found it a bit strange to say the least.

James's new relationship went even more public in the beginning of October when he started a blog, which he called "The View From Here."

"Welcome friends to my new blog, 'The View From Here.' What should you expect from this site? Well, just about anything. Most of what you will find here will come from my daily talk shows . . . but you're also going to get some extra insight into my daily life . . . sometimes it's exciting . . . sometimes it's downright boring. I look forward to hearing your thoughts as well. Enjoy the blog!"

He described how he and Julie Webber had gotten together:

"Sixteen years ago at the Cole County Fair I made a life-long friend. Her name is Julie. I would be hard pressed to name anyone who was [a] closer friend. Sure I had friends who I spent more time with, but Julie was someone who really knew me. Most of our friends treated us like brother and sister.

"College, jobs, marriages took us in different directions for over a decade. . . . [But] I was amazed to find how much we had grown together through our individual life experiences, even though we were apart for so long. And while no one knows what the future holds . . . I can only thank God, as the Irish blessing goes, for holding us both in the palm of his hand until we were able to meet again."

James continued to chronicle his romance with Julie on his blog as the weeks went by. She lived in St. Louis, about a two-hour drive from Jefferson City, and at one point James even talked about doing one of his shows from an affiliate station in St. Louis so that he could spend more time with his new flame.

As fall crept up on the Midwest, James Keown was miles away from the police investigation into his wife's murder, getting more and more comfortable in his new relationship. To those around him, it seemed that he was settling into a regular routine of someone with a busy job and long-distance relationship. Friends noted that James seemed to be getting his life back after the tragic death of his wife.

"Sunday, I went to St. Louis to see my friend Julie. Sometimes the best days are the days where you do very little. Jewels and I spent most of the afternoon sitting around her condo, listening to music and playing with Lilly, her new black lab. . . ."

James and Julie went to eat that weekend at a local bar.

"While there was no snow outside, the chill in our bones from the autumn wind quickly dissipated as we sat against the wall [and] laughed, shared stories, and just enjoyed each other's company. We might have come for the stew, but we quickly discovered that the best thing on the menu was companionship."

James's flair for writing continued as he chronicled another weekend with Julie and her puppy, Lilly.

"I make no bones about it, fall is my favorite time of the year. This weekend is a perfect example of why I feel this way. Friday, I made my way to St. Louis to spend the weekend with the girls—Julie and Lilly the puppy. . . . Walking underneath the tall trees near the duck pond, you forget that you're in the middle of one of the largest cities in America. Time slows down. You feel as if all your concerns are left at the gate when you walk in. The goal is not to get from one end of the park to the other. The goal is just to be in the park. Lafayette Park contains so many twists and turns that you can meander along— which allows it to be a unique experience every time you go through."

His budding relationship with Julie Webber wasn't the only thing that was going well for James in the fall of that year. His *Party Line* talk show for KLIK was growing in popularity, and listeners were getting frequent updates and recaps of the show on James's blog. James often wrote several posts a day on the blog, which featured a photo of James—sitting cross-legged and holding a baseball bat—that appeared to have been taken by a professional photographer.

At times, his blog posts were a bit self-promoting, such as his claim that he broke part of the story about former CIA operative Valerie Plame Wilson before the national media.

"Let me start by saying that I don't want this blog

to turn into a self-indulging ego trip . . . but you'll have to give me this one. Who says a little talk show in the middle of flyover country can't get the big stories. . . . On Monday's show I shared that I learned the investigation was starting to look closer at the Vice President himself and that there has even been hushed talk in D.C. about who might replace Cheney should he have to step down. I gave some details about a conversation that Libby and Cheney had in 2003 about Wilson. It is this conversation that has people talking about the Vice President's involvement in this matter.

"Well, what should appear in the *New York Times* less than 24 hours later. A story that mirrors the news we brought you on the radio. You can read the *Times* account. I just hope Special Prosecutor Fitzgerald doesn't ask me for my sources like he did Novak and Judith Miller! More importantly, how did I get this story before everyone else on the planet . . . luck, hard-nosed investigative reporting, unmatched sources??? Uh, try I bought the guy who told me the story a beer at a bar in D.C. last month. The special prosecutor might have subpoena power . . . but I have the power of Budweiser . . . and that will get them to talk every time."

Just before Halloween, the crew from the station decided to try a murder-mystery theme-party game. The party centered around a Chicago Mob boss who went missing after he was released from prison and was then found murdered. James dressed up as Eddie "Socks" R. Gyle, a character described as a rich, smart, handsome deal maker.

"Well, they clearly didn't typecast me," James wrote later on his blog.

In the same blog post, James discussed what it was like playing a different character.

"It often takes a game like this to break down barriers with some co-workers or friends. You spend so much time playing a particular role at work or home that it's hard to break out of your shell. Then you get thrown into a mix where your boss is no longer your boss—he's now a crooked D.A. who you are trying to bribe. Something amazing happens when you're busy trying to act out a character—the real character inside you starts to come out in little bits."

James went home that night to his mother's house, on Covey Lane, where he stayed up until 1:30 a.m. watching the third game of the World Series. By all appearances, to those who were around him that fall, life was going well for James Keown—he had a good job, a regular crowd of friends, and a new girlfriend.

"When did life get this busy?" James asked on one blog post. "I can still remember a simpler time—a time when I would sit around and ask the question, 'what am I going to do tonight?' I call them my 'salad days.' Truthfully, I don't really know what 'salad days' means—it's a phrase some of my relatives use to talk about easier times. My 'salad days' have clearly passed me by."

Although he spent most weekends in St. Louis visiting Julie Webber, James made time during the third weekend of October to take his sister Shawna's son to the Harvest Fest in Jefferson City. The two hung out at the Halloween-themed spooky village and stopped to get kettle corn and caramel apples from the street vendors. James seemed the ideal fun uncle as he took the little boy to the bouncy house and to see a giant inflated pumpkin.

It seemed that things just couldn't get any better for James that fall. Because of the popularity of his *Party*

Line show, the station decided to add a second afternoon show with James at the mic. The second daily installment of *Party Line* kicked off at the end of October, and James celebrated the end of his first week of the afternoon show by going out with a group of station employees to a swanky piano bar in Columbia called the Penguin. The bar was known for being more upscale than many of the college hangouts in Columbia and for its unique approach to running a piano bar that included two dueling pianos.

The group included program director Brian Wilson, Matt LaCasse, and several of the women from the station. It was also the first time that James brought Julie Webber to meet Matt and the other station employees.

The group got to the bar early and got a prime table near the front, where they all got in on the fun singing along to the songs. As the rowdy group sang and drank, Matt LaCasse observed that James and Julie seemed like a typical couple out for a night with friends. James sat with his arm around the pretty blond throughout the night and referred to her several times throughout the night as his girlfriend. The two seemed to enjoy each other's company but weren't over-the-top in terms of public displays of affection. Matt was happy for James. He was a little surprised that his friend had been willing to get into a relationship so soon after his wife had passed away, but at the same time he knew that James was young, in his early thirties. He had lost his wife at the start of his life, and Matt told himself there was no reason why James shouldn't try to find a new partner. It wasn't necessarily what Matt would have done, but it seemed to make sense for James.

As the night drew to a close, Matt said good night to James and Julie after exchanging pleasantries about how nice it was to meet her.

"I'll see you later," Matt said as he left.

It was the last time Matt saw James Keown in person. He had no way of knowing that a grand jury in Middlesex County, Massachusetts, had just returned an indictment against Keown, charging him with first-degree murder in the death of his wife. The indictment was under seal, meaning it was not made public. But there were two men who knew about the indictment, and by the end of the weekend, they were boarding a plane at Boston's Logan International Airport bound for St. Louis.

CHAPTER 27

As dawn broke on the morning of November 7, 2005, Waltham detective Jon Bailey knew he was the closest he had ever come to being an undercover cop. He and Lieutenant Jim Connolly had quietly slipped into the small hotel on the outskirts of downtown Jefferson City, Missouri. They stayed in position until they were ready to make the next move in their carefully orchestrated plan. One wrong step could jeopardize everything they had worked toward over the past fourteen months. Both men were keenly aware of the delicate nature of the operation.

Bailey was still amazed that Jefferson City, where there didn't even seem to be a restaurant open after six o'clock in the evening, was the state capital. Earlier in the day, they had driven across mile after mile of open farmland dotted with old farmhouses, few road signs, and still fewer vehicles. The main road from St. Louis to Jefferson City was characterized by triple-X-rated adult video shops, churches, and roadside barbecue shacks.

After dinner that night, for which they'd driven to an out-of-the-way chain restaurant, they went to scope out the KLIK building and get a sense of the exit locations and layout of the building. Back at their hotel, the two went over the plan to arrest James the next morning while he was at the radio station. After more than a year, James Keown was almost within their reach. But Bailey knew all too well that the signed arrest warrant he held in his hand was only one piece of a very large puzzle—a puzzle he still didn't have all the pieces to and wasn't sure he ever would.

None of the local police knew that they were in town. Bailey and Connolly were breaking unwritten police protocol by not notifying local police that they were there and preparing to arrest one of their citizens. Connolly arranged for officers from the local U.S. Marshal's Office to meet them in the hotel lobby at 8 a.m. the next morning, where he would fill them in on the details at that time. After that, they would head to the Jefferson City Police Station and bring the local authorities in on the plan. Just having the warrant didn't mean that they would arrest James, as they were still concerned that he might get tipped off to their presence there and run. They had no idea how far his influence and connections went in the city, especially because local prosecutor Bill Tackett was a regular guest on the show each week. Both investigators were well aware that James was connected to many of the city's top politicians and businessmen. They couldn't risk even the slightest chance that he might get a tip that the two Massachusetts investigators were in town, especially because James had recently confided to the Willmores that he had a plan to flee to Prague if he felt the police were moving in on him. The Willmores had shared the details of the conversation with Bailey and Connolly, as they felt the police should be aware of it.

Bailey thought back to all of the people who had told him during this investigation that James was too good at covering himself—too skilled, too careful. But Bailey was like a dog on a scent. He'd first caught a whiff of it in the Newton-Wellesley Hospital in September of 2004. It was the scent of a guilty man, but Bailey had nothing to back it up at the time other than a feeling in his gut. Bailey always thought back to that first night at the hospital when James had been so upbeat, asking the detectives whether they wanted a glass of water or a soda, while a few floors up his wife was in a coma, her life slipping away with each minute that passed. Every lead Bailey followed seemed to point directly back to James. Now, more than a year later, James was within his grasp, as was justice for Julie.

Bailey suspected that most people he and Connolly had interviewed for the case would be shocked by the arrest. Dozens and dozens of interviews with those who knew James well had failed to elicit suspicions that James could somehow be involved. No one had a bad thing to say about the guy. Sure, he had a tendency to exaggerate from time to time, even stretch the truth; some would even say *lie*. But he always had an explanation for their questions. And they all also said that James was always a loving husband, devoted to his poor wife whose health had been failing for months.

And now, as the two men drove in separate SUVs, each with a U.S. Marshal, an arrest warrant for James in hand, Bailey still wasn't sure they would get him.

The radio in each SUV was tuned to 1240 AM, where

James's voice could be heard loud and clear over the airwaves. As long as they could hear James on the radio, they knew where he was. Their plan to arrest James on the air had nothing to do with making a big splash with the media, but more practically, it meant that they could guarantee his exact location and coordinate a quick and tidy arrest.

The two investigators listened to James's voice as they drove, knowing he was still inside the KLIK studio, next to the Capital Plaza Mall, when they arrived. Behind the marshals, two female detectives from Jefferson City, Carla Kilgore and Julie Sparks, rode in another unmarked car. After meeting with the U.S. Marshals in the hotel lobby, Bailey and Connolly had driven to the Jefferson City Police Station, where the detective division supervisor assigned Kilgore and Sparks to assist them.

The three unmarked cars parked in front of the tiny one-story brick building that housed the KLIK studio. Given the location of the arrest, which was out of Connolly and Bailey's jurisdiction in Massachusetts, the U.S. Marshals were the ones with the power to serve the actual arrest warrant on James. Only one of the U.S. Marshals went inside, along with Bailey, Connolly, and Detective Carla Kilgore. The other U.S. Marshal and Jefferson City patrolman Julie Sparks positioned themselves outside the back door of the studio.

As the four officers walked into the lobby of the building, Stephanie Boltz, the station's receptionist, was sitting behind a desk in the lobby.

"Is James Keown here?" Connolly asked her.

"Yes, he's in the studio. Are you his guests for today?"

"No," the marshal replied. "But he's going to be our guest."

"Where is the studio?" Bailey asked, and Boltz pointed to the stairs.

They did not hesitate, racing down the stairs almost as soon as she pointed in that direction.

We're going to pull this off, Bailey thought. *We have to.*

At the bottom of the stairs, he could see the "on air" light over the studio door. And then, almost like he knew they were coming, James Keown hurried out of the studio into the narrow hallway.

He's seen us, Bailey thought. *He's making a run for it!*

He wondered if the receptionist had called to announce their arrival.

But James didn't even seem to see the officers at that point. He turned and called to a man with large glasses in the studio.

"Hey, Dean, could you cover for me?"

Was he taking a bathroom break? Bailey wondered. He didn't have time to ponder the question as Connolly nodded at him.

It was time.

Bailey and Connolly crossed the hallway in two steps, each taking one of James's arms and pushing him back up against the wall. The look on James's face was akin to a deer in headlights—he knew he was caught.

"James, do you remember us?" Connolly asked.

James nodded.

"Do you know why we're here?"

James looked down. And for the first time since he'd known him, Bailey thought the redheaded talk-show host seemed nervous.

"Yes, I do."

Those were the last words he spoke to the two detectives, who opened the back door to let the two officers stationed there know the arrest had been made. For the first time since Bailey and Connolly had been on the case, James Keown, the man who always had an explanation for everything, had nothing to say.

Dean Morgan, however, had plenty to say, whether he liked it or not.

Oh shit, Dean thought to himself. *The rumors were right.*

But he didn't have time to think about those rumors. Or the fact that his friend James, the person who had made the last months the best, most fun, and most rewarding of his radio career, had just been hauled away in handcuffs. The thirty-second break was almost over, and he was going to have to go on air in James's place.

As he sat in the control room, Dean realized he had no idea what to talk about. There was no way he was going to mention that James had just been arrested. But luckily, James had left a stack of notes he had written out as preparation for that morning on the desk inside the studio.

Dean sat down, and plugged in his headphones.

And the show went on.

Dean didn't take any listener calls during the show, not wanting to answer questions about where James was. He also worried that news of James's arrest had probably leaked out by then, and he didn't want to respond to that on air, especially because he didn't know what was going on.

Dean signed off from the morning edition of *Party Line*, leaned back in his chair, and breathed a sigh of relief. He had survived.

Then he realized that someone was going to have to fill in for the afternoon show.

Down the hall, in a small office inside the station, Betsy Dudenhoeffer's best friend, Jocelyn Knaebel, picked up the phone and dialed Betsy's number. Betsy struggled to hear Jocelyn, who was whispering as she delivered the news that James had just been arrested.

Oh my God, Betsy thought. Her husband had been right.

CHAPTER 28

Ryan Smith walked his beat every day. For the ambitious young reporter, who had worked his way up to the afternoon daily paper in Missouri's capital after working at a small weekly paper, and then a small daily paper, it was an awesome beat. He covered cops, courts, and county government and had no shortage of juicy stories to write about. Jefferson City was historically known as a sleepy midwestern town in terms of murder cases to report on, with local and state politics dominating the front page. But since he'd taken over the cops and courts beat, Ryan's co-workers often joked that the Illinois native had brought a bad-luck streak with him in terms of crime, as the city saw a handful of murders in only a few months. With a prosecuting attorney, Bill Tackett, who was known as being extremely media-friendly, Ryan had a plum job.

The *Jefferson City News Tribune* was located directly across the street from the Cole County Courthouse, two blocks from the police department, and another block from the fire department. It wasn't uncommon for Ryan to walk over to cover a meeting or arraignment in the court, then rush back across the street to write up his story by deadline for the afternoon paper. After he got off deadline, he usually walked back around his beat, cultivating sources in the police station and courthouse, with hopes of finding future stories to follow up on.

When news of James Keown's arrest trickled into the small midwestern newsroom, Ryan had only very, very limited information, but he dropped what he was doing. The morning edition of *Party Line* was always on somewhere in the newsroom, and Ryan had heard someone remark earlier that morning that James had left in the middle of his show. It seemed a little strange, but Ryan hadn't spent a lot of time thinking about what it meant. Shortly after that, a call came into the newsroom that James had been arrested. It took just minutes for Ryan to run across the street to the massive gray stone courthouse.

Ryan knew James from around town, and the two media men covered some of the same meetings. At the time, efforts were under way to build a new justice center for Jefferson City. Ryan had covered a series of public forums on the plan and often saw James there. Newspaper reporters often looked at reporters in television or radio as being somewhat egotistical, stereotyping them as people who just liked to hear themselves talk, and after meeting James a few times, Ryan put him into that category.

It wasn't that James wasn't a nice guy to talk to; he had a good sense of humor and was always friendly.

But in Ryan's opinion, he had a tendency to be a bit of a blowhard, always quick to point out that he knew inside details about everyone, and everything, in Jefferson City.

Ryan had gone out for drinks a few times with James and some of the other local reporters but had never gotten to know him that well. Still, as he raced across the street to the courthouse, along with veteran reporter Bob Watson, he realized he hadn't quite processed the fact that he was about to cover the case of a colleague. They were the first media to arrive, and no one inside the courthouse was releasing any information. The two went outside to wait and practically jumped James's old mentor Warren Krech when he came walking down the street. Warren looked devastated to Ryan, and the young reporter held back from pushing the veteran radioman for a long interview.

Krech had little more information than Ryan did as he described police swooping into the KLIK building during a commercial break and putting handcuffs on James.

"We're all still shocked," said Krech, his face somber as he walked into the courthouse, like someone going to a funeral.

Ryan watched as Detective Jon Bailey and Lieutenant Jim Connolly walked into the courthouse, but the two Massachusetts police officers weren't releasing any information either. After the arrest, they had taken James to the Jefferson City Police Station, where he was booked before being transported to a holding cell in the county jail, which sat in the basement of the courthouse.

A short time later in the courthouse, Bailey and Connolly went to sit next to Julie Keown's parents, Jack and Nancy Oldag, who had driven more than three hours from their farm to watch their former son-in-law face the judge. As he walked toward the Oldags, Bailey observed that for the first time since he'd known her, Nancy Oldag looked excited. He had grown used to her down-to-earth, stoic midwestern manner over the past fourteen months. He knew there had been times Nancy and Jack had thought this day would never come, and now that it was here, they were ready to see James held responsible for what he'd done.

For Bailey there was an excitement but also a sense of relief that they had finally caught up to James. He knew that James had believed that he was simply going to leave the area if he caught wind that the police were coming for him. Bailey recalled the story James had told about fleeing to Prague if the police came for him.

That sense of excitement didn't carry over to the other side of the courtroom, however, where James's mother, Betty Keown, sat perfectly made up and dressed, next to James's sister Shawna. Betty was visibly shaken up as she sat waiting for her son to appear on a video monitor in the front of the courtroom, where he would be arraigned from the jail cell before Cole County Associate Judge Thomas L. Sodergren. Next to her Shawna looked really angry.

James was arraigned as a fugitive from justice from Massachusetts, where he was now facing a charge of first-degree murder. As he watched James on the monitor, Ryan was surprised by James's reaction as the charges were read by the court clerk. He had a grim look on his face, almost stoic. It was the same reaction Ryan had seen on the faces of numerous other defendants, but for some reason, he had expected James to look different, more visibly upset, but he showed no emotion. James waived extradition and the judge indicated that he would be transported back to Massachusetts.

———————

"Can I hug you now?" Nancy asked Bailey after the arraignment.

"You can, but this is only the first step. We're not there yet," he cautioned her, pointing out that just getting an arrest didn't mean they would be able to get a conviction.

By the time the arraignment was over, the court was packed with local media and a television crew. The throng of media followed Betty and Shawna Keown outside. Ryan was working up the nerve to talk to the two when a young reporter, who appeared to be a college student from the college-operated radio station, approached James's mother. The student didn't have the tact that a more seasoned reporter would have in approaching a family member obviously going through a tough situation but did open the door for the other media to ask questions of Betty and Shawna. The two had been able to speak briefly with James via the video monitor.

"He told me he wasn't guilty of anything," Betty told the group. "He said, 'Mom, don't worry about this, it won't hang over our heads anymore. Let's get it out of there and over with. It'll be OK in the end.'"

Shawna, who was just twenty-one years old, defended her much-older brother to the media, saying that the true story about Julie's death would come out.

"I believe he's innocent," she said. "If I didn't think he was, I wouldn't be here."

Betty added, "There's no way my son could murder someone, especially his wife. They loved each other."

The Oldags avoided the media after the arraignment and did not offer any comments when called by reporters later that day.

_____

Jon Bailey and Jim Connolly walked out of the court-house, doing their best to avoid the media, when Warren Krech walked over to them and introduced himself as a longtime friend of James, who had first met him when James had interned at KLIK starting when he was twelve years old. When James returned to the job at the local station earlier that year, Krech had been pleased but found it strange. He knew that James's wife had died from kidney disease, but the AM station was a local station, and James was a "big market" guy who was really overqualified for the job, which paid about thirty thousand.

Still, most people seemed to attribute the move to Julie's death and James's need to return home to get back on his feet, Krech told the detectives.

Bailey had already heard a lot of the same sentiment from the other radio people in Jefferson City, but as Krech went on, something he said caught the detectives' attention. James had recently started dating a girl named Julie Webber, whose parents lived near the radio station. Julie herself lived in St. Louis, about two hours away, and James had confided to Warren that he wanted to start doing two of his shows each week from the KMOX station in St. Louis so that he could be near Julie.

Bailey had suspected there was a new woman in James's life, but up until that point, he and Connolly hadn't been able to find out her name. The investigators had not been aware of James's blog, where he detailed his relationship with Julie.

_____

Across the street, inside the tiny newspaper office, Ryan Smith sat down to write the story. He removed himself from the emotion of writing about someone he knew, taking an almost clinical approach to the case. It was shocking, but he found himself thinking back to a conversation he'd had with another reporter a few months prior. The other reporter, a longtime journalist in Jefferson City, always seemed to have the true inside line on things, unlike James, who just put on a show of having the inside scoop. During a whispered conversation, the other reporter told Ryan that he'd heard Julie Keown had died under mysterious circumstances and that James might be involved. At the time, Ryan thought it sounded a little strange but brushed it off as a rumor.

———————————

Across the street, James sat in his cell at the Cole County Jail. He tried to use his connections in Jefferson City, asking for Deputy Sheriff Marc Haycock by name. Haycock had worked as a part-time on-air personality at KLIK until earlier that year. He'd left KLIK in June for a change of pace and got the job with the sheriff's department.

"I want to talk about what happened," James told Marc, confiding that he thought the arrest earlier that day was a joke. But he didn't linger on the charges against him and instead engaged Marc in general chitchat and small talk about the conditions in the jail.

Marc found himself feeling uncomfortable as he stood outside the cell. Not once had James told his former co-worker that he had not poisoned his wife. Why wasn't he pleading his innocence?

———————————

Christina Liles was just finishing shopping when she got a call on her cell phone from Nancy Oldag that afternoon. Tears ran down Christina's face as she stood in the checkout line and realized the meaning of what Nancy told her. She was simply overwhelmed, especially after the amount of time that had passed since Julie's death. There was finally going to be justice for Julie. James was finally going to face the court for the crime that investigators, Julie's family, and friends like Christina had come to believe he committed.

CHAPTER 29

Matt LaCasse was on his way to an interview with the county clerk about the next day's elections when he got a call from the business manager at the station. She had something important to tell him.

"I really don't want to tell you this on the phone," she began.

Matt began to worry that he'd been let go, but the manager continued, "James was just arrested for first-degree murder of his wife."

"You're fucking kidding me," Matt swore.

Matt was completely floored by the news. He couldn't think straight. He just couldn't believe that this was true. Hearing that James, his best friend and co-worker, had been arrested was like being informed that the sky was not really blue. He immediately told himself that the police must have the wrong person. He was sure that the mistake would be cleared up quickly. There was no way that

James could be a murderer, especially his wife's murderer, the wife who James spoke of in glowing, reverent terms.

But he didn't have time to linger on the thought. Back at the station, Matt was told he had to read the story about James's arrest over the air. His boss told him that he knew how Matt felt but that it was his job, and he had to be professional and go on air with the news—all the news.

Matt hated reading the story, but he did his job, and then he muddled through the rest of the day. That night he gathered with some of the other employees and talked about the arrest. Like him, no one could believe that James was responsible for Julie's death. Matt could not count the number of times he shook his head and uttered, "What the fuck."

James Keown had been Matt's closest friend the past few months, and he couldn't fathom the reality of the situation. Why would James lie about how his wife had died? And why would Matt have even thought to question what James had told him? James was so sincere, so sad, so seemingly honest when he talked about Julie's death.

_____

Lene Johansen had gotten a call that afternoon from Tony Messenger, of the *Columbia Daily Tribune*, with the news. Like Matt, Lene thought of herself as someone who had a good sense of people and whether they were truthful. She never saw this coming. She found herself scouring the Internet and the news wire for details of the arrest. But details were few in those early hours, which only led to more speculation about what was really going on.

_____

Later that afternoon, both the Missouri and Massachusetts press got more information about the case when

Middlesex District Attorney Martha Coakley held a press
conference. As she stood before the eager press, Coakley was flanked by Waltham Police chief Edward Drew,
Detective Captain Richard Forte, and Ed Forster, from
the Massachusetts State Police. Coakley began with the
basic facts of the arrest earlier that day. "James Keown,
whose date of birth is May 17, 1974, was arrested for the
first-degree murder of his wife, Julie Oldag Keown, who
at thirty-one years of age died on September 4, 2004."

The petite blond prosecutor told reporters that James
was accused of slowly poisoning his wife with ethylene
glycol. "Ethylene glycol is a fairly thick, syrupy, sweet-
tasting substance. It will induce initially conditions that
approximate someone who is under the influence of alcohol, but, when mixed with this liquid [i.e., Gatorade],
would be undetectable to taste, and by and large, would
also be absorbed into the system pretty quickly because
of the high sugar content."

Coakley outlined some of James's lies during the press
conference. "Investigators also learned that the defendant, contrary to the belief of his wife and others, was not
enrolled at the Harvard Business School, but had merely
enrolled at the Harvard extension school in a particular
course involving the Internet, for which he received a
failing grade."

The prosecutor continued, "At this time, the motive—
if there is one—appears to be financial. It was pretty
clear that [Julie] did not understand what was happening
to her or that she was being poisoned."

———————————

At the *Jefferson City News Tribune*, Ryan Smith and
Bob Watson quickly found that James Keown's financial
troubles had started even before he'd moved to Massachusetts. They reported on a case filed against James for

an outstanding credit-card bill of $8,521.41. It was the same case that Christina Liles had found just after her friend's murder the previous September.

James's co-workers at KLIK were not allowed to speak to the media seeking comment on the case, but Scott Boltz, the marketing manager for the radio station's parent company Cumulus Broadasting, did shed some insight into their reaction.

"It's devastating for us," Boltz said. "It was just devastating for our staffers and the community at large. He showed up for work every day. He worked hard."

The case was soon picked up by the national media, and *Nancy Grace* ran a segment on the arrest that same evening. As Coakley had told reporters that James Keown's motive was financial, reporters were questioning what he was spending his money on. Did he have a drug problem? A gambling addiction? Have a secret life? They were the same questions that Jon Bailey and Jim Connolly had asked themselves during their investigation as they tried to find the missing pieces of the puzzle. They were answers the two investigators realized they might never know.

Many members of the press in Jefferson City and Columbia, Missouri, were questioning the strength of the case against James, as was defense attorney Adam Kretowicz, a Boston-area criminal defense attorney who James had hired the previous year when he stopped speaking with police after a meeting with police that did not go as James had hoped. The details of that meeting were never revealed publicly. Kretowicz had handled a host of high-profile cases over the years, and in the first twenty-four hours after James's arrest, he worked to cast doubt on the strength of the prosecution's case, pointing to the fourteen-month-long investigation.

"There's no new [medical] information that they have now that they haven't had twelve months ago," he said. "I haven't seen the pathology report. But I have been told by the district attorney's office that this was found in her system very early on, around September of 2004."

Kretowicz said that James and Julie Keown were both working and had no more debts than any other young couple just starting out. He said he was upset that the case was already being tried in the media and not the courtroom.

James's reason for moving to Waltham was not an attempt to move his wife away from her family so that he could poison her, but much less sinister, the defense attorney said. The couple had honeymooned on Cape Cod and enjoyed the area. But there was another reason for the move.

"While in the Midwest, they did not have any children. They felt that they were being constantly surrounded and asked questions about, when are they going to have children? They needed a break from the family. The other reason is that he had a friend who he had worked for in Chicago that was now working at a radio station in Boston, and he was offered a job here to work there as well. There were many reasons why they moved here," Kretowicz said.

As for the radio talk-show host's alleged admission to the elite Harvard Business School, the defense attorney suggested that Julie knew her husband was not attending the school.

"He did take a continuing education class at Harvard, which he dropped out of because of how much work he had. Now, in terms of telling people that he was going to

Harvard Business School, it's my understanding that both he and his wife made those assertions to family members to help lessen the impact of moving away from such a close family," Kretowicz said.

He did not have an explanation for why James went to such elaborate lengths to convince Tammy Blossom of his acceptance to Harvard. The defense attorney maintained that his client was innocent and had been deeply in love with his wife.

He wasn't the only one who maintained that the police had the wrong man. A number of James's friends and co-workers, like Matt LaCasse and Betsy Dudenhoeffer, were convinced police had the wrong man. They started to speculate that the arrest was a political move by Coakley, who was in the running for attorney general, to make herself look good.

Tony Messenger, of the *Columbia Daily Tribune*, was asked to take over James's *Party Line* show at KLIK, and he got an unusual call that first day. James's mother, Betty Keown, called in to the show to defend her son. She told Messenger and the listeners that she knew he was innocent and that they would all come to the same conclusion in time. But Betty said she'd known something was up in the month after Julie's death; the police were interviewing everyone except for her, and she had wondered if the police considered her son a suspect in the case.

Betty told the listeners that she could not believe that her son was capable of such a cold-blooded act. But just the same, she felt she'd had to ask him about it. So she'd asked James outright if he had killed his wife.

He'd started crying and asked his mother how she could believe such a thing. He loved his wife. He could never have hurt her. And Betty believed him.

"We shall make it through this," Betty said. "This is my son."

Messenger gave a recap to his listeners after Betty Keown's call concluded.

"A shocking day here in Jefferson City. I'm filling in for James Keown, who was arrested on this show yesterday, charged with the murder of his wife in September 2004.

"He is in Cole County Jail. We just had his mother on the phone. She indicated that he will probably be sent to Boston at some point in the coming days. She's been told when, but didn't want to share that with us. I don't blame her. Lots of phone calls lighting up, people wanting to talk about this case."

Members of the area press were blindsided by the arrest, and many gathered at McNally's Pub the next day to discuss the charges. Dean Morgan felt every eye in the place was on him when he joined the journalists, who were deep in discussion about James Keown as they nursed their cocktails. Everyone wanted to know about the arrest. What had it been like from where Dean was sitting? What did James do? How did he look? What did he say?

Many of them questioned how they had not seen this coming. Some claimed they had been suspicious of James all along. Others continued to circulate the theory that the arrest was a publicity move by Coakley to bolster her campaign for attorney general in Massachusetts.

———————————

Mike McCartney, who had worked with James at that first radio station job in Kansas City so many years ago, had an "out-of-body experience" when he heard about James's arrest. And then, like everyone else had done, he found himself thinking about whether there had been clues that James was capable of doing something like this.

McCartney knew that there was another side of James, and he knew it was not always nice. Sure, James had been a rising star in the radio station back then, but there were those who'd always been leery of him. James worked well with the management, but he kept tabs on the employees for them, too. A lot of people felt that James was a snitch, that he had a really sneaky, snakelike side to him.

"If he didn't like you, he'd find a way to nail you," McCartney said.

If there was anything going on at the station, like someone getting fired or even a potential sale of the station, James knew all of the details. Some of his co-workers started to distrust James. They stopped sharing information with him. But he still seemed to know everything, and no one could figure out how or why he knew the information.

But one day James told McCartney his secret—he knew how to hack into the company voice-mail system. He listened to everyone's messages, from the mailroom people to the upper management.

"You better watch that," McCartney told James.

James shrugged him off and continued his practice of listening to the messages, but it didn't seem to matter. He never got caught. Management at the radio station seemed to love him. McCartney felt like that made James bolder and more confident, and perhaps it made him think he could pull off coming back to Missouri after his wife's murder.

"He knew how to get out of things, and he got away with them," McCartney said. "I think he got around here and was like, 'I'm going to give it a shot.'"

CHAPTER 30

Detective Jon Bailey and Lieutenant Jim Connolly had the name of James Keown's current girlfriend, Julie Webber, but they still had to find her. They found her the day after James was arrested.

It seemed more than a little eerie that his new girlfriend had the same first name as his wife and that James called her "new Julie" to his friends. With the help of an intern in the detective bureau back in Waltham, Jon Bailey was able to get Julie's phone number in St. Louis and put in a call to her phone.

No answer. It went to the answering machine. Bailey debated for a split second whether he should leave a message. But with James behind bars in Jefferson City, he decided Julie probably knew some of what was going on.

Bailey identified himself on the answering machine.

"You've probably heard, or if you haven't, you will

hear shortly, James Keown was arrested today," Bailey began. "I understand you'd been dating him for a while and I'd like to talk to you."

Given the reaction that Bailey had gotten from many of James's friends and acquaintances—that the police had the wrong man—he wasn't expecting Julie Webber to call him back as quickly as she did. She agreed to sit down with detectives, and a meeting was set up for the following day at her apartment in St. Louis.

On November 9, 2005, Bailey and Connolly found themselves in an upscale section of St. Louis, with well-maintained old buildings and streets. It reminded Bailey of Boston with its manicured landscaping, quaint side-walks, and restored brownstones. It was early evening as the two Massachusetts investigators rang the front doorbell.

There was no response.

They waited.

"I think we got stood up," Bailey remarked to his part-ner, and the two turned to walk back to their rental car.

Just as they were about to leave, the door opened. Bai-ley found himself looking at an attractive young woman with strawberry blonde hair. She invited them in, and they followed her up to her apartment, on the second floor. As they walked into her place, Julie introduced them to a male friend in her living room.

"I hope you don't mind, but I would feel more comfort-able with someone else here," she said as they sat down.

The two investigators filled Julie in on some of the details of the case against James—the details that had been made public with the indictment and arrest. They explained that they had been investigating James for quite some time, and they had gathered enough evidence to arrest him for murdering his wife.

"We're looking to see what he told you as far as how Julie died," Bailey began.

As Julie told the detectives about her relationship with James, she had the look of someone whose whole world was crashing down. She was clearly a very intelligent young woman, and Bailey was not surprised that James had dated her. She seemed like his type. He got the impression that Julie Webber had really liked James and was having a hard time with the news of his arrest.

Julie explained that she had known James since high school in Jefferson City, although she'd been a year behind him. Before James returned to Jefferson City after his wife's death, Julie hadn't seen him since her own wedding, on April 29, 2000. James had served as the emcee for the wedding. She was since divorced.

Julie knew that James was back in Jefferson City because her mother had seen Betty Keown over the summer of 2005. Betty had filled Julie's mother in on details of her daughter-in-law's death.

James and Julie started dating about a month before his arrest, after he'd called her on the phone and asked her out, she told the detectives. Julie lived in St. Louis, and James often drove out to visit her on the weekends, something he chronicled on his blog.

James hadn't talked much about how his wife had died other than a brief mention that it had been a result of kidney disease. Julie hadn't pushed for any specific details, she told the investigators, because she hadn't wanted to pry. She'd told herself that if he wanted to tell her more, he would.

And then, about a week before his arrest, James confessed much more about his wife's death, Julie said. The two were out at dinner when James grew serious. He said he was going to tell her something that he'd never told anyone else about his wife's death.

She had committed suicide.

To Julie, it seemed like James was breaking down as the details spilled from his lips. She was taken aback but listened quietly as he continued. His wife had been very sick for a long time. Her doctors told her she would never be able to have children and would eventually die from kidney failure.

"Did you help her commit suicide?" Julie had asked.

James had shaken his head. "No, all I wanted to do was help her get better."

His wife, he gravely explained, had taken ethylene glycol. He had gone to the grocery store, and when he returned, he found her in bed, almost unresponsive. She refused his attempts to take her to the hospital. Eventually he took her there anyway, despite her protests.

"Does anyone know about this?" Julie asked James.

He shook his head again before confiding that his mother and Julie's parents knew the truth, but Julie's parents didn't believe it and blamed him for their daughter's death.

James was surprised that his wife had died from ethylene glycol poisoning because there wasn't even any antifreeze in the house. He didn't know where she could have found the deadly poison.

Julie asked if his wife had left a note for him. She hadn't, he said, but she did leave him an anniversary card under the keyboard at his computer. He went on to explain that his wife's life insurance wouldn't pay out because the death was a suicide. As a result, he was dead broke from not only hospital bills, but the funeral expenses. Bailey knew that, actually, James had not paid for either, and the funeral had been paid for entirely by a close friend of Julie's. He chalked it up to just another lie that James had told yet another person about his wife's death.

It was a lie that Julie Webber hadn't seen coming. Julie recalled that as they left the restaurant, she thought to herself, *OK, that's the real story, and I'm OK with that.* She was glad that James had trusted her enough to tell her the truth.

Julie told them that James had never told her much about his time at Harvard, but she did know that he had been going to school there when his wife died. She wasn't sure what he'd been doing for work at the time.

Bailey and Connolly were now giving her another truth—one far more frightening. They told her what they could, including that James had not gone to Harvard. Bailey wanted her to know that she wasn't alone in falling for James's lies and stories.

Julie was shocked and seemed truly sad that James was not who she'd believed him to be. Bailey wasn't surprised by her reaction. All of the women who he and Connolly had interviewed about James spoke about his charming personality. He was a gentleman to the women, and it was clear that he had been to Julie Webber as well.

The two wrapped up their interview and thanked Julie for speaking with them. After they got in the car, Bailey turned to Connolly and voiced the thought on both of their minds.

"If he gets away with this, he's not going to stop," he said. "We probably just saved her life."

———————————

Later, after James had been transported to Cambridge Jail, in Massachusetts, Betty Keown phoned her son. Her message was cryptic, but there was no doubt James got the meaning. "Just so you know, the police got to St. Louis. She won't be calling you."

And she didn't. James had three names on his approved

list of callers in the Massachusetts jail—Julie Webber; Brian Wilson, the program director at KLIK; and his mother, Betty. The only person he ever heard from was his mother.

CHAPTER 31

Detective Jon Bailey and Lieutenant Jim Connolly stayed in Missouri for two days interviewing employees of the radio station, while James Keown sat in the Cole County Jail.

Although the radio employees had been "gagged" by the station's management in terms of talking with any of the local or national media about the story, they were given the go-ahead to speak with investigators. The one caveat to the interviews was that Scott Boltz, the marketing manager for Cumulus Broadcasting, KLIK's parent company, had to sit in on all interviews with station employees. That was fine with the two investigators, and they began the round of interviews. Boltz was married to Stephanie Boltz, the receptionist at KLIK who had let the police into the station the day that James was arrested.

The detectives began with Brian Wilson, director at KLIK. Wilson told investigators that James said that he returned to Jefferson City to "regroup" and heal following his wife's death, which he'd told Wilson had been from either liver disease or liver cancer. As it turned out, Wilson was the only person at the station whom James had confided to about the police investigation into his wife's death. James told Wilson in February of that year that the police might be contacting him in regard to what he called a routine investigation into Julie's death. Brian Wilson was vaguely aware that James had attended Harvard but couldn't remember who told him that.

Jocelyn Knaebel, Betsy Dudenhoeffer's best friend, who worked in sales for the radio station, told investigators that James told her that his wife had died unexpectedly when they were living in Massachusetts, where they had moved so that he could take classes at Harvard Law School (yet another tweak to the tale). He had just started taking classes when his wife became sick, he'd said, and was unable to continue after her death, so he moved home to Missouri.

James hadn't spoken with all of his new co-workers about his wife's death. KLIK production director Jack Murphy told investigators that James never mentioned his wife's death; he told Murphy that he'd left a job in Boston to return to Missouri in order to get back into radio.

Dean Morgan, who had known James the longest of any of the station employees, recalled talking about the Terry Schiavo case with James and the emotional aspect of having to decide when or if to take someone off life support. Schiavo had lived in a persistent vegetative state for seven years before her husband, Michael, finally received a court ruling in March of 2005 that allowed him to have her removed from life support. Terry Schiavo died on March 31, 2005. James told Dean that he'd had to make the same decision for his wife, but he did not elaborate. His wife, he said, had died from kidney failure. But on other occasions when they were out with a group, Dean heard James say that his wife had kidney cancer. He thought it was odd that James changed his story, but he never questioned it. James never said anything to Dean about why he'd moved to Boston, and Dean had simply assumed that James was working in radio there.

He did know that James had attended Harvard. James wore Harvard shirts and had a Harvard bumper sticker on his Ford Expedition, an SUV he later got rid of because it used too much gas. At one point, James did tell Dean that both he and Bill Gates had something in common because neither of them had actually graduated from Harvard.

The investigators headed to Columbia to interview employees of the sister station, KFRU. The human resources manager for the stations, Mindy Wolf, told Bailey and Connolly that James Keown had contacted her in October or November of 2004 about getting a job. He'd told her that his wife had recently died and he was looking to move back to Missouri. He did not mention how she'd died or that he was supposedly attending Harvard. Wolf explained that a program director position had been offered to James but they never got a response from him. The job was then offered to Brian Wilson.

Matt LaCasse was still reeling from the shock of James's arrest and couldn't bring himself to believe that his friend was guilty of the charges against him. When he was interviewed by Bailey and Connolly, LaCasse gave them very minimal information. He explained that James told him that Julie had died from kidney failure or kidney cancer, which he'd assumed meant the same thing. He knew that James went to Harvard because one day when James was wearing a Harvard shirt, he told Matt it was from his time at the elite East Coast institution.

James had decided to move back to Missouri, he'd told Matt, after talking it over with his then boss following Julie's death. His boss had supposedly asked him, "What's keeping you here?" to which James said he responded, "My job." He then decided to leave that job and "find himself" by returning to his roots in the Midwest. Matt knew that James hadn't initially been doing well financially upon his return to Missouri, as he often bummed lunch money from Matt.

James told another morning-show host a completely different version of how his wife had died. He told her that Julie became sick in Kansas City, not Boston, and James immediately took her to a doctor in Kansas City and that doctor told her to return in two weeks, but she never made it back. She was admitted to a hospital in Kansas City where she died on a Thursday from either kidney failure or liver disease. James shared with the young woman that his wife was buried in Kansas City.

At one point, the young co-worker had tried to set James up on a date with her friend who lived in New York City. The setup never went anywhere, but the woman in New York later told her that James had confided that his wife suffered from a terminal illness she had had since childhood. Another time, James told the woman in New York that he'd traveled to Washington, D.C., to work on a radio spot for XM radio that would air in December of 2005. Other station employees heard that James went to Washington to meet up with Warren Krech's son, who helped him with a website.

Although the interviews were interesting, they didn't give Jon Bailey or Jim Connolly anything of evidentiary value. They were just more examples of James telling lies and twisting the truth. They also showed the investigators how well James had fooled everyone around him in the year after Julie's death; some of his co-workers seemed to almost idolize James as a larger-than-life media personality. Bailey just didn't understand it.

Bailey and Connolly planned to fly out of St. Louis to Boston on November 9, 2005, with James. They picked him up at the Cole County Jail in their rental car, before starting the two-hour drive northeast to St. Louis. James sat in the front passenger seat next to Bailey, who drove. Connolly sat behind Bailey in the rear of the car.

As they drove, James said nothing, and they all listened to the radio. Bailey could not believe the commercial that came over the radio as they drove—it was for antifreeze. He looked over at James, who had no reaction, then cast his eyes to the rearview mirror and met Connolly's gaze; Connolly's eyes widened in disbelief. The two gave each other a look that they both knew meant they could not believe the irony of the commercial playing at that exact moment. James sat looking out the window, saying nothing for the rest of the ride to the airport.

When they got to the airport in St. Louis, the investigators notified the airline that they had a prisoner in custody. They made every effort to remain inconspicuous and not draw attention to the situation. They did not display their police badges or guns, though James was wearing handcuffs that were attached, or shackled, to his waist. The police covered the shackles with his sweater.

The airline asked that they take any leg irons off James before boarding the plane, which they did. They were allowed to board the plane first and sat about ten rows from the rear of the plane. Bailey had James take the window seat, while he took the aisle in the two-seat row. Connolly sat on the other side of the plane, three rows behind them, to keep an eye on things.

As he had in the car, James sat silently, looking out his

window as the rolling farmland of his home state faded away. If the case went as investigators hoped, it would be the last time that James would ever see Missouri, except in the recesses of his mind. When the stewardess came down the aisle for the in-flight drink and snack, James declined.

Although they had been the first to board in St. Louis, the three were the last to deplane at Boston's Logan International Airport. The media was camped out in the terminal waiting to snap a photo of the talk-show host in handcuffs, but police were not looking to create a show at this point. They placed leg irons on James before getting off the plane and met several state police and Waltham police cruisers on the tarmac. James was helped into the back of a Waltham police cruiser, while Bailey climbed into the passenger seat in the front. James remained silent during the drive from Boston to the Waltham Police Department, where he was fingerprinted and photographed during the booking procedure. He ended his day in a cell at the Cambridge Jail, where he waited, alone and hungry, to make his first appearance in a Massachusetts courtroom.

CHAPTER 32

James was brought into the Middlesex County Superior Court in Cambridge the next morning. Dressed in a gray V-necked sweater, he looked more like the students he once sought to be included with at the Harvard Business School than an accused murderer. The prestigious university was only miles away from the courtroom he appeared in on November 10, 2005, but given his situation, there was little chance James would ever walk through the campus again.

He was officially arraigned on the charge of first-degree murder before Judge Catherine White, a well-respected judge with almost two decades of service at the superior court level. During her term as a judge, she had served on the court's Alternative Dispute Resolution Subcommittee as well as the advisory committee for the Judicial Institute. Later that year, the Massachusetts Academy of

Trial Attorneys presented her with their Judge of the Year Award.

Judge White was not the only esteemed legal mind in the courtroom that morning. James was now represented by his newly appointed attorney, J. W. Carney Jr., an extremely experienced and well-known defense attorney in Massachusetts courtrooms. Bespectacled, with a thick, short gray beard, Carney stood next to his new client as the red-haired talk-show personality said the words "Not guilty" when asked by Judge White how he wanted to plead to the charge of first-degree murder.

Assistant District Attorney Lynn Rooney gave an offer of proof in the case, laying out Julie Keown's admission to the emergency room at the Newton-Wellesley Hospital on September 4, 2004, and her death in that same hospital on September 8.

Carney insisted that his client was innocent and told reporters that James was still mourning his wife's passing. He also cast doubt on the strength of the prosecution's case.

"It's always suspect when the prosecutors need a year to get enough evidence to even obtain an indictment," he said.

Jack and Nancy Oldag sat in the front row of the courtroom, next to Detective Jon Bailey, and watched the proceedings, as they had in Jefferson City. A few days later, Jack read a prepared statement during a press conference in a room at the district attorney's office.

"We will miss hearing her laugh and seeing her smile for the rest of our lives," Jack read. "It is now time for Julie to receive the justice and dignity she truly deserves."

James Keown had been arrested and brought back to Massachusetts, but that did not guarantee a conviction.

He did, after all, have a very capable defense team working on his case in J. W. Carney and attorney Janice Bassil. Carney, who had a prestigious Park Plaza office, had been practicing in Massachusetts since 1978. From 1978 until 1983, he was an attorney with the Massachusetts Defenders Committee. From 1983 until 1988, he was an assistant district attorney in Middlesex County. He'd been involved with thousands of felony and murder cases during his time practicing, and James would have been hard-pressed to find a more experienced attorney to defend him, or one with more of an affinity for taking on tough, high-profile criminal cases in the Boston area.

After his financial troubles, which left negative balances in his bank accounts, James was deemed "indigent," meaning that he was eligible to receive a court-appointed attorney because he could not pay for an attorney himself. Carney was appointed to James Keown's case through what is known as "the murder list" in Massachusetts, a list of attorneys qualified to take indigent clients charged with murder. The attorneys on this list were paid one hundred dollars per hour at the time Carney took on Keown's case, eight times less than Carney's going rate at his practice.

The case was on *Nancy Grace* again that night, as it had been after the arrest in Jefferson City. The pundits pontificated on the merits of the case as they knew it, predicting that it would be a tough sell to a jury. They forecast that the case would come down to the medical testimony of the prosecution and defense medical experts.

Bill Tackett, the Cole County prosecutor who'd spent every Tuesday that summer on James's radio show, tried to downplay the extent of his relationship with James after the arrest. He said he'd only arrived about five minutes before the *Tuesdays with Tackett* show and left immediately after. He hadn't hung around and engaged in personal chitchat with James, he insisted.

"We talked extensively about the various murder cases, whatever it was that was happening, whether it was national or whether it was within my office. But other than that, I mean, he was just a talk-show host. They come and go," Tackett said.

He analyzed and discussed the case, just as he had discussed other criminal cases with James Keown during their weekly radio show. Now that he'd heard James's claim that Julie had just happened to pick up a container of antifreeze and drink it while out for a walk, Tackett seemed unconvinced.

"That's a toughie to sell. I'm not saying it can't be sold. I just don't know. You know, people look at just the commonsense end of this. Do you walk down the street, pick up an open container, and just drink it? I think that's tough. But, that being said, hey, you know, it's up to the jury," Tackett said.

There were months and months of research and preparation ahead for both the defense and prosecution. It would be at least a year, possibly more, before a jury heard the details of James's case and his arguments in his own defense.

CHAPTER 33

Detective Jon Bailey continued to conduct follow-up interviews with James Keown's friends and co-workers in the week after his arrest. Most of the information he collected, however, though examples of James's lying and con-man ways, were not things that would be admissible during the trial.

From his desk in the Waltham Police Department, Jon put in a phone call to Ellen Schenk, an anchor at radio station KMBZ in Missouri, who used to work with James. Schenk had always thought that James, or JP as she knew him, had the look of success—he always wore a Rolex watch and a three-piece suit. She'd seen him driving the Jaguar. JP was just the sort of person she expected to end up at a major radio network.

Schenk had last seen James in person when he came into the KMBZ radio station in early 2004. At the time, he told her that he was working at Harvard, and she'd gotten the impression from the way he spoke that he was teaching there. She recalled that during an earlier conversation, James had told her that he attended Harvard, so Schenk assumed that was how he went on to get the teaching position. It seemed a little off at first, but knowing JP's ability to network, Schenk realized that if anyone could move from radio broadcasting to teaching at Harvard, it was him.

James kept in touch with Schenk from time to time, and during a phone conversation in 2004, he told her that his wife might need a kidney transplant. Schenk assumed at the time that James told her this because he knew that her husband had a liver transplant. She expected James to ask her some questions about what to expect with an organ transplant, but he never did. The next time she heard from him was a phone call in which he broke the news of his wife's death. He told her that the doctors had found ethylene glycol in Julie's system, and he'd sounded surprised by the discovery.

Eileen White, an ICU nurse who'd worked with Julie at Liberty Hospital, told Detective Bailey that she and her husband went out to dinner with the Keowns before they moved to Boston. During dinner conversation that night, the Keowns told Eileen and her husband that the Learning Exchange was paying for James to go to Harvard, but they planned to return to the Kansas City area after he finished his degree. Eileen remembered the conversation well because her twelve-year-old daughter hoped to someday attend Harvard Law School and was excited to hear that James was at the prestigious institution.

Lene Johansen, meanwhile, started writing about the case on her blog on November 13, in a post she called

"James Keown: Digesting the Shock." She wrote about how she believed that James had returned to Missouri to be close to his family and figure out what to do with his life after his wife's death. She felt he had drowned the grief over his wife's death in his work during his time in Jefferson City.

The reality of James's arrest forced Lene and the other journalists to reexamine their own interactions with James and their role as reporters. "By default, the journalists among us have accepted the accusation. That is what we do as reporters; we assume the worst and hope for the best. The charge does not gel with the reality of the James we know, but we have to assume that he did this to protect our professional integrity and to protect our own feelings," Lene wrote. "I am a journalist and my duty is to the facts. There are so many facts I don't know in this case, but I do have some facts that I learned through an intense friendship that lasted me three months this spring. James Keown is a person that is immensely vulnerable right now, and I care about him. He has been nothing but sweet to me."

Lene wasn't the only one blogging about the case. James's younger sister, Shawna Keown, started her own blog after her brother's was pulled by the hosting company when it received word of his arrest.

"I don't know if anyone will read my blog since it's not on anyone's site, but I just want people to e-mail me if they feel they have comments to make that they can't make on James Keown's blog site anymore."

When police collected James's belongings from the Learning Exchange, they found several documents from a company called Orion Digital, which was the company James's friend Troy Rivas operated. They were mostly invoices for electronic equipment that James claimed he was buying for the Learning Exchange.

Bailey sent Troy copies of the documents to review, and on November 15, Bailey called Troy to follow up on the documents and what they might mean. The first thing Troy told Bailey was that the documents, though they carried his company name, had not been generated by him or his company. They were fakes. He had never sold any equipment to the Learning Exchange and was at a loss for what the invoices meant.

One of the documents was a proposal in the amount of $50,000 to $65,000 that was written by a woman named Jennifer Thompson. The name was familiar to Troy because it was his wife's maiden name, but she did not use it anymore. Jennifer Rivas looked at the document and confirmed to Bailey that she had never seen it before. In addition, the letterheads on both of the documents were not from Orion Digital, she told the detective.

The letter allegedly from Jennifer was written in response to a "request for proposal" for work at the Learning Exchange. "As I stated during our conversation on Monday, I am confident that Orion Digital can provide the following assistance to the Learning Exchange by early August of this year," the letter began. Among work that Orion Digital was supposedly offering was consultation on the design of the new website, archiving of the current website, making suggestions on news aggregator services, and developing tools to connect those selected services to the new site.

Bailey suspected that James had made the letterheads using templates on his computer, just as he had made the Harvard Business School acceptance letter and the bogus résumés he'd given to Tim Trabon and the Learning Exchange. It seemed that James had tried to use Orion Digital as a cover to embezzle money from the Learning

Exchange. He designed the letterhead for Orion Digital and sent out the invoice for the "equipment" the company received. Whether the Learning Exchange received any equipment was unknown. Bailey learned that the non-profit was not interested in pursuing criminal charges against James at the time; they felt the scandal would be too damaging to their ability to fund-raise. If potential donors caught wind of the Orion Digital scam, they might not be willing to donate in the future.

Bailey found himself pondering the issue, which was not the first such con job James had pulled off. He had managed to collect money that should have gone to Wetsu Creative and Jason Jett for the website design at the Learning Exchange by sending the fake invoices from Interactive Methods. Bailey and Connolly had managed to piece together how James had laid out that scam, too. He used a fake bid from a company where he once worked as the high bid on the website design project, then added a lower bid from his own company, Interactive Methods. After the project was awarded to Interactive Methods, he brought on his friend Jason Jett to do the real design work, but he never paid him.

And then there was the nearly $10,000 in moving expenses that Tim Trabon had paid to a moving company that didn't even exist when James relocated to Kansas City. This was starting to add up to a lot of money. But where had it all gone? There were negative balances in James's bank accounts when Julie died, and $20,000 of credit-card debt. Where had James been spending this money? As he had done many times already, Bailey rolled over the possibilities in his head—girlfriend, boyfriend, drug problem, gambling addiction? So far, there was no evidence to support any of those theories.

By all accounts, James had been broke when he returned to Missouri after his wife's death, too broke to even pay for the funeral. And so broke that, as Jennifer Rivas told the detectives, he'd stayed with friends, like Jennifer and Troy, because he didn't have anyplace to live.

Jennifer Rivas also recounted to Detective Bailey some things she remembered from the time James stayed with her and her husband after Julie's death. He was trying to get back on his feet in Missouri, find a job, and rent an apartment. At one point, James went into the kitchen to get a drink and remarked, "I guess it's safe here," as he took a beer from the refrigerator. At the time, Jennifer thought that the police were watching James to see if he had any bad habits like drinking or smoking. Jennifer also told Bailey about a statement James made prior to his wife's funeral the year before. Jennifer and Troy were at the home of Robert and Caren Patterson with James, who told them he would go to Europe if he had the chance. Later, at the funeral, Jennifer watched James and thought he seemed "disconnected," like he was hiding something. He wasn't spending time with Jack and Nancy Oldag as she would have expected at such a time. He was distant.

When James got the job with Tim Trabon, he told Jennifer and Troy that he had a good plan for the new job. "If you establish a relationship with payroll, you're all set," he told the couple.

Shortly after that, James rented the expensive loft apartment overlooking the river in Kansas City. James's friends and co-workers admired the trendy loft, but some wondered how he could afford the place. Detective Bailey didn't know how James paid the rent, but he did know how James got the lease, much in the same way he got paid on a number of other occasions: he used forgery. The letters of reference he provided to the landlord were from friends and acquaintances who confirmed they had never written or signed the letters. And then there was the lease itself. Investigators determined that James had forged his mother's signature on the lease agreement, signing her name as the person who was responsible for the apartment. When confronted with her signature on the lease, Betty told investigators that it was not her signature but that her son had permission to sign her name. Bailey felt her statement was just another instance where Betty Keown tried to protect or cover up for her son, and he suspected it would not be the last.

───────────

When Bailey contacted Betsy Dudenhoeffer on November 15, she was adamant that the police had arrested the wrong person. She relayed basic information to Bailey about her childhood friend but volunteered nothing extra. She had nothing of evidentiary value to offer the investigator. She was just yet another friend of James's whom Bailey felt had been conned by the accused killer.

But two days later, Betsy would call Bailey back with information that would change the course of the investigation.

After his arrest, James wrote several letters to Betsy from his Massachusetts jail cell. He was upbeat and never mentioned the case. It seemed to Betsy that James was in denial about how serious his situation was, as he referred to his jail cell as his "dorm room," then talked about getting together with "the guys on his hall" for Bible study.

In other letters, he talked about the weather, one time telling Betsy how he loved the winters in New England, or about what he planned to do when he went home.

"I can't wait to get back to Jefferson City and share a glass of wine with you," he wrote.

At one point he mentioned another high-profile inmate, Neil Entwistle, who was awaiting trial on charges that he murdered his wife, Rachel, and infant daughter,

Lillian. Entwistle was later convicted on both counts and is serving a life sentence in prison.

"I wish you could meet him, he's such a nice guy," James told Betsy about Entwistle. "These guys here are all great guys. We have a lot of fun."

Shortly after his arrest, James made an unusual request of his friend.

"Can you do me a favor?" he wrote. "Can you go to the radio station and get my computer?"

Betsy still worked as an advertising representative for KLIK, and no doubt James knew she had access to the station, including his office. He went on to explain to Betsy that he was sure the station would let him have his belongings. Betsy declined. She just didn't feel right about the request.

A few days later, James's mother called Betsy. James had called his mother and instructed her to call Betsy, Betty Keown explained. She asked Betsy if she would find out from Brian Wilson if it was OK to take some of James's belongings from the station. Specifically, James wanted her to get his personal laptop, a red binder that had some financial papers inside it, and a hard drive from his work computer.

Betsy had known Betty since she was a child. Her parents used to socialize with Jim and Betty when she was younger, and she felt genuine sympathy for what James's mother must have been feeling after her son's arrest. Betsy was still having a hard time digesting the shock of his arrest herself; she just couldn't connect the crime James was charged with to the person she had known for most of her life. When the police came to interview her just after his arrest, she had been adamant when she told them they had the wrong person. The James she knew from her childhood could never do this.

Still, she didn't feel comfortable with the request. Betsy

apologized to Betty but turned her down. She just didn't want to get involved, she explained.

Betsy kept thinking about the request, however, first from James and then from his mother. Something wasn't right about the situation. The next day she saw Jason Jett, the college friend whom James had used as a cover for his bogus website design job at the Learning Exchange, and told him about the request from Betty. Jason urged Betsy to tell the police.

———————————

At 1:30 p.m., November 17, 2005, Betsy picked up the phone and called Detective Bailey. Bailey was a little surprised to hear from her, because just the week before Betsy had been an ardent supporter of James's. And though he didn't get the impression that she was wavering in her support of her childhood friend, she just seemed to want the investigators to know that James was looking for those items.

As Betsy told Bailey about the items that James wanted from the office, she mentioned the laptop. He perked up at the mention of the computer, especially because he knew that James had a computer they hadn't been able to secure as evidence. Could this be the computer he was looking for?

This has to be it, Bailey thought. *Why else would James be so concerned about getting it? But why would he want the hard drive from the desktop computer he used at the radio station? That didn't make any sense.* Bailey didn't think that James was careless enough to have actually searched for something incriminating on the work computer.

What was on that laptop? Was it the key to prosecuting James? Did it have any clues about where he spent all the money he'd swindled out of his former employers?

Bailey thought the computer had to have something important on it.

Bailey immediately called Lieutenant Jim Connolly and filled him in on the conversation he'd had with Betsy. The two knew that time was of the essence, so Connolly called Brian Wilson at KLIK. He explained to Wilson that he wanted to obtain the laptop and hard drive from James's work computer.

Wilson gave Connolly some surprising news. And it wasn't news that the seasoned investigator wanted to hear: Betty Keown had already picked up the Sony VAIO laptop and the hard drive from the radio station.

Connolly called Bailey with the information. The two investigators knew that by the time they got a search warrant and a flight to Missouri, it might be too late. They were concerned that crucial evidence in the case might be destroyed if they didn't act fast. There was a reason James wanted those computers so desperately. And now that they were aware of the computers' existence, the two investigators wanted them, too.

CHAPTER 34

November 22, 2005

Massachusetts State Investigator Lieutenant Jim Connolly was anxious to get the laptop and hard drive that James Keown had left in Jefferson City, Missouri. He would need help if he was going to get to the computer before it was compromised.

He needed someone already in Jefferson City to assist, so he put in a call to Carla Kilgore—the Jefferson City detective who had helped when they arrested James at the station just weeks before—to ask if she could help obtain and execute a search warrant at Betty Keown's house for the computers. He explained to Kilgore that he was looking specifically for the Sony VAIO laptop computer.

Connolly filled Kilgore in on the background of the laptop over the phone and by e-mail. He e-mailed her an unsigned affidavit to use in applying for a search warrant, just as he had done with Reed Buente for the Learning

Exchange warrant. However, Kilgore did not use the template for the warrant as Buente had done, a decision that the defense would later jump on during pretrial wrangling. Instead, she went immediately to Assistant Prosecutor Kurt Valentine with the information Connolly had e-mailed her for use in applying for the search warrant. A search warrant was drawn up based on Connolly's affidavit and Kilgore's verbal explanation to the prosecutor of what Connolly had told her about the investigation. Kilgore did not cut and paste Connolly's affidavit into the application for the warrant but incorporated the information into the warrant.

The warrant was approved by a judge at 1:30 p.m. on November 22, 2005.

Later that afternoon, Kilgore drove to Betty Keown's house to serve the warrant. The well-manicured area behind the country club was not a neighborhood that the city's police typically responded to for this type of situation. But then, nothing about the case against James Keown had been typical.

Kilgore was accompanied by another uniformed officer and a Cole County sheriff's deputy. When she got to the house, Kilgore knocked at the front door. There was no answer. While the deputy and uniformed officer stayed by the front door, Kilgore walked around back. A sliding-glass door at the rear of the house was unlocked. She pushed it open and called out.

"Jefferson City Police, is anyone home? We have a search warrant for the premises."

There was no answer.

Kilgore walked into the house, went to the front door, and let the other two officers inside. She started her search on the top floor, where there were two bedrooms. One was a large master bedroom, with a large bathroom and walk-in closet. She knew she was looking for four boxes that had been removed from the KLIK radio station, specifically the laptop computer. She didn't see the laptop, but inside a closet, under some clothes on hangers, Kilgore spied two boxes without lids. As she got closer, she looked inside and saw that they appeared to have business-type materials inside. She brought the boxes down to the first floor before continuing her search.

The three went through the entire house and could not find the laptop. Kilgore found a number for James's sister Shawna Keown and called her to ask about getting in touch with Betty Keown. Shawna set up a three-way call with Betty, who explained that she was out grocery shopping but would be there shortly.

About ten minutes passed before Betty arrived at the home. Kilgore explained that she was looking for four boxes that Betty had retrieved from the KLIK offices after her son was arrested.

Betty replied that two of them were upstairs and led Kilgore to the upstairs bedroom where she had already found the two boxes in the closet. Kilgore asked about the other two boxes.

"I beat you to it," Betty replied, telling the female officer that she had already sent the other two boxes, including the Sony VAIO laptop, to her son's attorney, J. W. Carney, in Boston.

"Do you have anything to prove that?" Kilgore asked.

Betty walked away and returned with a receipt from the post office that detailed the shipping. She'd mailed a package off to Carney on November 18, four days before Carla Kilgore arrived with the search warrant, and one day after Betsy Dudenhoeffer had declined to help. Though Betty showed Kilgore the dated slip, there was no way for her to prove what was actually shipped in those boxes. As a result, Kilgore continued her search to make sure the items were not still there in the house.

The two remaining boxes Kilgore found at the house had little of evidentiary value. There were some picture frames, a desktop nameplate, and other miscellaneous office decorations. In a second upstairs bedroom, Kilgore found a desktop computer that Betty Keown told her was not hooked up and had not been used by either James or her. It looked like the bedroom had been used as an office. Kilgore did not take the desktop computer during the search.

Betty Keown explained it wasn't her idea to take the items from the KLIK station after her son's arrest. She claimed that she had received a call from KLIK receptionist Stephanie Boltz about a week after James's arrest and that Boltz had asked her to pick up James's belongings. Betty went over that afternoon and picked up a box with the Sony laptop and some books and papers.

A week after that, Betty got another call from Stephanie Boltz. Apparently James had left some belongings in the Columbia office of the radio station, and those would need to be picked up as well. Betty returned to the KLIK station building in Jefferson City for the other boxes, which were sealed with tape. She took them home and put them upstairs in her son's closet.

Betty went on to explain that her son had called her to ask if she would send the laptop computer and the hard drive from the desktop computer in his bedroom to his attorney in Boston. Betty asked Shawna's fiancé to help with removing the hard drive from the computer, which he did with a screwdriver.

The computers were in Boston already. Despite her quick response, Kilgore left Betty's house empty-handed. And with that, the investigation was back on the East Coast, where Jon Bailey and Jim Connolly were waiting.

Connolly immediately filled Assistant District Attorney Lynn Rooney in on the issue with the laptop. Rooney and J. W. Carney had known each other for decades; he had trained her when he was the director of trial attorney training in Middlesex County, and the two had enjoyed a very cordial professional relationship since then. After Rooney learned about the laptop Betty Keown had sent to the defense attorney, she put in a phone call to her longtime colleague.

Rooney began by telling Carney that she understood that he had the laptop and a hard drive. Carney responded that he knew she had a warrant for the items. The defense attorney felt that the appropriate response in his role as James's attorney was to hold on to the items and preserve them in their present condition until there was a formal court order to turn them over. Carney assured Rooney that he would not access the computer or allow anyone else to do so, and the prosecutor accepted his word that he would not. Rooney explained that she would seek a court order to take possession of the computer, and Carney agreed to that. Following the phone conversation, Carney placed the box from Betty Keown inside a credenza in his office. He told his staff not to touch the box.

On December 7, 2005, Rooney filed a Motion for an Order to Turn Over Certain Items of the Defendant's Personal Property in the Custody of the Defendant's Attorney. On January 4, 2006, after a hearing, a judge ordered that the property be turned over to the state. State Trooper Michael Banks went to pick up the laptop and what he thought would be the hard drive from the other computer from Carney's office. The "hard drive" turned out to be just a floppy disk that had been removed from a disk drive on the computer. J. W. Carney contacted Betty Keown about the mix-up with the hard drive after the court's order in early January of 2006. Betty took the computer to a computer store where someone removed the hard drive, then sent it to Carney, who turned it over to the state.

Both the Sony VAIO laptop and hard drive were placed in a state police evidence locker, where they were held until early that summer, their contents unknown to everyone but James Keown. As it turned out, some of the information on the computer had been deleted, no doubt to try to cover up what the laptop had been used for.

But police would eventually find out anyway, and the result was shocking.

CHAPTER 35

The Sony VAIO laptop and the hard drive sat in storage for months at the Massachusetts State Police Detective Evidence Locker, where Detective Jon Bailey and Lieutenant Jim Connolly could only guess at what information or clues they might contain. James, meanwhile, was still locked away in jail waiting for the case to move toward trial.

In early June of 2006, Connolly obtained a warrant to have a forensic analysis done on both the laptop and hard drive that had been handed over to the state by J. W. Carney six months prior.

The two were given to forensic computer expert Andrew Winrow along with the list of search terms. Winrow had worked as a computer forensic specialist for three years at the time, and though he'd initially worked for the Middlesex County District Attorney's Office, he had gone on to a similar job with the state attorney general's

office. Winrow's expertise involved acquiring, authen-
ticating, searching, and analyzing computer evidence,
electronic information stored on a computer, and electronic stored media as well as compact discs. Among the
terms Winrow was asked to look for were *methylmalonic
academia*, *propionic acid*, *ethylene glycol*, *antifreeze and
poison*, *Lynn Turner*, *Court TV*, *Forensic Files*, *polygraph*,
Waltham Police, and *Massachusetts State Police*. Other
search terms included *Harvard*, *forgery*, *accidental*, and
death.

The prosecution and police investigators would not
find out what was on the laptop or the hard drive until
later in the summer of 2006. Because of the manner in
which the computers came to police, through J. W. Carney,
the defense attorney wanted the opportunity to view the
information that Winrow found on the computer first, to
protect any attorney-client privileged materials.

During an August 2006 meeting between Carney,
Assistant District Attorney Nat Yeager, Jim Connolly,
and Winrow, an agreement was reached about the contents of the laptop. It was agreed that Winrow and Carney
would look at a copy of the hard drive alone. Winrow was
told not to speak to anyone about what he saw on that
hard drive without a court order. After viewing the material on the hard drive, Carney believed that it was directly
connected to the terms laid out in the search warrant,
specifically that it included computer searches done by
someone, presumably James, before Julie Keown died.

Winrow was considered an expert witness for the prosecution because of his experience assisting law enforcement and prosecutors in investigating computer crime
cases. His forensic analysis had a number of steps. He
began by making an exact bit-by-bit read-only copy of
the original hard drive. As a forensic specialist, he knew
it was never a good idea to work off the original hard

drive in case of a hardware failure. The original hard drive was "write protected," which meant that it could not be altered at any stage of the investigation. The copy of the hard drive was made as a "read-only" copy so that it could not be changed either.

The second step was to authenticate the computer using EnCase, a software program that ran a mathematical checksum, or error check. Winrow's third step was the actual analysis of the computer, when he searched the hard drive for anything that might be relevant to the case. He used the EnCase program to enter fifty search terms that investigators had provided, and he was given a list of all "hits" found on the computer for things related to search terms like *poison*, *kidney dysfunction*, and *ethylene glycol*.

The search on the laptop hard drive and the hard drive from the second computer took several months. The number of hits on some of the search terms was daunting. For example, Winrow entered the word *Sprite*, because of James Keown's statement to investigators about getting Julie a bottle of Sprite that last weekend of her life; he got 20,980 hits.

Among the other items Winrow found stored on the computer was a picture of a bottle of potassium ferricyanide. The chemical itself was only slightly toxic, but when mixed with an acid in its aqueous form, the resulting solution yielded toxic hydrogen cyanide gas. Potassium ferricyanide was used in the foiled terrorist attempt in Italy in 2002 in which four Moroccan nationalists were arrested with nine pounds of the chemical and a map of water pipes leading to the U.S. Embassy in Rome. It was thought that they planned to dump the chemical into the water supply, though that would not have been toxic. Whether James had discovered this detail about the chemical during his search was not known, but it gave prosecutors some evidence that he had been researching poisonous chemicals on his laptop.

But cyanide wasn't the only poison James Keown researched on the laptop. Winrow found that James did almost all of his searches via the popular search engine Google.com.

Although someone could try to delete a search term or result, with the idea being that it couldn't be found, the software Winrow used enabled him to locate even deleted items. When a file was on the hard drive of the computer, it was stored in a specific allocated area. When deleted, the actual data from that file is still on the computer but is moved to an area known as unallocated space. That unallocated space remained as long as it wasn't overwritten by new files.

The unallocated space on the hard drive of James Keown's computer proved to be a major find for the prosecution's case. Files that James had clearly tried to delete from the computer included a search for *The Anarchist Cookbook* on August 17, 2004, and August 18, 2004, just weeks before Julie Keown's death. The file was huge and included information on everything from making bombs and poisons to killing someone with your hands, as well as other illegal activities. Another search included the word *chloroform*. A search on Google for homemade poisons was also done on August 17 and August 18.

In the end, Winrow found that someone had used the laptop to search for poison twenty different times before Julie Keown's death. The evidence seemed overwhelming.

Prosecutors now had a witness in Julie's former coworker Sam Shoemaker, who would testify that James Keown had suggested his wife ingested antifreeze from a Gatorade bottle; another witness, Heather LeBlanc, who testified that James was making Julie drink Gatorade when she did not want to; and the fact that someone had searched for antifreeze and ethylene glycol poisoning on James's laptop computer, a computer used solely by one person—James Keown.

But whether a jury would hear the results from the computer analysis remained to be seen. James Keown's defense team filed a thick motion in Middlesex County Superior Court contesting the computer evidence. They would argue that the computers had not been seized properly, and as such, any evidence on those computers should be suppressed, meaning the evidence would not be admitted in court.

CHAPTER 36

The defense team that contested the computer search evidence was a new one for James Keown.

Attorney J. W. Carney had withdrawn from the case after the computer forensic analysis was completed. He and his partner, Janice Bassil, cited irreconcilable differences with their client when they ended their representation in November of 2006.

Carney later stated in an affidavit that he withdrew because he was concerned that prosecutors had obtained the evidence in part as a result of his own acts or omissions and because he was now likely to be a witness in the case.

In place of Carney and Bassil, two veteran criminal defense lawyers—Matthew Feinberg and Matthew Kamholtz—were appointed by the Committee for Public Counsel Services through the so-called murder list to represent James Keown on November 21, 2006. Feinberg was a former public defender for the Legal Aid Society in New York City and a former legal director of the Civil Liberties Union of Massachusetts. Kamholtz had more than twenty years of experience trying criminal cases and was a frequent lecturer in the area of criminal defense.

The two attorneys received seven boxes of documents related to the case, which they later said took six months to review and organize. There was no way they would be ready for trial by the February 26, 2007, trial date that had been set in the case.

Feinberg and Kamholtz filed three different motions to suppress evidence in the case in early 2007, motions that would not be heard by a judge until a lengthy hearing lasting more than a week that summer. In their motions, the defense asked Judge Sandra Hamlin to rule in favor of suppressing evidence found during the search of James and Julie Keown's Waltham duplex on September 7 and 8, 2004; the search at the Learning Exchange in January of 2005; and the search at Betty Keown's home in November of 2005.

In support of the motion to suppress, they filed an affidavit from James Keown, in which the accused murderer claimed he never gave his consent for the police to search the duplex. James's lengthy statement differed considerably from the version of events that police had provided. Sergeant Ed Forster, of the Massachusetts State Police, and Sergeant Brian Lambert, of the Waltham Police Department, indicated in their reports that James had not been considered a suspect during their first interview with him at the Newton-Wellesley Hospital. They also maintained that he voluntarily agreed to let them search both the Waltham duplex and his Ford Expedition.

James now disagreed with all of those statements in an affidavit filed with the motions. He now claimed that he felt the police considered him a suspect from the first night they met him in the Newton-Wellesley Hospital, and he contradicted police statements about how it was that he decided to go to the duplex during their first search. James suggested that he was forced to be present for the search, despite the fact that he had given Ted Willmore the keys to the house and had initially opted to stay at the hospital, which the police had agreed to at the time.

"I told them I didn't want to leave the hospital due to Julie's condition. They responded that they would be searching my house that night. They never mentioned getting a warrant and I understood that they would search my house whether I consented or not, or whether I was there or not. I was intimidated and felt I had no choice but to go with them to the house," James said.

Although police were under the impression that Ted Willmore had volunteered to go with James to the duplex for the search, James said the police told him that Willmore needed to go with them because they didn't know what they were looking for.

James claimed that the police began searching the duplex before he had even arrived and that he did not sign a consent form authorizing the search until it was under way. This directly contradicted statements by police, who said that James authorized Ted Willmore to be present for the search, as he wanted to stay at the hospital with Julie. He maintained that he did not willingly sign the consent form. "When I signed the form, I did not feel I had any choice," James said.

James later stated that the police also searched his car that same night before he even signed an amended consent form including the car.

Although police, including detectives Jon Bailey and Stephen Taranto, observed that James had not appeared upset about his wife's death, James said he *was* upset. "I was in shock due to Julie's death," he said.

He insisted that he had not wanted to leave the hospital on September 8, 2004, the day his wife died, but that police had made him in order to get his wife's computers. His statements were in direct contradiction to police statements and observations made that day.

Those computers, which had been issued by the Cerner Corporation, contained Julie Keown's searches for how to get well. James, through his attorneys, said that although he'd signed the consent form authorizing the search of the computers, he now questioned whether he had the authority to give that consent, since the computers were the property of the Cerner Corporation.

James went on to challenge the warrant that resulted in police gathering his belongings at the Learning Exchange offices in Kansas City. James claimed that his personal belongings were locked in a private office and that his laptop was password protected. Tammy Blossom, he now said, had assured him she would mail these belongings to him but never did. Although Blossom and the others at the company maintained that James had abandoned the property, James felt otherwise.

James blamed the Massachusetts police for the decision by Tim Trabon to fire him. "I believe I was terminated from that job because police in Massachusetts contacted my employer and told him I was under suspicion for having murdered my wife. I was very upset and went into a deep depression."

Because of this depression, James said, he moved to stay with his mother in Jefferson City at the end of November 2004.

The affidavit contained even more statements that investigators knew were obvious lies. James claimed that he and his mother had packed "most of his belongings" from the Waltham duplex when he moved back to Missouri following Julie's death. Bailey and Connolly were a bit surprised by this claim because when they searched the duplex in March of 2005, they found nearly all of the couple's belongings still inside.

James challenged the March 2005 search as well, saying that police would have no reason to look inside the window at the rear of the duplex as Jon Bailey had done. Bailey maintained that he was able to see the boxes marked *James's Computer* from the lawn adjacent to the porch, without stepping onto the porch.

James swore in the affidavit that he was surprised when his landlord in Massachusetts changed the locks on the duplex. James had every intention of gathering any belongings still left in the apartment and claimed that he never gave the landlord permission to enter the residence.

Lastly, the defense challenged the search warrant executed at Betty Keown's home after James was arrested. James stated that he had the expectation that the rooms he used in his mother's house were private, as was the office space he used at the KLIK station.

"I had not seen the search warrant and did not know any of the details regarding it. I was told by Mr. Carney that even though he had to turn over the Sony laptop and hard drive to the prosecutor, we would still have the right to challenge their use at trial by filing a motion to suppress at the proper time," James stated. "I did not specifically authorize Mr. Carney to give anything to the prosecution. Rather, I accepted what he said about what he was obligated to do, and that we would be filing a motion to suppress."

James indicated that he had discussed the potential presence of documents on the computers that might be protected by attorney-client privilege. Carney told him that there would be a procedure in place to identify the attorney-client materials and to make sure the prosecution had no access to them.

When Carney approached him in October of 2006 with an agreement regarding the computer hard drive and how any attorney-client files would be dealt with, James said he went along with the agreement based on Carney's advice.

An affidavit was also filed from James's mother, Betty Keown, about the Sony laptop. Betty again claimed that it was Stephanie Boltz at the radio station, not herself, who had initiated picking up her son's belongings from the station. Betty stated that she went to the station and picked up a laptop computer, a radio, some pictures, and a coat. About two weeks later, she received another phone call from Boltz, who told her that there were additional items, which had been packed into three boxes. Betty then went back to the station and picked up those boxes as well as a bicycle. She put all of the boxes in James's bedroom upstairs.

About one week after that, Betty said, she got a phone call from attorney J. W. Carney asking her to send some of the items she'd picked up from KLIK, including the laptop computer and the hard drive from the desktop computer in the upstairs room.

Betty admitted she did not have computer skills and so had asked her daughter Shawna and Shawna's fiancé to help remove the hard drive. She then mailed the laptop and what she thought was the hard drive to Carney in Boston.

Betty detailed in the affidavit her account of the search warrant that was executed at her home on November 22, 2005. She was at Walmart when Shawna called to tell her the police were at the house and looking for the boxes Betty had picked up at KLIK. Betty said that although police told her the house had been unlocked when they arrived, she did not feel that was the case.

"I never leave the house with the doors open," Betty said in the affidavit.

Betty returned from her shopping trip to Walmart and found the officers inside her house. "I saw the warrant on the table but I was too upset to read it," she said. "It was clear to me that they had already been through the house as one of the boxes I had brought from KLIK was downstairs, not upstairs in James's bedroom where I had left the three boxes." Betty's statement about three boxes also was inconsistent with the search warrant executed by the Jefferson City Police, which mentioned four boxes.

The police asked Betty about the location of the laptop James left at the radio station. Betty informed the police she had already mailed the laptop to Carney.

Betty explained that Carney had then called her in January of 2006 regarding the missing hard drive on the desktop computer that James kept in the house. She had in fact sent him a disk drive, so she went to a computer store for help in removing the real hard drive.

As was the case with the laptop, she mailed it right off to Carney, determined to help her son however possible.

CHAPTER 37

Assistant District Attorney Nat Yeager had been flattered to be given the job of prosecuting James Keown after former prosecutor Lynn Rooney left when she was appointed as a judge in the Dedham District Court on April 12, 2006.

Yeager was a graduate of the New England School of Law, where he'd served as the editor in chief of *The New England Law Review*. He had worked in the Middlesex County District Attorney's Office since 1996. Yeager truly felt he could make a difference through practicing law, but in the case of James Keown, that meant getting to trial. And by February of 2007, the new defense attorneys on the case were asking for more time to prepare for the trial, citing their late appointment to the case and conflicts with other trials on their schedule. Yeager was growing frustrated with the delays, and he expressed this to the court, along with the frustration of Julie Keown's family members, who were traveling from Missouri to see the case to its end. Assistant District Attorney Steve Hoffman, who had been on the case already, remained as part of the prosecution's team.

The defense wanted more time to prepare for what was expected to be a seven-day hearing on the three different motions they had filed asking the judge to suppress computer evidence. Yeager sent letters pressing them to end the delays in the case and insisting that if the hearing was continued, all of the attorneys should commit to a date and stick to it. He pointed to the logistics of coordinating the schedules of the witnesses who would need to come from out of state, including Missouri, to testify.

"As to the trial date, as you are aware, I have made clear from the beginning that I want to try the case this year," Yeager wrote to the defense. "I absolutely respect that you have an obligation to digest all of the evidence in the case. As you delve into the case, however, I think that the amount of paper is misleading. It is, after all, only February. I would urge you to consider moving the case forward, rather than further out. I remain available in both September and October."

The defense disagreed, saying in any murder case they needed two years from the date of their appointment to adequately prepare for trial. James Keown's defense attorneys held firm in their request to push the trial date out, despite the requests from prosecutor Yeager. In September of 2007, they filed a motion to continue the trial to no earlier than June of 2008. At the time, the trial was scheduled for November 13, 2007.

In support of their request, attorneys Feinberg and Kamholtz pointed out again their late appointment to the case and the fact that Judge Hamlin had not yet issued an order following the extended evidentiary hearing earlier that summer. They held their position that the warrant served by Detective Carla Kilgore in Jefferson City was invalid, which would mean none of the evidence from the Sony VAIO laptop would be heard by a jury.

"There is little doubt the result of the motion to suppress will have great impact for both sides," the defense wrote.

The defense argued further that a series of what they felt were critical discovery issues still needed to be resolved. They raised the issue of a delay in receiving forensic copies of all of the computer hard drives in the case, including the two Dell laptops from Julie's work, the Toshiba laptop from the Learning Exchange, and the two other computers taken from the Waltham duplex in March of 2005. The defense had received copies of the Dell computers' hard drives as well as the Sony laptop in mid-July of 2007. They were still waiting for copies of the Toshiba and the computer hard drive from the March search of the duplex.

Computer analyst Andrew Winrow testified during the suppression hearings that summer that it took him three months to analyze the computers. The defense expected their analysis would take even longer.

But it wasn't just the computer hard drives that the defense said it still needed. They told the judge they needed copies of the call to the police business line made by Lynn Nuti in September of 2004; the video from the Waltham police from when James Keown was booked; and the audio from one of James's radio shows at KLIK.

The defense was also having trouble finding a nephrologist to serve as their expert in kidney disease and function. That expert, when located, would be asked to review slides of tissue taken from Julie Keown's kidneys during the autopsy. The prosecution medical expert believed those slides showed oxalate crystals, which were signs of ethylene glycol poisoning. The defense wanted a chance to have their own expert confirm or deny this conclusion.

The defense urged the judge to continue the case in order for them to properly represent James Keown.

"If the defendant is forced to go to trial in November 2007, the undersigned counsel say unequivocally they will not be able to provide effective representation. The defendant will be greatly prejudiced if counsel is not given adequate time to prepare this most complex of cases."

Once again, prosecutor Nat Yeager objected and asked the court to move the case to trial sooner rather than later. James had been sitting in jail waiting for trial the entire time. The case had already been pending for two years, and Julie Keown's family was tired of waiting. They had communicated this to not only Yeager, but to Kara Grant and Susie Marshall, the victim witness advocates in the case. They were tired of making travel plans and then having to change them at the last minute. They wanted justice for Julie.

Nevertheless, on September 19, 2007, Judge Kenneth Fishman, who was at the time assigned the case, ruled in favor of the defense motion to continue the trial. In his decision he cited the need to resolve the suppression issues as well as the conflicts with other trials the defense team was scheduled to try. The judge moved the trial to March 3, 2008.

To say that prosecutor Nat Yeager was visibly irritated when the defense asked for another delay in the case during a February 19, 2008, hearing before a new judge on the case, Judge Geraldine Hines, was an understatement.

"We have been in this courtroom on multiple occasions when counsel has asked for continuances. This case has gone on and on with counsel's deliberate intentions to continue this matter," Yeager said.

But the defense claimed it was not their fault that the case was being continued yet again, pointing to the delay in getting a ruling on the suppression issues from Judge Hamlin. "The reality is that she held on to the case for six months. Somehow, a justice of this court took a long time to decide this case," Feinberg told Judge Hines.

The defense had received word that Hamlin had denied their motions to suppress but needed her written decision before they could appeal the decision to the state's court of appeals. "I simply want to have an appropriate and fair amount of time. We're talking about a complex series of events pursuant to the search of computers. If this wasn't an issue, we would be ready to go on March 3," Feinberg told the judge.

Hines didn't make a ruling on continuing the trial until the following week, when she set a new trial date of March 31. "I'm going to respect your rights under the rule. I want to see your client get the fair shake he's entitled to, nothing more, nothing less," the judge told the defense.

Finally, the prosecution and defense reported to Middlesex County Superior Court on March 31, 2008, where they began the slow process of jury selection. They sorted through one hundred and fifty potential jurors before they agreed on ten men and six women to hear the case. Three years after his arrest at the KLIK studio, James Keown was finally going to stand trial. The defense team's appeal of Judge Hamlin's decision on the suppression issues had been denied by the higher court. The decision guaranteed that the jury would hear perhaps the most damning piece of evidence the prosecution had: the results of James Keown's Google searches on his Sony VAIO laptop.

But then an almost inconceivable turn of events occurred after the jury was selected in the case. Word trickled out that the opening statements, which were set for April 6, 2008, were delayed because one of the key defense witnesses was undergoing a medical evaluation. The defense's kidney expert, Dr. Richard Hellman, was undergoing emergency surgery and would not be well enough to travel before the end of the anticipated three-week trial. Hellman was a critical witness for the defense, who had already reviewed extensive medical evidence in the case. Without him, the trial could not go on. As a result, Judge Hines declared a mistrial, and a new trial date was scheduled for Wednesday, June 11, 2008.

James Keown's former journalist colleagues in Missouri waited to see what would happen when the trial finally started. Lene Johansen wrote about the upcoming trial and her desire for closure on her blog. Her early support for James had started to waver. Lene pointed out that, like others who knew James, she was having a hard time reconciling the person she knew with an accused murderer. By this point, those who knew James had figured out that the stories he told different people didn't match, but she questioned whether being a liar made him a murderer as well.

As news of the mistrial made its way to Missouri, James's younger sister, Shawna Keown, wrote to Lene Johansen, who was now living outside of Washington, D.C., through a comment she posted on Lene's blog.

"I just wanted to say thank you for the card that you sent to James the other day. It was very thoughtful and from what I have read hopefully sincere. Hopefully this case can get going and then he can come home because truly in my heart I don't believe he did this. Not just because he's my brother either like everyone thinks, but just because," Shawna wrote.

Lene was confused because she had not sent James any card or had any contact with him since his arrest. "Are you sure he said I sent one? I would not even know where to send it, and I don't know he would want one from me," Lene wrote back. "I wish and hope and pray you are right Shawna, that he did not do this. The James I know would never do this. However, I have met too many people that turned out to be someone other than I thought, and he did guard something. I thought it was his grief at the time, but now I do not know what it was. We just have to be patient and wait to let the court process run the course. . . . Please Shawna, I know you love him for being the funny, jovial James we knew and liked, not just for being your brother. But don't get blinded by hope. I have learned to prepare for the worst and hope for the best, and you should do that too, for yourself, for your mother and for James."

They had another two months ahead of them before there would be a resolution in the case. Jury selection for the second time finally got under way in June, before Judge Sandra Hamlin, who had previously been on the case, which was temporarily handled that same year by Judge Hines.

James Keown sat between his two defense attorneys, wearing a dark suit and tie but with shackles on his ankles. Jury selection was tedious, as a number of the jurors had read about the case in the local media and felt they knew too much to be impartial. Others pointed to the timing of the trial, just as many schools were letting out for summer vacation, as a reason they could not serve on the jury.

Eventually, it would be a jury of ten women and six men who would hear the evidence in the case of James Keown, who would be the third murder defendant in the country to stand trial for poisoning a spouse with ethylene glycol in just a two-year period. After the trial concluded, four of the sixteen jurors would be designated as alternates, meaning they would not actually get to deliberate.

Some wondered if James had read about the other, highly publicized cases of Lynn Turner and Mark Jensen. Lieutenant Connolly had determined early on in the investigation that a cable television special about the Lynn Turner case had aired around the same time that Julie started getting sick in 2004 and had suggested in an affidavit in the case that James had seen the show.

Former 911 operator Lynn Turner had been convicted in March of 2007 of murdering her boyfriend, Randy Thompson, with antifreeze. By the time Turner was finally brought to trial for Thompson's murder she had already been convicted of killing her husband, Glenn Turner, by the same method in 1995. Just months before James Keown's trial began, in February 2008, a Wisconsin man, Mark Jensen, was convicted of murdering his wife, also named Julie, by poisoning her with ethylene glycol.

There were a number of similarities among the cases in both the manner in which the victims were poisoned (by ingesting antifreeze from a sweet-tasting food) and the approach the prosecuting attorneys would take during trial (suggesting the motive was financial, in that both victims had life insurance policies in which the surviving significant other or spouse was the beneficiary).

Turner was just twenty-five years old when her husband, Glenn, a police officer, went to the emergency room with flulike symptoms. He was dead by the following day. At the time Turner had been having an affair with Randy Thompson, a firefighter, who went to an emergency room six years later, in 2001, complaining of a stomachache and constant vomiting. That night, Turner had made him some Jell-O, which prosecutors alleged she'd used to disguise the taste of the antifreeze. Thompson was dead by the next day. As in James Keown's case, prosecutors pointed to financial gain as one motive for the killings. Turner collected about $153,000 in insurance benefits after her husband's death and $36,000 from Thompson's death.

Turner could have faced the death penalty in Thompson's murder but was instead sentenced to life in a Georgia prison without the possibility of parole. The charge of first-degree murder James was facing carried the sentence of life in prison without the possibility of parole. There was no death penalty in Massachusetts, and some observers of Keown's case wondered aloud if that was the reason he had chosen to move Julie away from Missouri, a state that had reinstated the death penalty in 1989. The Massachusetts legislature had rejected a bill to reinstate the death penalty only months before, on November 7, 2007.

The prosecution in James Keown's case would face the same challenge as prosecutors in Turner's case in that no one actually saw James put antifreeze into his wife's food. In Turner's case, the prosecution argued that despite the lack of an eyewitness, she was the last person with both of the men before they became ill and the last person to give them anything to eat or drink.

Mark Jensen was already serving a life sentence for the 1998 murder of his wife, Julie. Although Detective Jon Bailey and Lieutenant Jim Connolly had always suspected there was something more to James Keown's motives than the money problems, they'd never found evidence of an affair; but in the case of Mark Jensen, authorities discovered that Jensen was having an affair and had poisoned his wife, Julie Jensen, to be with his mistress.

Some observers also noted the eerie coincidence of two women named Julie being poisoned by ethylene glycol allegedly at the hands of their husbands. There were some other similarities between the two cases in the tack that the defense team would take. Similar to what Keown's attorneys planned, Jensen's attorneys argued that Julie Jensen had been depressed and suicidal and had ingested the antifreeze on her own. But the similarities didn't end there. Prosecutors in the Jensen case found that someone had searched the Internet on the family computer for antifreeze and ethylene glycol a week before Julie Jensen's death. The user also looked at oxalic acid, the ethylene glycol metabolite that causes crystals to form in human kidneys, as well as an article on poisoning treatments and a man who accidentally swallowed antifreeze.

Mark Jensen had also searched for *The Anarchist Cookbook*, including a section that suggested visiting a garden center to buy fertilizer to make homemade bombs. The computer forensic expert in Keown's case was expected to testify that someone had searched for the same deadly cookbook on James Keown's laptop before Julie Keown died.

Jensen's case was delayed for years as attorneys argued over whether to allow the prosecution to introduce a letter that Julie Jensen had written before her death. In the letter, Julie pointed the finger at her husband, saying if she was found dead that he was the one who killed her. The jury in Jensen's case eventually got to hear the letter, just as the jurors in Keown's case would hear the e-mails Julie Keown sent to her friends in the weeks before her death.

As it turned out, James Keown would not be the only husband in Massachusetts who went on trial that June for allegedly murdering his wife. One columnist for the *Boston Herald* noted that a perfect storm of murder trials was lined up in June of 2008 in the new Middlesex County Superior Court, in Woburn, Massachusetts. James Brescia went to trial in early June for hiring a hit man to kill his estranged wife's boyfriend. Ironically, Brescia was represented by Keown's second defense attorney, J. W. Carney. He was found guilty.

Both national and international press converged on the courthouse to cover the highly publicized trial of Briton Neil Entwistle, who was eventually convicted of murdering his wife and infant daughter. Entwistle's defense had tried to convince the jury that his wife, Rachel, had been suicidal and had killed not only herself, but also their infant daughter, Lillian. The suicidal-wife defense did not work for Neil Entwistle, however, and as they looked forward to James Keown's trial, the prosecution and members of Julie Keown's family were hoping the jury wouldn't buy it in James Keown's case either.

CHAPTER 38

Prosecutor Nat Yeager had been waiting for months to bring the case against James Keown to trial. With the delays behind him, Yeager would finally get his chance to outline the details of the case that he, and the investigators, felt were proof that James Keown had murdered his wife in a horrific, and premeditated, fashion.

Yeager stood before the jury on the morning of Monday, June 16, 2008, and described James as a master of deception who had fooled not only his wife, but also his family, friends, and doctors. James had created an elaborate web of lies, a house of cards that had come crashing down after he was fired from the Learning Exchange. His Jaguar had been repossessed after he failed to make the payments, he was behind on his rent, and his wife, Julie, had no idea of any of their problems.

Yeager told the jury that they would hear from both

witnesses and experts about how James Keown had researched poisons over the Internet in the months before his wife's death.

It was a slow, painful, torturous death, Yeager told the jury. Julie Keown's last days of life were unbearably painful as her kidneys shut down, while the one person who knew what was wrong with her—James Keown—said nothing and watched as she became weaker and weaker.

Yeager acknowledged that Julie had a preexisting kidney disease but said that disease had nothing to do with her excruciating death. But James had attacked this underlying weakness in his wife and used it to his advantage as he cold-bloodedly poisoned her with ethylene glycol in order to collect on her $250,000 life insurance policy. At the end of the trial, after hearing all of the evidence, the jury would have no choice but to find James guilty.

The defense disagreed.

Defense attorney Matthew Feinberg pointed out that the investigators had no direct evidence linking James Keown to the poison. There was no antifreeze in their duplex. As far as the defense was concerned, it was a mystery as to how Julie had ingested the syrupy substance. It could have been an accident, Feinberg said, but he suggested another scenario—suicide.

Feinberg told the jury that witnesses would tell them how Julie Keown became distraught in the last months of her life. After her preexisting kidney disease was discovered, she felt guilty because she thought she was a burden to James.

"The Commonwealth's entire case is built on circumstantial evidence. The Commonwealth is asking you to make a leap of faith," Feinberg said. "In place of proof . . . the Commonwealth is going to pile on evidence to persuade you he had a motive to kill his wife."

Feinberg described James and Julie as having a loving and supportive relationship. James, he said, had made some mistakes and told some lies, but he did not kill his wife.

"We all have things in our past that we're not proud of, and James Keown is no different," said Feinberg.

But that didn't make him a murderer, the defense maintained.

The trial got under way with medical testimony. Dr. Heather Tarrant, a youthful blond who had completed her emergency-department residency earlier that year at Brown University, was working in the Newton-Wellesley Hospital's emergency department on September 4, 2004, when Julie was brought in by James. Tarrant testified that doctors were initially baffled by her symptoms. Julie became unresponsive and did not react to visual, audio, or physical stimulus. The doctor told the jury how she worked to stabilize Julie Keown's breathing in the emergency room that night.

Dr. Kevin Rankins testified about his observations of Julie Keown during her August 20, 2004, stay in the hospital and his suspicions about James, who was answering most of the questions for his wife. Rankins told the jury about James's unusual question regarding what the hospital would do if Julie's death was ruled an accident.

Medical Examiner Dr. Faryl Sandler had performed the autopsy but did not declare the death a homicide for a year. The defense challenged her investigation into the death, suggesting that it was not science, but suggestions from police that had influenced her ruling. They asked the medical examiner about the possibility that Julie had committed suicide, which Sandler said the evidence did not support.

"In a suicide, usually the evidence is there because there's no reason to hide it. The substance that the deceased took is usually there. This is not a painless way to die," Sandler said.

The prosecution introduced testimony they felt would show how James got his wife to drink the antifreeze. Julie's former co-worker Samuel Shoemaker detailed the conversation in which James told him Julie likely got the antifreeze from drinking discarded antifreeze from a Gatorade bottle. Shoemaker also testified that James told him he had to lock Julie in the house because her medications made her act "goofy."

Julie's mother, Nancy Oldag, testified on direct examination that James had offered a similar explanation to her.

"[He said] she might have possibly picked up a bottle that someone drained their radiator in," Nancy testified. "He said he kind of scolded Julie for taking off without telling him."

But on cross-examination, Feinberg questioned why the Oldags thought Julie's poisoning was the result of foul play and not accidental ingestion or even suicide.

"You decided this was a matter for police. And you decided there was no way in your mind that Julie committed suicide? . . . [Or] that was a possibility in your mind?" asked Feinberg.

"Yes," Nancy acknowledged. "Anything's possible."

The trial included conflicting testimony from two opposing medical experts specializing in kidney disease— Dr. Hasan Bazari for the prosecution and Dr. Richard Hellman for the defense.

Dr. Bazari was on staff at Massachusetts General Hospital and Harvard Medical, and he had reviewed Julie Keown's medical records prior to trial. He felt that evidence of scar tissue on Julie's kidneys indicated that she had been poisoned with a lesser amount of ethylene glycol in the weeks prior to her final, fatal dose.

Bazari explained to the jury that within three to eight

hours after being ingested, antifreeze skews the body's acidic balance. This causes the person to act as if he or she is drunk, often slurring his or her speech and having trouble walking. As the ethylene glycol spread through Julie Keown's body, it metabolized and formed crystals in the kidneys, causing toxins that, if not treated with an antibody, cause death. Dr. Bazari had found a massive amount of oxalate crystal deposits in the tissue sample he reviewed from Julie's kidney.

There was an absence of the crystals and scarring in the blood vessels, which demonstrated that the presence of oxalate crystals elsewhere in her body would not be explained by a hereditary disease. When she died, Julie was suffering from a mild form of kidney disease called focal segmental glomerulosclerosis, which accounted for test results that showed elevated protein levels and blood in her urine during prior doctors' visits in the late 1990s. The preexisting condition did not, however, account for the level of kidney decline seen when Julie went to the hospital on either August 20, 2004, or September 4, 2004, the doctor determined. The condition had nothing to do with her death.

Although Julie Keown had been given the antibody after her admission to the emergency room on September 4, 2004, it was too late to reverse the effects of the poison coursing through her body. The antibody was not administered until almost nine hours after she arrived at the hospital, which Bazari said could have affected her outcome.

"They were able to eliminate all the ethylene glycol from her body, but by the time that was done, she had met brain death," Bazari said. "There's no doubt in my mind that she would have had an opportunity to be treated and allowed to live on if she had [been brought in] earlier."

On cross-examination, Feinberg suggested that Julie's preexisting kidney condition made her reaction to the ethylene glycol worse. He asked Bazari if it would take a longer time for the crystals to dissipate once the antidote was given. Bazari responded that the crystals would have built up to a higher level than in a person without a pre-existing kidney condition.

The defense again brought up the possibility of suicide and had Bazari tell the jury about the case of a twenty-seven-year-old man who had drunk antifreeze in an effort to kill himself. Though Bazari did not state an opinion on whether Julie Keown could have done the same, Feinberg was successful in planting the seed with the jury.

Dr. Richard Hellman, the defense kidney expert, questioned whether diarrhea, not ethylene glycol, could have been the reason the acidic balance in Julie's body was out of balance on her first hospital visit. Hellman explained that diarrhea can cause hypoglycemic acid to form.

"So maybe that was a factor. I don't know, but it's a question. I have questions about that particular situation," said Hellman.

Though Dr. Hellman did not dispute that Julie Keown had died from ethylene glycol poisoning, his testimony attempted to create some doubt among the jurors about the accuracy of her diagnosis and what, if any, impact that had on her outcome. He also suggested that some of the drugs Julie had been prescribed might have caused her to become depressed, an attempt by the defense to bolster their suicide theory. Hellman told the jury that a steroid prescribed by Dr. Julia Neuringer, who treated Julie in the weeks before her death at Newton-Wellesley Hospital, might have caused side effects such as lack of muscle control, fatigue, moodiness, and psychosis.

Dr. Julia Neuringer testified that she determined early on that Julie's kidneys were not fully functioning. When she reviewed a CT scan of Julie's kidneys in August of 2004, Neuringer was shocked at their poor condition. At the time, she told Julie that she had a chronic kidney disease and would eventually need dialysis and then possibly a transplant.

Neuringer was the first to diagnose the condition known as focal segmental glomerulosclerosis, despite Julie's history of having the abnormal urine samples in the 1990s. The doctor explained that Julie had been taking Prilosec, a drug that decreases acid in the stomach, and she at first suspected that Julie's kidney decline might have been the result of an allergic reaction to the Prilosec. Thinking the decline in her kidney function was because of an allergic reaction to Prilosec, Neuringer prescribed an anti-inflammatory steroid, which the defense worked to suggest was a reason for Julie Keown's depressed mood and potential suicide. But the doctor didn't feel this was the case. She testified that she had asked Julie if she was having suicidal thoughts, and the young woman had said she was not. The doctor was satisfied with Julie's answer and believed her.

Neuringer told the jury that she had a sense that there was something else that she hadn't pinpointed that caused the rapid decline in Julie's kidney function.

"I personally did not feel as though the [acidity level] was due to ethylene glycol," Neuringer testified. "Nothing really fit. . . . I could not explain the first set of labs."

Neuringer testified that Julie's acidity levels were not nearly as high as the other extreme forms of antifreeze intoxication she had seen. She eventually decided that Julie must have ingested a small amount of antifreeze the first time, or the acidity tests were taken at the tail end of ingestion.

"What you're telling us is that you were wrong?" Feinberg asked during cross-examination.

"I don't think I was wrong then. What I'm telling you is if I had the correct [medical] history, I would have made the correct diagnosis," replied Dr. Neuringer.

Dr. Grazyna Galicka-Piskorska testified that she had been on call at Newton-Wellesley Hospital during Labor Day weekend of 2004. The kidney doctor told the jury that she received a call from James Keown at 10 a.m. on September 4 about Julie Keown's worsening condition.

Galicka-Piskorska testified that she advised James to bring Julie to the hospital right away, but it wasn't until nearly twelve hours later that the couple arrived in the emergency room. The ER doctor felt that Julie was suffering from ethylene glycol poisoning and asked James Keown if they had any products, such as antifreeze, that might contain the poison in their home. Galicka-Piskorska said James Keown told her that nothing containing ethylene glycol was in or around their home.

The defense's suicide theory took a hit during the doctor's testimony when she said that James had told her Julie was not suicidal at the time. James also told the doctor that it was Julie, not him, who was behind their delay in arriving at the hospital that day; Julie had wanted to rest at home and had not wanted to go to the hospital, he said.

Those twelve hours made all the difference in Julie Keown's outcome. All of the medical experts agreed that Julie would almost certainly still be alive if James had brought her to the hospital earlier on September 4, 2004.

CHAPTER 39

By the time she prepared to testify in the trial, James Keown's former boss Tammy Blossom was ready to put the situation behind her. It had been almost four years since she and the other administrators at the Learning Exchange had uncovered James's lies and fired him. Blossom had since left the Learning Exchange and had moved to a new job and home in Nebraska with her family. She was ready to close this chapter after the trial.

As the first week of the trial continued, Blossom took the stand to tell the jury about how James had deceived her and the others at the Learning Exchange. She testified about how the company fired James in July of 2004 after discovering the bogus website bills. She testified about James's claims of acceptance into Harvard Business School and her decision to allow him to telecommute. And she told the jury that the company had discovered some other things about James that led to his dismissal.

Assistant District Attorney Nat Yeager had Blossom read James's supposed letter of acceptance to Harvard in court.

On behalf of the Admissions Board, I would like to congratulate you on your acceptance to the Harvard Business School MBA Program.

The mission of the Harvard Business School MBA Program is to develop outstanding business leaders who will contribute to the well-being of society. Each year, our challenge is to select the highest potential leaders from an applicant pool of very talented candidates from around the world.

Our selection process emphasizes leadership potential, strong academic ability, and personal qualities and characteristics. Moreover, the MBA Admissions Board aspires to create a class with diverse backgrounds and global perspectives to add to the richness of both the BBS learning experience and the BBS community broadly.

At Harvard, you will join students who have been leaders in a variety of settings: in their extracurricular activities while at college or university, in their workplaces, and in their communities.

Over the coming weeks and months, you will receive a variety of information pertaining to your enrollment at Harvard. Please review each document carefully. My office is here to help you sort through any questions that may arise as you prepare to join us in Cambridge.

Congratulations again. We look forward to seeing you in the "Yard" this fall.

It was signed by Britt K. Dewey, director of admissions for Harvard Business School. Dewey testified later that day that the signature on the letter was not hers.

After watching the first days of the trial from the audience, Detective Jon Bailey testified. He had taken most of the evidence photos in the case and had to testify to that in order to have those photos admitted.

Bailey testified about the March 2005 search inside the Keowns' duplex. He told the jury that a "green substance" had been found on the shelf in a closet; when tested, it was found not to contain ethylene glycol. The defense hammered on Bailey about his decision to get the surveillance tapes from the CVS store on Harvard Street but not the CVS that was much closer to James and Julie's duplex. Bailey testified that he got the surveillance from the Harvard Street location because that was where James said he went. In addition, he confirmed with the pharmacy that it was the one James and Julie used to fill all of their prescriptions.

The defense focused on the investigators' search of the duplex, with Feinberg questioning why Massachusetts State Police lieutenant Ed Forster took some liquid-filled bottles for testing and not others, including two glasses of water and bottles of detergent.

Prosecution witness Alphonse Poklis, a professor of pathology at Virginia Commonwealth University, testified that other substances that could be used to poison unsuspecting people are harder to acquire than ethylene glycol. Poklis gave an overview of poisons including arsenic, methanol, ricin, chloroform, and acetone.

Poklis testified that ethylene glycol was something that could be ingested without the victim's knowledge initially because of the sweet taste, which meant it could be mixed in with food or drink. As part of his research in the case, he looked into whether there were other cases in which Gatorade had been suspected or identified as the vehicle for antifreeze poisoning. He thought it was a likely substance to mask the antifreeze, pointing out that it even came in a yellowish-green color very similar to antifreeze.

His testimony drew visible reaction from the jury when he told them that he had even tasted antifreeze, but he explained that he swished it around in his mouth and spit it out. "I didn't swallow it," he said, adding it tasted sweet and inconspicuous. "You can certainly get away with a couple of ounces mixed in there."

The defense questioned Poklis on why ethylene glycol would be a poison of choice when its presence could be easily identified through medical testing and when its symptoms were so obvious.

"There's almost no symptoms of a poison or a drug that does not mirror a natural illness. If you have suspicion, with today's technology, you can find out about anything," the prosecution expert testified.

He went on to explain that initially the symptoms of ethylene glycol poisoning could mimic a number of other natural illnesses.

Despite attempts by the defense to have the information excluded, the jury would hear what investigators found on James Keown's computers.

Prosecutor Nat Yeager set out to show the drastically different searches that had been done on James and Julie's computers. Julie was searching for ways to get better, ways to live with what she thought was just a preexisting kidney condition. James's searches were far more sinister.

Computer analyst Andrew Winrow, who had moved on from the Middlesex County District Attorney's Office during the trial delays, detailed the lengthy list of Google

searches James had conducted on his Sony VAIO laptop
from late July 2004 to August 2004. Though the laptop
hadn't been found until after his arrest, it provided perhaps the most damning evidence against James.

James had searched for "Readily available poisons"
and "Can you buy arsenic?" as well as for *The Anarchist
Cookbook*, by William Powell, which includes recipes
for both explosives and poisons. Winrow's analysis also
found a web page dealing with forensic toxicology as well
as searches for how to make or buy ricin. Other searches
had included the words *antifreeze*, *human*, and *death*.

The searches seemed to provide a direct link between
James Keown and the ethylene glycol eventually used to
murder Julie. But the defense team offered another theory about the searches: perhaps Julie had been doing the
searches herself.

Attorney Matthew Kamholtz questioned Winrow whether
the computer had any user-created passwords. When Winrow said he didn't recall, Kamholtz said that it was possible
then for anyone to access the computer and that "you can't
tell us who is sitting at the keyboard."

Winrow admitted that he could not.

Kamholtz also raised the possibility that the search
words were on the computer for another reason.

"I could inadvertently click on a link and go some-
place I didn't intend to go," Kamholtz suggested.

Nat Yeager attempted to rebut the defense suggestion
by using a blackboard that had the names of twenty-four
different Google searches for information about poisons
found on James Keown's laptop computer. They included
phrases such as "how to make ricin from castor beans."
Yeager urged the jury to consider how far-fetched the
defense theory was.

"I would have to go to each one of these inadvertently
twenty-four different times," Yeager said.

State Trooper David McSweeney, the computer foren-sics expert who'd analyzed the two Dell laptops issued to Julie Keown by Cerner Corporation, testified about an e-mail Julie had sent to her husband just a week before her death. The September 1, 2004, e-mail had questions that Julie wanted to remember to ask Dr. Julia Neuringer at Newton-Wellesley Hospital.

The e-mails gave the jury a sense of Julie speaking to them about her condition.

"Shouldn't I talk to a transplant coordinator, shouldn't I do this?"

"How long should I expect to live on my current kid-ney function?"

"What is the problem with my kidney?"

McSweeney testified that Julie also searched on her computer in that last week of her life for information on how to deal and live with kidney ailments. She also wanted to find out about the possibility of getting preg-nant and searched for "Pregnancy with 55 percent kidney function."

There was one thing missing from Julie Keown's computer—any searches on how to make or purchase poisons.

It wasn't only the searches on her computers that gave the jury a sense of the young woman. They also got to hear from Julie in her own words through the e-mails she'd sent to friends like Heather LeBlanc and Jill Lawson. As with the searches on the computer, the e-mails suggested that Julie was trying to get well and was concerned about how her worsening condition was affecting her husband.

The defense hoped to use the e-mails to show that Julie and James had a good relationship. The e-mails to friends gave the jury a chance to hear Julie's thoughts about their move to Waltham and her belief that James had been given the full scholarship to the Harvard Business School.

Prosecutor Nat Yeager called Deborah Jordan, an official with the Hartford Insurance Company, to introduce details of the life insurance policy in Julie Keown's name. Jordan testified that the policy included a $50,000 basic life policy, a $150,000 supplemental insurance policy, and $50,000 accidental death and dismemberment policy, for a total of $250,000. Though to some it seemed implausible that James went to so much effort to murder his wife for $250,000, the prosecution felt the promise of the policy amid James's crumbling financial picture was what led him to carry out the murder.

Yeager had more witnesses to illustrate the couple's financial troubles. Patrick Byrne, a financial investigator for the Middlesex County District Attorney's Office who'd analyzed the Keowns' records, testified that James had received a notice that his electricity would be shut off because of $452 in unpaid bills. Gas to the duplex was also slated to be disconnected. And James owed $360 on his cell-phone bill. Although James and Julie had three different bank accounts at the time, there were negative or zero balances in all of them. James had no job and no income, yet his attorney suggested during cross-examination that the prosecution was making too much of his financial difficulties. Matthew Feinberg asked Byrne if he had looked at the couple's retirement accounts, which Byrne testified he did not.

Although most of the Keowns' friends and acquaintances whom Detective Bailey and Lieutenant Connolly interviewed during their investigation had initially stood by James, some had changed their minds by the time of the trial. Ted Willmore, whose wife, Leila, had been fearful in the early days of the investigation that James would be wrongfully accused, testified about how he came to believe James was responsible for Julie's death. It was conversations with James after Julie's passing that started to make Ted and Leila wonder if James could be capable of murder. In one specific conversation, Ted testified that he came right out and asked James in November of 2004 if he was worried that the police suspected him of killing Julie. James said he thought it was possible that he might get indicted, but that the case was all circumstantial, so there was no chance he'd be convicted. On cross-examination, Ted admitted that after that conversation, he started to doubt James's innocence, and the couple no longer felt the desire to support him as they had been before, as a friend whom they had thought of as going through an unbelievably painful time.

Another witness who was damaging to the defense theory of suicide was a woman whom Julie had planned to meet up with the week after she died. The woman had successfully lived through a kidney transplant and gone on to have a child. If Julie had really been planning to kill herself, why would she have gone to such great lengths to set up the meeting?

And then there was the question of how James got Julie to drink the syrupy antifreeze. In addition to Sam Shoemaker's testimony that James told him Julie must have drunk antifreeze from a Gatorade bottle, there was testimony about Julie actually drinking Gatorade during her illness. Jill Lawson, her friend and co-worker from Cerner, testified that Julie told her James was trying to get her to drink Gatorade. Julie did not want to drink the Gatorade, she told Jill, because her stomach could not handle the citrus taste. And Julie's best friend, Heather LeBlanc, heard James in the background while she was on the phone with Julie telling his wife to drink her Gatorade.

Heather further disputed the defense theory that Julie was suicidal, pointing to her friend's demeanor during a visit with her the month before she died. Julie wanted to have a baby and was optimistic about getting well.

"She was ready to tackle things, she was ready, as she would say, to 'kick butt' and ready to move on with life," Heather testified.

By the end of the second week of the trial, there were a number of people in the courtroom who wanted to move on with their lives as well—Jon Bailey, Jack and Nancy Oldag, Heather LeBlanc. Moving on for them meant having the jury find James guilty and bringing justice to Julie. They were getting closer, as the defense rested their case on a Thursday afternoon without calling any witnesses. James Keown would not speak in his own defense, nor would anyone other than his defense team, who would get their last chance to argue his case during closing arguments the judge had scheduled for Monday morning.

CHAPTER 40

Detective Jon Bailey sat in the back row of the court-room next to Lieutenant Jim Connolly where he had watched the trial every day for the past two weeks. He knew the evidence pointed to James Keown. He knew that there were no other suspects. He felt that the computer searches on James's laptop, combined with the inconsistencies in his story, combined with his financial troubles, made a strong case. But he also knew that it would ultimately be up to the twelve men and women sitting in the jury box to decide.

Prosecutor Nat Yeager had always been realistic when talking about the potential for a guilty verdict in the case. He would never say that it was a definite that James would be found guilty. The one thing he did say to Jack and Nancy Oldag was that he was committed to the case.

"I will promise you one thing, I will do the best I can for you," Yeager told the couple.

The prosecutor would later say that he knew going into the trial that the computer search results and medical testimony would be the key to getting a conviction. The challenge was bringing that medical testimony to a level that didn't overwhelm the jury. He knew that good defense attorneys could use a lot of complex information to cast doubt on the strength of the prosecution's case. To be successful, Yeager would have to find a way to speak as clearly and concisely as possible about the medical evidence in the case. He also knew that the computer evidence was the strongest, but he also knew that he had to be wary of making his argument too technical for the jury.

Yeager was by nature a laid-back individual, but he had the attention of everyone in the courtroom that morning as he told the jury that James Keown had deliberately, methodically, and cold-bloodedly poisoned his wife. He started with September 8, 2004, the day that doctors confirmed that Julie Keown had ethylene glycol in her system, and worked backward. He knew that the jury's natural tendency was to be skeptical of trial lawyers, and he wanted the evidence to speak to them.

Yeager compared the months in the summer of 2004 to a house of cards crashing down on James Keown. He had been fired from his job at the Learning Exchange. He lied about his acceptance to Harvard. He was deeply in debt and saw only one way out—murdering his wife to get her $250,000 life insurance policy.

"This was not a crime of passion," he said. "It was the exact opposite."

The computer searches showed how James came to the decision to use antifreeze but also how Julie wanted to get well. Yeager placed two poster boards in front of the jury, one with the computer searches that James Keown had made in the weeks before his wife's death, and the other with the searches Julie Keown made during those same weeks. They represented two polar opposites—death or life.

Testimony from Sam Shoemaker and Heather Le-Blanc showed that James put the poison-laced Gatorade in his wife's hands and made her drink, despite her reluctance to do so, despite the fact that she didn't even like Gatorade.

Julie Keown wanted to get well, and her husband told her that drinking the Gatorade would replenish her, make her feel better after being sick, make her well.

And so she drank it. And when she was so sick that she could no longer stand and her limbs were numb, James purposefully delayed taking her to the hospital for almost twelve hours.

"Access, motive, and the defendant's conduct tell you that the defendant murdered his wife," Yeager told the jury.

The most powerful part of Yeager's closing argument came at the end, when Yeager talked about James's decision to move back to Missouri after his wife's death. Yeager told the jury about the things James left behind. Photos of each item were displayed on a large monitor at the front of the courtroom as he spoke.

He left behind Julie's wedding dress. He left their wedding photo album. A new big-screen TV. An expensive sleigh bed. Tools. The seat from his Ford Expedition, completely intact in the basement. Even Julie's wedding ring.

Yeager slowly walked back toward the prosecution table, leaving the photo of the ring up on the monitor.

"He left everything behind," Yeager said. He then picked up the Sony VAIO laptop: the laptop on which

James had searched for ways to kill Julie; the laptop on which he had received an e-mail from Julie with questions for her doctor; the laptop that his mother tried to keep away from the police.

"He left it all behind—but not that Sony VAIO," Yeager told the jury as he carried the laptop across the courtroom and laid it down in front of them.

He spoke so softly in his last statement that everyone in the courtroom seemed to lean forward a bit in their seats to hear him.

Middlesex District Attorney Gerry Leone sat in the audience during the closing arguments and later called Yeager's closings one of the most outstanding closing arguments he'd ever seen. The use of Julie Keown's e-mails, her own words, really gave the sense that Julie was speaking to the jury.

Defense attorney Matthew Feinberg stood before the jury and argued that there was some crucial evidence lacking in the case—proof that James Keown had given his wife antifreeze. There was no evidence of ethylene glycol in the couple's duplex. Forensic testing showed no traces of poison in or around the residence.

The defense attorney rebutted the prosecution's position that James's financial situation had pushed him to murder his wife. The financial difficulties were not that serious, the defense attorney stated, and certainly not any different from many young couples living paycheck to paycheck.

"Their financial situation was not desperate," Feinberg said.

Feinberg again suggested that anyone could have made the searches on the computer, not only James, because the laptop did not have any network-protected passwords.

Really, Feinberg told the jury, the computer evidence was at best unreliable, as was the search that investigators had done of the couple's Waltham duplex. He reminded the jury of testimony that showed that investigators did not take all of the items from the apartment for testing, including the two glasses of water in the couple's bedroom.

Feinberg told the jury that the question of where or how Julie ingested ethylene glycol was a mystery that they would never know the answer to. But one thing was certain, he said, it had not come from James Keown.

———————

Before retiring to the deliberation room to decide James Keown's fate, the jury received lengthy instructions from Judge Sandra Hamlin about what they could and could not consider during their deliberations.

They were told that James Keown was presumed innocent until proven otherwise by the evidence as presented.

"The jury must bear in mind that the law never imposes on a defendant in a criminal case the burden or duty of calling any witnesses," the judge said. "This legal presumption of the defendant's innocence is not an idle theory to be discarded or disposed of by the jury by caprice, passion, or prejudice. Furthermore, the defendant is not to be found guilty on this indictment on suspicion or conjecture, but only on evidence produced and admitted before the jury in this courtroom."

They were instructed to only consider evidence that had been properly admitted in the case. Evidence consisted of the sworn testimony of the witnesses, the exhibits, and anything that was read out loud in court and agreed to by both sides as fact.

"Opening statements and closing arguments of counsel are not evidence; they are only intended to assist you in understanding the evidence and the contentions of the parties. If any reference by the court or by counsel, either in opening or in closing remarks, does not coincide with your own recollection of the evidence, it is your recollection which should control during your deliberations," Hamlin told the jurors.

The judge went on to explain the difference between direct and circumstantial evidence. The jurors were told that direct evidence is the testimony of a witness asserting actual knowledge of a fact that he or she saw, felt, heard, or gained from some other scene.

"Circumstantial evidence is founded upon the basis of observed facts and experiences that require the establishment of a connection between known facts and the facts sought to be proved. In order to establish this connection, the jury is permitted to draw from what are known as reasonable inferences from the known facts or direct testimony that you believe," the judge explained.

If the jury had any reasonable doubt that James was guilty, they had to find him not guilty.

Once she dispatched with what were the more standard jury instructions, Hamlin gave the jury instructions related specifically to James Keown's case. The instructions had been agreed upon by both the defense and prosecution.

The jury was told that they needed to take special care when considering any statements that James Keown had made to either the Waltham police or the Massachusetts State Police. "Before you may consider any such statements by the defendant, you must make a preliminary determination. You may consider such statements in your deliberations only if the Commonwealth has proved beyond a reasonable doubt that the defendant made the statements and that he made them voluntarily, freely, and rationally," Hamlin said.

In determining whether James made the statements on his own accord, the jury was told to consider all of the surrounding circumstances. Where did the conversations take place? What was the nature of the conversations? How long were the conversations? What was James Keown's physical or mental condition at the time?

In regard to the first interview James Keown gave police at the Newton-Wellesley Hospital, which police called an informational interview, the jury could not consider the absence of Miranda rights during that interview as meaning James's statements were not voluntary.

The judge detailed how the jury should consider testimony about James's employment with the Learning Exchange, bogus admission to Harvard Business School, financial situation, and the life insurance policy.

"You may not take that evidence as a substitute for proof that the defendant committed the murder charged here, or that he has a criminal personality. However, you may consider the incidents solely to assist you in evaluating the defendant's state of mind, his intent, and his motive. I repeat, you may consider such evidence for the limited and sole purpose of the defendant's state of mind, his intent, and his motive."

The judge went on to discuss evidence introduced by the prosecution intended to show that James was conscious of being guilty. These included statements about the life insurance policy and statements to Ted Willmore about what would happen if the police arrested him. "If the Commonwealth has proven that the defendant made such statements and acted in such ways, you are permitted to consider whether such statements and actions indicate feelings of guilt by the defendant and whether, in turn, such feelings of guilt tend to show actual guilt on this murder charge," the judge said.

The jury was instructed how to consider the e-mails

written by Julie Keown and statements she made to different people before her death. Statements made to medical providers could be considered as evidence. Statements to friends and family or in e-mails could be considered by the jury as they considered Julie Keown's state of mind.

Once they had considered all of the evidence, the jury was to consider the elements of the charge of first-degree murder. In Massachusetts, murder in the first degree was defined as the unlawful killing of a human being with deliberate premeditation and malice. Massachusetts law also gave juries the power to determine the degree of murder in a case. If they did not feel the evidence supported the charge of first-degree murder, they could find James guilty of a lesser degree of murder.

The prosecution had two ways to prove that James was guilty of first-degree murder. In the first instance, the jury would have to believe beyond a reasonable doubt that James either killed his wife with deliberate premeditation or with extreme atrocity or cruelty. To prove deliberate premeditation, the jury had to agree that all three elements of the charge had been met. They included that James committed the killing, that the killing was committed with malice, and that the killing was committed with deliberate premeditation.

To prove that James had murdered Julie with extreme atrocity or cruelty, the jury would have to agree that three other elements had been met. The first two elements were the same as those needed to prove deliberate premeditation, while the third element required that the jury agreed that James had committed the killing with extreme atrocity and cruelty.

"Extreme cruelty means that the defendant caused the death of the victim by a method that surpassed the cruelty inherent in any taking of human life. Extreme atrocity means an act that is extremely wicked or brutal, appalling, horrifying, or utterly revolting. You must determine whether the method or mode of killing is so shocking as to amount to murder by extreme atrocity or cruelty," the judge told the jurors.

———————————

There was one detail the jurors would not be allowed to consider during their deliberations. Though they had heard about James's screen name of "Keyser Soze" on the laptop issued to him by Trabon Solutions, they could not speculate on the meaning or significance of the name.

After spending four years of his life and career learning about James Keown, there was no doubt in Detective Jon Bailey's mind, however, that the choice of Keyser Soze was significant. For Bailey, it was a chilling look inside James's mind and who he really was. To him, if you understood Keyser Soze, you understood James Keown.

The last line in the film had stuck with Bailey for years—"The greatest trick the Devil ever pulled was convincing the world he didn't exist."

To Bailey that devil did exist, and his name was James Keown.

CHAPTER 41

The jury deliberated for a day and a half. They had two weeks of testimony and more than two hundred pieces of evidence to go over in the deliberation room.

As they deliberated, everyone else waited. They waited in the courthouse in Woburn and in their homes or offices in Missouri for some word on a verdict.

Lana Koon-Anderson and a handful of former Cerner employees who had known Julie Keown had all been glued to the computer those past two weeks for news of the trial. Lana could not count the number of times she hit refresh on the *Waltham Daily News* website the morning of July 2, 2008. Like Julie's family and friends in the courtroom, the women were holding out hope that James Keown would be found guilty and held accountable for the murder.

Finally a bulletin appeared on the website stating that a verdict had been reached.

Detective Jon Bailey and Lieutenant Jim Connolly were in the Middlesex County District Attorney's Office with prosecutor Nat Yeager when a call came into the office about the verdict. They didn't talk about the case, or the verdict, as they made their way upstairs from the office to the courtroom.

Bailey never thought that James would be found not guilty, but there was always the potential for a hung jury. All it took was one juror who did not agree with the rest about James's guilt or innocence.

Bailey headed to his regular seat in the back row of the courtroom where he had watched the trial every day. Connolly filed in next to him, as did a number of other people who had worked on the case—the victim witness advocates Kara Grant and Susie Marshall; computer analyst Andrew Winrow; Ed Forster, of the state police; and District Attorney Gerry Leone. The trial hadn't been widely attended, with most courtroom spectators opting to watch the more high-profile Neil Entwistle trial up the hall. But Judge Hamlin's courtroom was packed that afternoon. It seemed that as word circulated through the courthouse, everyone who was able to do so came to watch.

Bailey watched as James Keown was brought back into the courtroom and to the defense table, where he sat waiting to learn his fate. He was dressed in a black suit, light blue shirt, and coordinating striped blue tie, his red hair cropped short in the standard jailhouse haircut. The jury foreman stood and announced that they, the jury, had reached a verdict. It was unanimous.

Guilty.

James Keown was guilty of first-degree murder in the poisoning death of his wife, Julie.

James closed his eyes and briefly bowed his head. But aside from that, there was no visible sign of emotion from the once-outgoing radio talk-show host. He had finally become the center of attention in the news world, though the ending was not what he expected. Betty Keown, his only courtroom supporter, sat alone, stoically clutching her Bible as she had throughout the trial, her makeup as perfect as the night Bailey and Connolly had interviewed her as she'd sat in her pink bathrobe. Like her son, Betty Keown had learned to put her best face forward, no matter how dire the situation.

The courtroom was quiet; no one else seemed to react visibly. Relief flooded Bailey as he heard the word *guilty*. The jury had found James guilty, and he had done his part to help them reach that conclusion and find justice for Julie, the wholesome young woman with the open smile whom he felt he now knew, despite having never met her while she was alive.

————————————

In front of her computer across the country, Lana Koon-Anderson pumped her fist in the air and yelled "Yes!" when she saw the verdict on the computer monitor.

A woman behind Lana who also knew Julie didn't mince words. "Good job, he needs to rot in hell," she called out.

————————————

Four years after they lost their daughter, Jack and Nancy Oldag finally saw her killer held accountable. And they were finally able to tell James how they felt. Nancy read a prepared statement before sentencing, occasionally looking at James. As she looked at him, Nancy realized that the person she saw on the other side of the courtroom was not the person she thought her daughter had married.

She really didn't know who he was at that moment. What she did know for sure was that losing Julie had been like losing the light from their lives, Nancy said, and there was only one person to blame—James.

"In my mind, James is no longer a person. He is just a mass of flesh and bones taking up space on this earth. No real person would ever do such an evil thing," Nancy said, with her husband standing by her side. "I will be forever grateful to the justice system for bringing this self-involved evil monster to court and to reveal to everyone what kind of person he really is. I feel like a storm has come through my life, my home, my family."

James was stoic as he listened to his former mother-in-law's words. The only sign of emotion came as he looked at his mother in the audience and told her he would be OK.

Jack Oldag's voice choked with emotion as he read his statement. "My wife and I were always so proud of our kids. Now he has taken half of that away from us"— he paused to compose himself before continuing—"in one of the most cowardly and brutal ways possible. It is difficult to think of the suffering she endured."

Judge Sandra Hamlin prepared to hand down the life sentence without the possibility of parole, but after listening to the shocking testimony in the case, she opted to address James Keown first. The judge expressed her horror at the manner in which he had chosen to kill his wife.

"The way in which this defendant secretly and methodically planned and carried out the poisoning of his wife and allowed her to suffer so horribly and die such a slow and painful death makes this court feel that I am truly in the presence of an evil person," Judge Hamlin said as she looked down from the bench at James.

District Attorney Gerry Leone made a brief statement to the press after the conviction and sentencing.

"James Keown was a liar and a failure and, because

of that, he executed a sadistic plan to poison his wife and obtain her life insurance money," Leone said. "He compounded the pain for Julie's family by trying to claim that Julie committed suicide—a claim that had no basis in evidence, facts, or reality. While this verdict will not bring Julie back, we hope it provides some solace to her family that the man responsible for these cowardly and reprehensible crimes will spend the rest of his life in prison."

———————

Thousands of miles from the courtroom, Christina Liles felt a true sense of relief when she heard the guilty verdict. She had spent the day glued to the network news station waiting for a verdict. She knew there was a slim chance that James might be found not guilty. She sat and prayed for Jack and Nancy Oldag and cried when she heard the word *guilty*. She immediately called Nancy's cell phone and left her a message, letting her know she had heard the news and was so happy for the resolution. She only hoped Julie's parents could find some peace now that James had been convicted.

———————

Betsy Dudenhoeffer had come to a point months before where she felt that James was guilty, before the trial had even occurred. Hearing the verdict reinforced that feeling as well as the deep hurt she felt at being lied to by James. Despite the time that had passed, and the guilty verdict, Betsy felt that she knew the truth but still could not come to grips with the mind-boggling reality of the situation— that the James she had known her entire life was not the real James.

Two days later, on July 4, 2008, Betsy got a phone call. She heard the operator ask if she would accept a collect call from James Keown. She accepted the charges. Betsy felt in her heart that James was calling to apologize. She wanted to believe he was going to tell her he was sorry for the lies, for what he'd done, for involving her in the case. Instead he started proclaiming his innocence.

"Betsy, don't listen to what everyone's saying, it's not me," James pleaded.

Betsy told James never to call her again, then hung up the phone and closed the book on him.

After James's arrest, Betsy had begun having dinner with his mother once a week to make Betty Keown feel better, never letting on to Betty that she was starting to have doubts about James. But having known the family since she was a child, Betsy felt that making sure Betty was OK was the right thing to do. During one of those dinners, Betsy asked the other woman if she felt like going to the gambling boats, as she knew from James that his mother enjoyed going.

Betty looked at Betsy with a look of complete confusion.

"I don't gamble, Betsy," she replied, shocked.

Betsy thought back to the wads of cash James said he'd won on the gambling boats with his mother. His mother, he'd insisted at the time, loved to gamble. Betsy realized this was just another example of James spinning a story for her benefit, but she didn't know why.

Some questioned if it was James's fear of being seen for who he really was by his wife that drove him to murder. He created a successful persona for not only Julie, but everyone around him—he portrayed himself as an upwardly mobile young professional with connections to an impressive dossier of important executives and politicians. He was James Keown, the voice of ESPN Radio, the big deal, the big talker, the man who always had the perfect résumé for every new job he applied for and was going places in this world—the master of creating smoke and mirrors.

He was so good in fact at creating this other person that some might compare him to a chameleon, the lizard whose color changed based on whatever he was sitting next to, as a natural way to protect himself from the eyes of predators. Like the chameleon, James easily changed his colors to fit every situation, every job, every social group he encountered. But James's ability to change his colors, and transform himself so skillfully, left many wondering about his real personality. Who was he underneath that skin? He was so eager to tell about his connections with those in power, but could he really have been hiding from his connections something, or someone, much more sinister by changing his colors so often?

Most baffling to those involved with the case was why James had gone to such great lengths to kill Julie. Why not simply divorce her? It has been said that in the minds of some murderers, the decision to murder someone close to them is made to preserve themselves in the eyes of that person; in other words, it is better for that person to die than to see the murderer's real weaknesses and failures. That appeared to be the case with Julie, who remained the adoring and loving wife up until the end, never seeing her husband's true colors before her life slipped away.

EPILOGUE

Just over two months after James Keown was sentenced to life in prison for Julie's death, his former in-laws once again made the trip from Plattsburg, Missouri, to Boston. This time, their purpose was far different than the last. They made the trip in the name of peace for their daughter, to honor her memory, and to see Jon Bailey again.

On September 18, 2008, they attended a ceremony where a stone had been placed in Julie's memory in the Garden of Peace, a memorial that served as a living memorial to victims of homicide and violence, near the State House in downtown Boston on Somerset Street. The garden was a symbol of hope for peace and renewal in not only the Boston area, but the world.

At the center of the memorial, a dry streambed was filled with smooth river stones, each engraved with the name of a victim of homicide. At the beginning of the streambed sat a round black granite stone called Tragic Destiny, meant to represent the enormous weight of sadness and grief. The river stones wove through the garden until they reached a pool of water, where a sculpture called *Ibis Ascending* rose from the water.

The garden began with an idea by Paul Rober, a member of a group called Parents of Murdered Children who worked as an advocate for victims' rights after the murder of his son. In 1995, Rober went to the governor of Massachusetts, William Weld, with the idea for a garden on a state property. Rober and the group began the process of building support for the peace garden and raising money for the project. Rober became ill and passed away before the garden was completed, but another advocate, Beatrice Nessen, took over in his place. Catherine Melina, a landscape designer studying at Harvard, donated the design work for the garden, while artist Judy Kensley McKie, whose own son was murdered, designed the main sculpture in the water pool, *Ibis Ascending.*

When plans were approved by the Massachusetts legislature in 2000 to refurbish the Saltonstall state office building, they included plans to create and build the Garden of Peace. In 2004, the garden opened and began adding river stones in memory of murder victims. By the fall of 2008, there were 565 victims memorialized along the riverbed.

On Thursday, September 18, 2008, the Oldags arrived at the Garden of Peace, along with forty-five other families who lost a loved one to violence, for a ceremony honoring those victims. They were joined by Jon Bailey and his wife, Doreen, and Doreen's mother, Janice Aitchison; Middlesex district attorney Gerry Leone; and Susie Marshall and Kara Grant, the victim witness advocates from Leone's office who had been with them through the long ordeal.

Several family members who had lost relatives to homicides spoke during the ceremony, including Kim Odom, whose young son was killed by a stray bullet while walking through his Dorchester, Massachusetts, neighborhood in October of 2007 on his way home from playing basketball. Odom told the crowd she felt fortunate to be part of a place of such serenity and comfort. Melissa Gauthier, whose father was shot and killed in 2002, spoke of the sense of shared pain and support between the families as they stood together during the ceremony.

Some of the families stood quietly and attracted little attention, while others, like the family of Patrick Frye, stood out. In his memory, Frye's family wore yellow T-shirts with his favorite phrase printed on the back of the shirts: "It's a wrap. I love you too. Peace out." The family of Rebecca Payne, a twenty-two-year-old college student who had been shot in her Boston apartment earlier that year, placed a photo and a dozen candles on her stone.

Detective Jon Bailey and his wife and mother-in-law stood next to the Oldags and listened as Julie's name was read aloud during the ceremony: Julie Irene Oldag. The stone was for Julie and her memory, the bright light she'd brought into her parents' lives. It bore no reminder of her married name, of the person who had taken her life four years before.

For Bailey, who had been forever touched by his role in the case, the memorial seemed a fitting way to remember Julie. After the case was over, Bailey left the division. The emotional toll of the case had been enormous, and he did not want to go through something like that again. He returned to his post as the TRIAD officer for the department and got back to his roots. He had found justice for Julie and her family, but the elderly would always need his help. Still, he couldn't put the case, or

Julie's face, out of his mind. The picture of Julie that he put on his desk in the early weeks of the investigation remained on the wall. He couldn't bring himself to take it down.

Prosecutor Nat Yeager was named a Lawyer of the Year in 2008 by *Massachusetts Lawyers Weekly* for his work on the case. "Most prosecutors don't think in terms of victory," Yeager said when asked about his thoughts on securing the guilty verdict. "They think in terms of work they did as a team and whether they did the best they could do. But this is one of the biggest honors in terms of what I've been asked to work on."

Even years after she lost her dear friend, Christina Liles had moments where she found it hard to believe that Julie was really gone forever. "There are days I feel like this really didn't happen and I am going to see her again. I wish she could be here to share my life with me," Christina said.

And there are days that Christina felt Julie was still with her. After Julie's death, Christina found out she was pregnant again. She thought back to the birth of her daughter and Julie being by her side during the entire delivery. She knew that would not be the case this time around. On the day that Christina told her boss she was pregnant again, she went back and sat down at her desk. She had the strangest feeling that someone was giving her a huge hug. In her heart, she felt that it was Julie, still with her, still the caring nurse, watching over her.

Jack and Nancy Oldag stayed in Boston for several days after the memorial ceremony, and Jon Bailey offered to take them sightseeing. Over the past four years, he had really gotten to know the couple and felt a sort of friendship with them. He felt they should see some of the good things about the area, instead of just remembering Boston as the place where their daughter had died, where they had spent what seemed like months in a courtroom waiting for justice for her murder. He wanted to take them to the Bull and Finch Pub, made famous by the sitcom *Cheers*, and show them Faneuil Hall and the Boston Public Garden.

Several weeks before the trip, Bailey spoke to the couple by phone. He asked if they would like to see the prison where James was being housed, to find a sense of closure before returning to Missouri. Jack wanted to know if the prison was close to Boston.

"It's not too far, would you like to go?" Bailey asked.

Jack hesitated. "No, I don't think so."

Bailey sensed that Jack and Nancy did want to see the prison but were still a little unsure.

He was right.

The day after the ceremony at the Garden of Peace, Jack pulled him aside.

"I really think we need to see it," he told Bailey.

Bailey called the police station to get the exact address of the Massachusetts State Prison, in Shirley, then entered the address into the GPS in his car. The prison was about a one-hour drive west from Boston, out Route 2, a rural road spotted with fields, farms, and cows. New England had settled into the fall season, and the roadside farm stands they passed had pumpkins and apples out front on display.

Shirley was a small, historic town, with just over six thousand residents, and the prison was located on what had once been a Shaker settlement. The prison was a maximum-security prison designed for inmates who were not considered "career criminals" but who were serving life sentences. The common thought with some of these inmates was that they needed to be protected from the other inmates because they weren't physically tough or savvy to the ways of the prison culture, with the sentence handed down in a version of jailhouse justice far worse than the one handed down by the judge. James Keown would have little to worry about in terms of interacting with even the other prisoners in Shirley, as he was only allowed out of his cell for one hour a day, to get some exercise before he returned to a solitary life behind bars.

As they drove in Bailey's car, they talked about police work and how Bailey's father had also been a police officer. Nancy still had a lot of questions about her daughter's death. She wondered why James hadn't just left the marriage, why he went to such lengths to carry out murder. She still strongly felt that the wrong person had died on that September day four years ago.

Bailey told Jack and Nancy something he had shared several times throughout the case, his feeling that they were the nicest people he wished he never met. The same went for Julie, for by this time, Bailey felt like he knew her as if she were alive.

At the direction of the computerized voice on the GPS, Bailey made the last turn onto the road the prison was located on, turning by the Shirley Congregational Church, a quaint white church with red shutters. They drove through a residential neighborhood with modest single-family homes, looking ahead to catch a glimpse of the prison. Finally, just past a youth soccer field, the scenery opened up before them, and the prison nestled in a field that had clearly once been a farm. Just as Jefferson City had seemed like a state capital in the middle of nowhere, an unlikely location, the Massachusetts State Prison at Shirley seemed like a prison in a most unusual location.

And, as Jack Oldag noticed as he looked out the window, a rather ironic address.

He pointed out the name of the street in disbelief—Harvard Road. It was almost too much of a coincidence that

James's new home bore the name of the elite university he'd never really attended.

Jack turned to the others and remarked, "Well, I guess James finally made it to Harvard after all."